J. M. SYNGE : A BIBLIOGRAPHY OF PUBLISHED CRITICISM

PAUL M. LEVITT

J. M. SYNGE:
A BIBLIOGRAPHY OF
PUBLISHED
CRITICISM

IRISH UNIVERSITY PRESS
DUBLIN : IRELAND

© 1974 Paul M. Levitt

ISBN 0 7165 2155 5

All forms of micropublishing
© *Irish University Microforms   Dublin Ireland*

Irish University Press   Dublin   Ireland

Printed in the Republic of Ireland

ONCE AGAIN:
FOR MY MOTHER AND FATHER

Contents

ACKNOWLEDGEMENTS

For their generous and valuable help, I am indebted to: Eleanor Benjamin, Douglas Burger, Jane and Roger Clark, Roger Cox, Brigid Davis, Nancy Elliott, Laurel Hilton, Marcia Hoebreckx, Berel Lang, Sandra Levitt, Helen and Marvin Metz, Jack Ogilvy, Eugene Petriwsky, Elmer Poenack, Mary Sandoe, Lewis Sawin, Charles Vandersee, Gladys Weibel, Christopher J. Woods and Peggy Wrenn.

For their very substantial assistance, in a long and provoking search for materials, I am indebted to: William Donovan, Newspaper Service, The Chicago Public Library; Alf Mac Lochlainn, Keeper of Printed Books, National Library of Ireland; Mildred Nilon, Head of the Reference Department, Norlin Library, University of Colorado; and to the staffs of the Boston Herald Traveler Newspaper Reference Library, Boston Public Library, British Museum (Bloomsbury and Colindale), Chicago Historical Society Library, Free Library of Philadelphia, Harvard University Library, Library of Congress, Los Angeles Public Library, Massachusetts State Library, New York Public Library, Newberry Library, Rhode Island Historical Society Library, U.C.L.A. Library, and University of Illinois Library.

For a generous travel grant and for a faculty fellowship, I want to thank the Council on Research and Creative Work, University of Colorado.

For her help in preparing the manuscript for publication, I want to thank Katheryn L. Paullus. The errors that remain are, I regret, my own.

P.M.L.

INTRODUCTION

When Ellen Douglass Leyburn remarked that "students of Synge . . .
have chafed for years under the necessary limitations of the Bourgeois
biography" [*Modern Drama*, III (May 1960), 93], she might just as
well have said bibliography, for the same criticism is true of both.
Maurice Bourgeois's *John Millington Synge and the Irish Theatre*
appeared in 1913. It has a bibliographical appendix that includes the
primary works of J. M. Synge and presumably all the secondary works
Bourgeois was able to find. The Bourgeois bibliography, although awk-
wardly arranged, frequently inaccurate, and not always clearly documen-
ted, does have the virtue of being comprehensive: it not only includes
Synge's works and those of his critics (as well as unpublished and un-
printed material), it also includes a list of the best known paintings and
photographs of Synge, a bibliographical note on "the exegesis and non-
dramatic versions of the Deirdre saga", and a record of the first performances of Synge's plays in different countries and cities. The obvious
failing of the Bourgeois bibliography is, of course, that it concludes with
the year 1913.

The present bibliography is restricted to criticism of the works of
J. M. Synge and is designed to conclude with the year 1969, although
delays in publishing and other related matters have prompted me to
include some material for 1970-71. To those people whom I have
slighted by neglecting to include their work in this bibliography, I
apologize and plead that the omission was not intentional.

A few comments are probably in order about the documentation and
the organization of the material. (For specific categories see the table of
contents and for specific subjects the index.) In documenting books, I
have in some instances omitted page numbers. This is because the page
numbers are clearly listed in the index and are too numerous to repeat in
the entry. With periodicals, I have in every instance given the page
numbers for the complete article; and, as well, in those instances where
an article is cited several times because of the different subjects it treats,
I have given the particular pagination for those subjects in square
brackets. I have done this because in my own research I have often
wished, when coming upon a reference that only gives the pages quoted
from, that I could have the pages for the complete article.

With the newspapers there is a special problem. I have not organized
the newspapers according to the plan that I followed for the books and

periodicals because most newspaper collections today are preserved on microfilm, and one must take into account the problems of working with microfilm. Once a reader has placed a role of microfilm on a machine, he will more than likely want to read all of the material on that microfilm that pertains to his subject. The easiest way to read the material is by proceeding first by date (the earliest first), second by page number (page one before page two, when there are two or more articles in the same issue), and third by title, alphabetically (when there is more than one article on the same page in the same issue).

Moreover, since most newspapers in libraries in Western Europe and North America are catalogued by city of publication, I have organized the newspapers alphabetically by city of publication. This organization also preserves the coherence of related materials when a newspaper review or article or some event occasions a long series of articles as, for example, with the first production of *The Playboy of the Western World*. The Dublin newspapers ran weeks of related articles on *The Playboy* as play, Synge as artist, Yeats as director of the Abbey, and so on.

In order to avoid the confusion that often results from trying to decide what is a periodical and what is a newspaper, I have relied on the formal and legal distinction of how the item was, or is, registered at the General Post Office.

Raymond Williams's observation in 1952 that "Synge's plays . . . need evaluation as *texts,* with a temporary suspension of interest in the wider cultural issues, save only those which the texts themselves raise" [*Drama from Ibsen to Eliot,* p. 154] may be taken as applying not only to the plays but to all of Synge's works. In fact, the date 1952 provides a convenient watershed for Synge criticism. There had been, of course, some good criticism on Synge in general prior to 1952: W. B. Yeats, *Synge and the Ireland of His Time* (1911); Francis L. Bickley, *J. M. Synge and the Irish Dramatic Movement* (1912); Maurice Bourgeois, *John Millington Synge and the Irish Theatre* (1913); Lady Isabella Augusta Gregory, *Our Irish Theatre* (1913); John Masefield, *John M. Synge: A Few Personal Recollections with Biographical Notes* (1915); Ernest A. Boyd, *The Contemporary Drama of Ireland* (1918); Daniel Corkery, *Synge and Anglo-Irish Literature: A Study* (1931); W. G. Fay and Catherine Carswell, *The Fays of the Abbey Theatre* (1935); Una Ellis-Fermor, *The Irish Dramatic Movement* (1939); L. A. G. Strong, *John Millington Synge* (1941); Peter Kavanagh, *The Story of the Abbey Theatre* (1950); Lennox Robinson, *Ireland's Abbey Theatre* (1951). But on the whole, the reviewer for *The New Witness* [I (2 January 1913), 282-283] more accurately reflected, than did the exceptional book every few years, the state of Synge criticism for more than forty years when he observed:

> Synge is an easy artist to criticise in some respects, while in others he is difficult. He is easy to criticise because he himself in a few introductory remarks and comments said the most important things about his own drama. Critics can only repeat these, and Synge has said them so perfectly that amplification and glosses are more or less unnecessary. . . . The explanation is . . . that only this or that point remains to be amplified in writing about Synge, that critics quote inevitably the same passages and say the same things. Therefore if a critic is bent on saying something which shall be both new and true about Synge, his task is a difficult one.
>
> . . . When the critic has pointed out that it was among the Irish peasants that Synge found a speech which was fully flavoured as nut or apple and "a popular imagination that was fiery and magnificent and tender", when the story of how a hint from Yeats induced him to leave Paris and explore that forgotten field is told, and the relation of Synge's "Aran Islands" and his "Wicklow Papers" to the plays has been illustrated by quotations, all has been said that matters.

As a matter of fact, until the 1950s there were at least five subjects that most Synge critics never failed to mention: (1) Synge's Prefaces (*Playboy* in particular), (2) Synge's language, (3) *The Playboy of the Western World*, (4) *Riders to the Sea*, and (5) the story of how Yeats directed Synge to go to the Aran Islands.

The Preface to *Playboy* provided reviewers with an excuse to talk not about the play but about the Preface, or provided a stick with which to beat the "Ibsenite" drama. Those in the art-for-art's-sake movement, as well as those in the anti-Ibsenite camp, found a ready argument in Synge's assertion in the Preface to *The Tinker's Wedding* that "the drama is made serious . . . not by the degree in which it is taken up with problems that are serious in themselves, but by the degree in which it gives the nourishment . . . on which our imaginations live", and that "the drama, like the symphony, does not teach or prove anything." Most reviewers, however, like the one above from *The New Witness*, simply applied the Prefaces to the plays and thought that in the relationship between them they had discovered a truth that illuminated both the theory and the practice of Synge's art. Very few essayists focused in the Prefaces upon the real matter, which was for Synge, as Joseph Wood Krutch correctly points out, that

> The modern drama and all other forms of modern literature . . . had ceased to be great or even true literature because modern literature had ceased to be at once True and Beautiful. Indeed, to

most writers Beauty and Truth presented themselves as irreconcilables, between which a choice must be made. If you chose Beauty, you became an aesthete writing elaborately artificial works which were supposed to be beautiful but were admittedly not true. If, on the other hand, you declared your allegiance to Truth, you became a Naturalist and admitted that the supposed truth which you presented was ugly. But Homer and Shakespeare made no choice. Their works, like all true works of literature, are somehow both True and Beautiful.

This modern impasse, so Synge said, was the inevitable consequence of destroying the folk roots of literature.

[*"Modernism" in Modern Drama* (1953), pp. 94-95]

The Anglo-Irish dialect of Synge's plays has inspired philological studies, like A. G. van Hamel's "On Anglo-Irish Syntax" (1912), and has stirred up a controversy that has not ended about the beauty and authenticity of Synge's dramatic prose dialogue. There are the admirers: Clayton Hamilton, in a rather infelicitous phrase, speaks of Synge's "deathless eloquence" [*Conversations on Contemporary Drama* (1924), p. 7], and Edmund Wilson says that in Synge we have "perhaps the most authentic example of poetic drama which the modern stage has seen" [*Axel's Castle* (1931), p. 43]. And there are the sceptics: St. John Ervine in the 1920s calls Synge "an exhausted Elizabethan" and his language "the decorated wreck of a great tradition" [*The Organised Theatre* (1924), pp. 118, 85]. In another place, Ervine says that Synge's dialogue "is contrived stuff, withdrawn from reality and made into a pattern, pretty enough, but, after a time, tiresome and tedious" [*How to Write a Play* (1928), p. 20]. Owen Quinn in 1950 argues that Synge's language has "too much tongue" and "insufficient thought":

The freakish nature of Synge's work in general extenuates, to some extent, the mental flaccidity that gave rise to the dialogue. The English language is unsuited to the subtlety of the Irish mind . . . Synge tried to write "Irish" dialogue, and succeeded in exposing his work to Buck Mulligan's attempts at parody—a bad sign.

[*Envoy*, III: 11 (October 1950), 50]

The Playboy of the Western World, the most written about of all Synge subjects, and by discerning critics the most highly placed of Synge's plays, is to this day still villified and misunderstood; it still invites apology, and still inspires the *ad hominem* complaint that only a sick man could have written it. Henry MacKinnon Walbrook reviewing *The Playboy* at the Court Theatre in London in 1909, expressed an incomprehension typical of many early reviewers and sounded the political argument that caused Irish Nationalists to condemn the play violently.

A hearing of the late Mr. J. M. Synge's remarkable comedy, "The

Playboy of the Western World", has left us still in doubt as to the real purpose the author can have had in writing it. One who knew him well has told us that at the bottom of it was an irresponsible and irrepressible desire to provoke laughter at any cost, together with a tragic belief that such men and women as the characters in the play are all that have been left to Ireland after years of mis-government and emigration. It is hard to understand the play in the light of either explanation. It is really difficult, either in the theatre or the study, to laugh very enjoyably over the brutishness and cowardice of the men, and the coarseness of the women, here set forward as County Mayo types. If, however, it be the fact that emigration has really only left such human scum behind in the Island of Saints, then not only is Ireland in a bad way indeed, but it is as well that those of her leaders who flatter her should be confronted with this ghastly exposure of the sort of men and women for whom they are demanding nationhood and self-government.
[*Nights at the Play* (1911), pp. 107-108]

Sydney W. Carroll, fourteen years later in 1923, was even less restrained than Walbrook. Carroll said of the play:

If an Englishman had written this play he would have been shot within twenty-four hours of its production. And he would have deserved it. But because it comes from an Irish poet, because it is so genuinely Irish in its perversity, its sense of ridicule, its charged realism, its squalor, its shebeenery, and its curious streaks of romanticism, its black-hearted treachery to Irish ideals, it is hailed as Heaven-sent genius. The case of Ireland at this moment is being judged by the world. She stands at the tribunal of the nations and waits for her fate to be decided. And this is the moment selected by Irishmen to revive "The Playboy of the Western World". Well, well!
[*Some Dramatic Opinions* (1923), p. 69]

Carroll subsequently contended that the play was the work of a sick man.
"The Playboy" was the product of a great brain soured by illness, made morbid by disease. It is the kind of enigmatic rollick indulged in by a doomed consumptive—the feverish and forced joviality of a man faced with his own coffin.
[p. 70]

Patrick Kavanagh, writing in 1951, has a similar view, arguing that:
Those who rioted in the theatre at the "Playboy" were right though they lacked the intelligence to see why they were right. The pre-dominant note of Synge's writings is hate . . .
[*Envoy*, IV:16 (March 1951), 70]

The debate goes on. In a letter to the *Sunday Press* (Dublin), dated 7

December 1969, the writer objects to a showing in Dublin of a film version of *The Playboy*.

> When are [we] going to stop disgracing Ireland before the world by showing her up in such philistine light. I am thinking just at present of "The Playboy of the Western World", with its murderers, semi-drunken kitchen-inhabiting cursing crowd of uneducated peasants, a cinema showing of which I witnessed last week.
> [p. 18]

Riders to the Sea presents another situation. It is the one play of Synge's that consistently has inspired praise and admiration. Except for a few dissident voices charging that *Riders* was dour and depressing, the play has from the beginning been recognized for what it is: one of the most successful one-act plays in the language. The Reverend D. Fletcher's comment in 1912 that " 'Riders to the Sea' is one of the most perfect tragedies written in the English language" [*Transactions of the Rochdale Literary and Scientific Society*, XI (1912-1913), 103] may be too generous, but it sums up the view held by many about *Riders*. The classical restraint and resolution of the play has regularly attracted critical notice. Norman L. Robinson, writing in 1927, says that "Maurya's concluding words in the Play remind one . . . of the conclusion of a Greek tragedy" [*The Central Literary Magazine*, XXVIII (April 1927), 56]. Elizabeth Coxhead in 1962 makes virtually the same comment. "The forces which have brought [Maurya] beyond despair are those which bludgeon the protagonists in a Greek tragedy" [*J. M. Synge and Lady Gregory* (1962), pp. 15-16].

The sense of fate or inevitability that pervades *Riders* has over the years also been a favourite subject of reviewers and commentators. Ernest Boyd in 1911 observes:

> There is little uncertainty as to the fate of Bartley, for we know at once that he has gone to join his brothers in death. . . .
> [*The Contemporary Drama of Ireland* (1917), p. 96]

Francis Birrell in 1927 has a similar comment:

> "Riders to the Sea" grips the audience, but the author allows himself no adventitious aids. There is no element of surprise. Even the stupidest person must see what is going to happen almost in every detail, before the play is one quarter completed. It just pursues its inevitable way, and at the end is a complete and inevitable work of art.
> [*The Nation and Athenaeum*, 4 June 1927, p. 304]

T. R. Henn in 1956 puts forth the same view when he says:

> [*Riders*] is effective because the age-old sense of fatality is communicated simply and vividly, so that it becomes clear even to those

who do not know the Islands.
[*The Harvest of Tragedy* (1956), p. 202]
The one subject, it seems, that no critic ever neglects to mention is Synge's meeting Yeats in Paris. Not that critics dwell on this subject (on what is there to dwell?), but judging from the number of times that this story has been repeated, one has the impression that the name of Yeats is essential to the reputation of Synge.

In general, before the 1950s, Synge's non-dramatic prose (with the exception of the Prefaces) and his poetry were virtually ignored. His plays, with perhaps the exception of *Riders*, were regarded as expressions of Synge's own theories on the drama, as interesting linguistic specimens, as social and intellectual history, as anti-Irish tracts, as generic corruptions of comedy and tragedy, as expressions of the Abbey Theatre's folk-art ideal, as poems and not plays, as Yeatsian or Lady Gregorian, as myth, in short, as almost everything but plays.

For those interested in a comprehensive review of Synge criticism from the beginning through 1960, the introductory essay to Alan F. Price's *Synge and Anglo-Irish Drama*, entitled "A Survey of Criticism of Synge", provides an excellent review of commentary for which there is insufficient space in this brief introduction.

What is the state of Synge criticism since 1952? Raymond Williams, I think, would have to concede that Synge's plays are finally being analysed as dramatic texts according to legitimate dramatic criteria. Certainly the publication of the Oxford University Press *Collected Works* (1962-68) will now allow us to study the elements that went into the making of the plays and to have an overall view of the plays, poetry and non-dramatic prose—a view which, as Jeanne Flood observes, "will allow for the kind of study of Synge's development which has not so far been possible" [*Eire-Ireland*, III: 4 (Winter 1968), 143].

In addition to the *Collected Works*, there have been other significant publications: Gerard Fay, *The Abbey Theatre: Cradle of Genius* (1958); David H. Greene and Edward M. Stephens, *J. M. Synge: 1871-1909* (1959), which is the authorized biography; Robin Skelton, ed., *J. M. Synge: Translations* (1961); Alan F. Price, *Synge and Anglo-Irish Drama* (1961); Ann Saddlemyer, "A Share in the Dignity of the World; J. M. Synge's Aesthetic Theory", in Robin Skelton and Ann Saddlemyer, eds., *The World of W. B. Yeats* (1965); Robin Skelton, *The Writings of J. M. Synge* (1971); Ann Saddlemyer, ed., *J. M. Synge to Lady Gregory and W. B. Yeats* (1971); Ann Saddlemyer, ed., *Letters to Molly: John M. Synge to Maire O'Neill* (1971); Ann Saddlemyer, ed., *Theatre Business, Management of Men: The Letters of the First*

Abbey Theatre Directors (1971).

What Synge criticism still lacks are structural studies of the plays, in particular of *Deirdre of the Sorrows, In the Shadow of the Glen, The Tinker's Wedding,* and *The Well of the Saints.* What has been written about Synge's poetry is not without merit, especially the work by William Lyon Phelps [*The Bookman*, XLVII (March 1918), 63-66], Vivian de Sola Pinto [*Crisis in English Poetry* (1951), pp. 75-98], and Donald Davie [*The Dublin Magazine,* n.s. XXVII (January-March 1952), 32-38], but the surface has barely been scratched. The non-dramatic prose works have yet to receive serious attention as a body of literature independent of the plays. Virtually nothing has been written on Synge's work as a reviewer.

What is finally needed, of course, for any author, is intelligent criticism. After all the years of vitriol and tangential criticism, J. M. Synge especially deserves the best. It is in this conviction, and in the hope of assisting scholars, critics, students and anyone else interested in the world of J. M. Synge, that this bibliography is done.

Paul M. Levitt
Boulder, Colorado.

PART I

BOOKS AND PERIODICALS

BIBLIOGRAPHIES

Adelman, Irving, and Rita Dworkin. "Synge, John Millington, 1871-1909", *Modern Drama: A Checklist of Critical Literature on 20th Century Plays,* pp. 306-308. Metuchen, N.J., The Scarecrow Press, 1967.

Babler, O. F. "John Millington Synge in Czech Translations", *Notes and Queries* (London), CXCI (21 September 1946), 123-124.

Baker, Blanch M. "Synge, Edmund John Millington, 1871-1909", in *Theatre and Allied Arts: A Guide to Books Dealing with the History, Criticism, and Technic of the Drama and Theatre and Related Arts and Crafts,* p. 118. New York, H. W. Wilson, 1952.

Bourgeois, Maurice. *John Millington Synge and the Irish Theatre,* pp. 251-314. London, Constable, 1913.

Brown, Stephen James Meredith, ed. *A Guide to Books on Ireland: Part I. Prose Literature, Poetry, Music and Plays.* Dublin, Hodges, Figgis; London, Longmans, Green, 1912.

Coleman, Arthur, and Gary R. Tyler. "Synge, John", in *Drama Criticism: A Checklist of Interpretation since 1940 of English and American Plays,* I, 202-205. Denver, Colorado, Alan Swallow, 1966.

Dysinger, Robert E. "Additions to the John Millington Synge Collection", *Colby Library Quarterly* (Waterville, Maine), Ser. 4, No. 11 (August 1957), 192-194.

——————. "The John Millington Synge Collection at Colby College", *Colby Library Quarterly* (Waterville, Maine), Ser. 4, No. 9 (February 1957), 166-172.

Greene, David H. "An Adequate Text of J. M. Synge", *Modern Language Notes* (Baltimore), LXI (November 1946), 466-467.

Jochum, Klaus Peter S., *W. B. Yeats's Plays: An Annotated Checklist of Criticism.* Saarbrücken, Anglistisches Institut der Universität des Saarlandes, 1966.

"John Millington Synge at Colby", *Colby Library Quarterly* (Waterville, Maine), Ser. 4, No. 9 (February 1957), 157-158.

Lucas, Frank Laurence. "John Millington Synge", in *The Drama of Chekhov, Synge, Yeats, and Pirandello.* London, Cassell, 1963. [See pp. 149-166]

11

McGirr, Alice Thurston. "Reading List on John Millington Synge", *Bulletin of Bibliography* (Boston), VII (April 1913), 114-115.

MacManus, M. J. *A Bibliography of Books Written by John Millington Synge.* Bibliographies of Irish Authors, No. 4. Dublin, Talbot Press, 1930. [Reprinted from *The Dublin Magazine* (see below next entry)]

——————. "Bibliographies of Irish Authors, No. 4: John Millington Synge", *The Dublin Magazine*, n.s. V (October-December 1930), 47-51.

MacPhail, Ian. "John Millington Synge: Some Bibliographical Notes", *Irish Book* (Dublin), I (Spring 1959), 3-10.

——————, and M. Pollard, compilers. *John Millington Synge, 1871-1909: A Catalogue of an Exhibition Held at Trinity College Library Dublin on the Occasion of the Fiftieth Anniversary of His Death.* Dublin, Dolmen Press for the Friends of the Library of Trinity College, Dublin, April 1959.

Mikhail, Edward Halim. "Sixty Years of Synge Criticism, 1907-1967: A Selective Bibliography", *Bulletin of Bibliography and Magazine Notes* (Westwood, Mass.), XXVII: 1 (January-March 1970), 11-13; XXVII: 2 (April-June 1970), 53-56.

O Faolain, Sean. "John Millington Synge (1871-1909)", in *The Cambridge Bibliography of English Literature,* edited by F. W. Bateson, III, 1062-1063. Cambridge (England), Cambridge University Press; New York, Macmillan, 1940.

O'Hegarty, P. S. "Bibliographical Notes: The Abbey Theatre (Wolfhound) Series of Plays", *The Dublin Magazine*, n.s. XXII (April-June 1947), 41-42.

——————. "Some Notes on the Bibliography of J. M. Synge, Supplemental to Bourgeois and MacManus", *The Dublin Magazine*, n.s. XVII-XVIII (January-March 1942), 56-58.

Palmer, Helen H., and Anne Jane Dyson. "John Millington Synge", in *European Drama Criticism,* pp. 407-410. Hamden, Conn., The Shoe String Press, 1968.

Saul, George Brandon. "An Introductory Bibliography in Anglo-Irish Literature", *Bulletin of the New York Public Library* (New York), LVIII (September 1954), 429-435.

Triesch, Manfred. "Some Unpublished J. M. Synge Papers", *English Language Notes* (Boulder, Colorado), IV (September 1966), 49-51.

Trinity College, Dublin. "A Check-List of First Editions of Works by John Millington Synge and George William Russell", *T.C.D. Annual Bulletin* (1956), 4-9.

BIOGRAPHY

Ayling, Ronald. "Synge's First Love: Some South African Aspects", *English Studies in Africa* (Johannesburg), VI (September 1963), 173-185. [Reprinted in *Modern Drama*, VI (February 1964), 450-460]

Blake, Warren Barton. "John Synge and His Plays", *The Dial* (Chicago), L (16 January 1911), 37-41. [See pp. 37-39]

Bourgeois, Maurice. *John Millington Synge and the Irish Theatre.* London, Constable, 1913; reissued by Benjamin Blom, Bronx, New York, 1965.

Brooke, Stopford Augustus, and Thomas William Rolleston, eds. *A Treasury of Irish Poetry in the English Tongue,* pp. 596-598. Revised and enlarged edition, New York, Macmillan, 1932.

Brophy, Liam. "The 'Shocking' Synge", *The Word* (Donamon, Co. Roscommon), (March 1959), 6-8.

Browning, D. C. *Everyman's Dictionary of Literary Biography, English and American,* p. 664. Compiled after John W. Cousin, London, J. M. Dent; New York, E. P. Dutton, 1958; revised editions, 1960, 1962, 1963.

Carpenter, Bruce, ed. *A Book of Dramas: An Anthology of Nineteen Plays,* p. 1106. New York, Prentice-Hall, 1929.
[A brief biographical note]

Clark, Barrett Harper. *The British and American Drama of To-Day: Outlines for Their Study,* pp. 188-190. New York, Henry Holt, 1915.

——————. "John M. Synge", in *A Study of the Modern Drama,* pp. 336-337. New York and London, Appleton, 1925; revised edition, New York, Appleton-Century, 1938.

Colum, Padraic. "Memories of John M. Synge", *The Literary Review* [of the *New York Evening Post*] (New York), II (4 June 1921), 1-2.

——————. *The Road Round Ireland,* pp. 352-373. New York, Macmillan, 1926.

Corkery, Daniel. *Synge and Anglo-Irish Literature: A Study,* pp. 28-64. Dublin and Cork, Cork University Press; London, Longmans, Green, 1931.

Cosman, Max. "The Life and World of J. M. Synge", *The Commonweal* (New York), LXX (17 July 1959), 380-382. [A review of David H. Greene and Edward M. Stephens, *J. M. Synge: 1871-1909*]

Cousin, John W. *A Short Biographical Dictionary of English Literature.* Everyman's Library No. 449. London, J. M. Dent; New York, E. P. Dutton, [1910]; revised edition, London and Toronto, J. M. Dent; New York, E. P. Dutton, [1925]

Coxhead, Elizabeth. *Daughters of Erin: Five Women of the Irish Renascence.* London, Secker and Warburg, 1965. [Concerns relationship between Synge and Maire O'Neill]

Crosby, Robert R. [Review of David H. Greene and Edward M. Stephens, *J. M. Synge: 1871-1909*], *Quarterly Journal of Speech* (Iowa City, Iowa), XLV:3 (October 1959), 337-338.

Drew, Fraser. "The Irish Allegiances of an English Laureate: John Masefield and Ireland", *Eire-Ireland* (St. Paul, Minnesota), III:4 (Winter 1968), 24-34. [See pp. 25-27]

Fallon, Gabriel. "The Ageing Abbey—II", *The Irish Monthly* (Dublin), LXVI (May 1938), 339-344.

Fay, William George, and Catherine Carswell. *The Fays of the Abbey Theatre: An Autobiographical Record,* pp. 221-222. London, Rich and Cowan; New York, Harcourt, Brace, 1935.

Fraser, Russell A. "Ireland Made Him", *The Nation* (New York), CXC (20 February 1960), 171-173. [A review article of David H. Greene and Edward M. Stephens, *J. M. Synge: 1871-1909*]

"A Glimpse of Synge", *The American Playwright* (New York), II (March 1913), 101. [An incomplete quotation reprinted from W. B. Yeats, *The Cutting of an Agate*]

Greene, David H., and Edward M. Stephens. *J. M. Synge: 1871-1909.* New York, Macmillan, 1959.

Gregory, Lady Isabella Augusta. *Our Irish Theatre: A Chapter of Autobiography,* pp. 119-139. New York and London, G. P. Putnam's, 1913. [Reprinted from *The English Review* (see below, next entry)]

——————. "Synge", *The English Review* (London), XIII (March 1913), 556-566.

Gogarty, Oliver St. John. *As I Was Going Down Sackville Street: A Phantasy in Fact,* pp. 292-293, 299-300. London, Rich and Cowan; New York, Reynal and Hitchcock, 1937.

Henn, T. R. [Review of J. M. Synge, *The Autobiography of J. M. Synge,* constructed from the manuscripts by Alan Price], *The Modern Language Review* (Cambridge, England), LXII (April 1967), 325-326.

Holloway, Joseph. *Joseph Holloway's Abbey Theatre: A Selection from His Unpublished Journal, "Impressions of a Dublin Playgoer",* edited by Robert Hogan and Michael J. O'Neill. Carbondale and Edwardsville, Southern Illinois University Press; London and Amsterdam, Feffer and Simons, 1967.

Hone, J. M. "J. M. Synge", *Everyman* (London), II (15 August, 1913), 555.

"Ireland's Playwright", *The Independent* (New York), LXXXIII (27 September 1915), 433-434. [A review of John Masefield, *John M. Synge: A Few Personal Recollections with Biographical Notes*]

Krieger, Hans. *John Millington Synge, ein Dichter der "keltischen Renaissance"*, pp. 16-23. Inaugural Dissertation. Marburg, N. G. Elwert'sche, 1916.

Leyburn, Ellen Douglass. [Review of David H. Greene and Edward M. Stephens, *J. M. Synge: 1871-1909*], *Modern Drama* (Lawrence, Kansas), III (May 1960), 93-95.

Lucas, Frank Laurence. *The Drama of Chekhov, Synge, Yeats and Pirandello*, pp. 149-166. London, Cassell, 1963.

Lynch, Arthur. *My Life Story*, pp. 121, 148-150. London, John Long, 1924.

MacKenna, Stephen. *Journal and Letters of Stephen MacKenna*, edited with a memoir by E. R. Dodds and a preface by Padraic Colum. London, Constable, 1936; New York, William Morrow, 1937.

MacNeice, Louis. [Review article of David H. Greene and Edward M. Stephens, *J. M. Synge: 1871-1909*], *The London Magazine*, VII (August 1960), 70-73.

MacSiubhlaigh, Máire [Mary Walker], and Edward Kenny. *The Splendid Years: Recollections of M. Nic Shiubhlaigh*, as told to Edward Kenny, pp. 39-48, 53-56, 59, 62-63, 79-88, 106-107, 112. Dublin, James Duffy, 1955.

Masefield, John Edward. *A Book of Prose Selections*, pp. 77-78. London and New York, Macmillan, 1950. [Reprinted from *Recent Prose* (see below)]

—————. "John M. Synge", *Contemporary Review* (London), XCIX (April 1911), 470-478. [Reprinted in *John M. Synge: A Few Personal Recollections* (see below, next entry), and in *Recent Prose* (see below)]

—————. *John M. Synge: A Few Personal Recollections, with Biographical Notes*. Churchtown, Dundrum, Cuala Press; New York, Macmillan, 1915. [Reprinted in *Recent Prose* (see below, next entry)]

—————. *Recent Prose*, pp. 163-187. London, Heinemann, 1924.

—————. "Synge, John Millington (1871-1909)", *Dictionary of*

National Biography, Second Supplement, III, 468-471. New York, Macmillan; London, Smith, Elder, 1912.

Meyerfeld, Max. "Letters of John Millington Synge: From Material Supplied by Max Meyerfeld", *Yale Review* (New Haven), n.s. XIII (July 1924), 690-709. [See pp. 698-699]

Moore, George. *Hail and Farewell: A Trilogy: Vale,* pp. 194-219. New York, Appleton; London, Heinemann, 1914. [Most of this material was reprinted from *The English Review* (see below, next entry)]

——————. "Yeats, Lady Gregory, and Synge: II", *The English Review* (London), XVI (February 1914), 350-364.

Morgan, Arthur Eustace. *Tendencies of Modern English Drama.* London, Constable, 1924.

"Mr. Masefield's Recollections of John M. Synge", *The Dial* (Chicago), LX (16 March 1916), 285. [A review of John Masefield, *John M. Synge: A Few Personal Recollections with Biographical Notes*]

O'Connor, Brother Anthony Cyril. "Synge and National Drama", *Unitas: Revista de cultura y vida universitaria* (Manila), XXVII: 2 (April 1954), 294-346. [See pp. 301-309]

O'Donoghue, David James. *The Poets of Ireland: A Biographical and Bibliographical Dictionary of Irish Writers of English Verse,* p. 448. Dublin, Hodges Figgis; London, Oxford University Press, 1912.

O'Neill, Michael J. "Holloway on Synge's Last Days", *Modern Drama* (Lawrence, Kansas), VI (September 1963), 126-130. [Reprinted in the *Irish Digest* (see below, next entry)]

——————. "Last Days of J. M. Synge", *Irish Digest* (Dublin), LXXX (4 June 1964), 76-79.

Page, Curtis C., ed. *Drama: Synge's Riders to the Sea,* pp. 3-5. Casebooks for Objective Writing. Boston, Ginn, 1966.

Pocock, P. J. "Synge and the Photography of His Time", in J. M. Synge, *The Autobiography of J. M. Synge,* Constructed from the Manuscripts by Alan Price with Fourteen Photographs by J. M Synge and an Essay on Synge and the Photography of His Time by P. J. Pocock. Dublin, The Dolmen Press; London, Oxford University Press, 1965.

Price, Alan F. "Synge's Prose Writings: A First View of the Whole", *Modern Drama* (Lawrence, Kansas), XI (December 1968), 221-226.

Robinson, Lennox. *Ireland's Abbey Theatre: A History, 1899-1951,* pp. 34-36. London, Sidgwick and Jackson, 1951.

Ronsley, Joseph. *Yeats's Autobiography: Life as Symbolic Pattern,* pp. 123-128. Cambridge, Massachusetts, Harvard University Press, 1968.

Saddlemyer, Ann, ed. "Synge to MacKenna: The Mature Years", *The Massachusetts Review* (Amherst), V (Winter 1964), 279-296.

"The 'Saturday' on Synge", *The Irish Book Lover* (Dublin), II (March 1911), 126. [Extract from *The Saturday Review* (London), 27 March 1909, p. 388]

"Scrap Book", *The Irish Book Lover* (Dublin), III (September 1911), 31-32. [Extract from John Masefield's article in the *Contemporary Review* (London), XCIX (April 1911), 470-478.

Skelton, Robin. *J. M. Synge and His World*. London, Thames and Hudson, 1971.

—————, and David R. Clark. *Irish Renaissance*, A Gathering of Essays, Memoirs, Letters, and Dramatic Poetry from *The Massachusetts Review*, pp. 16, 18, 20, 65-79. Dublin, Dolmen; London, Oxford University Press, 1965. [Reprinted from *The Massachusetts Review* (Amherst), V (Winter 1964)]

Stephens, James. "Reminiscences of J. M. Synge", in *James, Seumas & Jacques: Unpublished Writings of James Stephens*, pp. 54-60. Chosen and edited with an introduction by Lloyd Frankenberg. London and New York, Macmillan, 1964.

Synge, (Rev.) Samuel. *Letters to My Daughter: Memories of John Millington Synge*. Dublin and Cork, Talbot Press, 1931.

Téry, Simone. "J. M. Synge et son oeuvre", *Revue Anglo-Américaine* (Paris), II (1924), 204-216. [See pp. 204-208]

Triesch, Manfred. "Some Unpublished J. M. Synge Papers", *English Language Notes* (Boulder, Colorado), IV (September 1966), 49-51.

Völker, Klaus. *Irisches Theater I: William Butler Yeats [und] John Millington Synge*. Friedrichs Dramatiker des Welttheaters, Band 29. Velber bei Hannover, Friedrich, 1967.

Yeats, Jack B. "With Synge in Connemara", in W. B. Yeats, *Synge and the Ireland of His Time by William Butler Yeats with a Note Concerning a Walk through Connemara with Him by Jack Butler Yeats*. Churchtown, Dundrum, Cuala Press, 1911.

Yeats, John Butler. *J. B. Yeats: Letters to His Son W. B. Yeats and Others, 1869-1922*, edited by Joseph Hone. London, Faber and Faber, 1944.

Yeats, William Butler. *Autobiographies*. London, Macmillan, 1955. [Consisting of "Reveries over Childhood and Youth", "The Trembling of the Veil", "Dramatis Pᴇrsonae", "Estrangement", "The Death of Synge" and "The Bount ᶜ Sweden".]

—————. *Autobiographies: Reveries over Childhood and Youth and*

The Trembling of the Veil, pp. 423-427. London, Macmillan, 1926. [The contents of the American edition, published in New York, Macmillan, 1927, are the same as those of the English edition]

—————. *The Autobiography of William Butler Yeats. Consisting of Reveries over Childhood and Youth. The Trembling of the Veil and Dramatis Personae*, pp. 292-295. New York, Macmillan, 1938.

—————. *The Cutting of an Agate*, pp. 111-113, 124-125, 128-129. New York, Macmillan, 1912. [London edition of 1919 is the same as the New York 1912 edition. Both editions include the following essays: "The Tragic Theatre" (pp. 25-35), "Preface to the First Edition of The Well of The Saints" (pp. 111-122), "Preface to the First Edition of John M. Synge's Poems and Translations" (pp. 123-129), "J. M. Synge and the Ireland of His Time" (pp. 130-176)]

—————. "The Death of Synge, and Other Pages from an Old Diary", *The Dial* (Chicago), LXXXIV (April 1928), 271-288. [The same article appears in *The London Mercury* (see below, next entry) with the title word "Pages" altered to "Passages"]

—————. "The Death of Synge, and Other Passages from an Old Diary", *The London Mercury*, XVII (April 1928), 637-651.

—————. *The Death of Synge, and Other Passages from an Old Diary*, pp. 10, 11, 12-13, 14-15, 15-16, 16-17, 18-19, 23-24. Dublin, Cuala Press, 1928.

—————. *Dramatis Personae, 1896-1902, Estrangement, The Death of Synge, The Bounty of Sweden*, pp. 185-186. London, Macmillan, 1936. [New York, Macmillan, 1936 edition: pp. 194-195]

—————. *Essays and Introductions*, pp. 238-239, 298-305, 306-310, 311-342, 515, 527, 528, 529. New York and London, Macmillan, 1961. [Includes the following essays: "Preface to the First Edition of *The Well of The Saints*" (pp. 298-305), "Preface to the First Edition of John M. Synge's *Poems and Translations*" (pp. 306-310), "J. M. Synge and the Ireland of His Time" (pp. 311-342)]

—————. "J. M. Synge and the Ireland of His Time", *The Forum* (New York), XLVI (August 1911), 179-200.

—————. "More Memories", *The Dial* (Chicago), LXXIII (September 1922), 283-302. [For Yeats's famous description of his meeting Synge in Paris, see pp. 298-301. Reprinted in *The Trembling of the Veil*, 1922; and in *Autobiographies*, 1926]

—————. "A People's Theatre: A Letter to Lady Gregory", *The Dial* (Chicago), LXVIII (April 1920), 458-468. [See pp. 461, 463, 464]

—————. *The Trembling of the Veil*, pp. 217-219. London, T. W. Laurie, 1922.

GENERAL DRAMATIC CRITICISM

Adams, J. Donald. "The Irish Dramatic Movement", *The Harvard Monthly* (Cambridge, Mass.), LIII (November 1911), 44-48. [See pp. 46-47]

Andrews, Charlton. *The Drama To-Day,* pp. 161-164. Philadelphia and London, J. B. Lippincott, 1913.

Armstrong, William Arthur. "Introduction: The Irish Dramatic Movement", in *Classic Irish Drama.* Penguin Play No. PL 54. Harmondsworth, Middlesex, Penguin, 1964. [See pp. 10-11]

Aufhauser, Annemarie. *Sind die Dramen von John Millington Synge durch französische Vorbilder beeinflusst?* Inaugural Dissertation. Würzburg, Richard Mayr, 1935.

Aughtry, Charles Edward, ed. "John Millington Synge (1871-1909)", in *Landmarks in Modern Drama: From Ibsen to Ionesco,* pp. 418-419. Boston, Houghton Mifflin, 1963.

Bateman, Reginald. "Synge—A Fragment", in *Reginald Bateman, Teacher and Soldier: A Memorial Volume of Selections from His Lectures and Other Writings,* pp. 85-91. London, printed for the University of Saskatchewan, Saskatoon, Canada and published for the university by H. Sotheran and Co., 1922.

Bellinger, Martha Fletcher. *A Short History of the Drama,* pp. 344-345. New York, Henry Holt, 1927.

Bennett, Charles A. "The Plays of John M. Synge", *Yale Review* (New Haven), n.s. I (January 1912), 192-205.

Bickley, Francis Lawrance. *J. M. Synge and the Irish Dramatic Movement,* pp. 32-48. London, Constable; Boston and New York, Houghton Mifflin, 1912.

──────. "Synge and the Drama", *The New Quarterly* (London), III (February 1910), 73-84.

Blake, Warren Barton. "A Great Irish Playwright", *The Theatre* (New York), XIII (June 1911), 202-204.

──────. "An Irish Playwright", *The Independent* (New York), LXX (13 April 1911), 792-793. [A review of J. W. Luce and Co. edition, *The Tinker's Wedding*]

Blake, Warren Barton. "John Synge and His Plays", *The Dial* (Chicago), L (16 January 1911), 37-41. [See pp. 39-41]

Block, Haskell M., and Robert G. Shedd, eds. "John Millington Synge (1871-1909)", and "The Playboy of the Western World", in *Masters of Modern Drama*, pp. 397-398, 404. New York, Random House, 1962.

Bourgeois, Maurice. *John Millington Synge and the Irish Theatre*. London, Constable, 1913; reissued by Benjamin Blom, Bronx, New York, 1965.

Bourniquel, Camille. *Ireland*, translated by John Fisher, pp. 159, 160-161, 162. London, Vista Books; New York Viking Press, 1960. [The French edition of *Irlande* (Paris, Editions du Seuil, 1955) corresponds with the above in paging]

Boyd, Ernest A. "The Abbey Theatre", *Irish Review* (Dublin), II (February 1913), 628-634. [See pp. 628-629]

————. "The Impulse to Folk Drama: J. M. Synge and Padraic Colum", in *The Contemporary Drama of Ireland*. Boston, Little, Brown, 1917; Dublin, Talbot Press; London, T. F. Unwin, 1918.

————. "J. M. Synge", in *Ireland's Literary Renaissance*, pp. 316-335. Dublin, Maunsel; London and New York, Knopf, 1916; revised edition, New York, 1922.

————. "Le Théâtre irlandais", *Revue de Paris*, V (September-October 1913), 191-205.

Bradbrook, Muriel Clara. *English Dramatic Form: A History of Its Development*, pp. 128, 130. London, Chatto and Windus; New York, Barnes and Noble, 1965.

Brown, Alan L. "John Millington Synge (1871-1909)", *The London Quarterly and Holborn Review*, CLXXV: 1 (January 1950), 44-49.

Brown, John R. [Review of Alan Price, *Synge and Anglo-Irish Drama*], *Modern Language Review* (London), LVII (July 1962), 434-435.

Brugsma, Rebecca Pauline Christine. *The Beginnings of the Irish Revival*, Part I, pp. 94-97. Groningen and Batavia, P. Noordhoff, [1933]. [Generally discusses *Shadow* and *Playboy*]

Brulé, A[ndré]. "John M. Synge: *Plays*", *Revue Anglo-Américaine* (Paris), XI (October 1933), 61-63. [Review of G. Allen and Unwin, revised collected edition (1932), *The Works of John M. Synge*]

Bryant, Sophie (Willock). *The Genius of the Gael: A Study in Celtic Psychology and Its Manifestations*, pp. 188-193. London, T. F. Unwin, 1913.

Burton, Richard. "An Irish Playwright—Gladstone and Religion", *The Bellman* (Minneapolis), X (24 June 1911), 786. [Review of J. W.

Luce and Co. editions, *The Aran Islands, The Tinker's Wedding,* and *Riders to the Sea*]

Byrne, Dawson. *The Story of Ireland's National Theatre: The Abbey Theatre, Dublin.* Dublin, Talbot Press, 1929.

Cahalan, Thomas, and Paul A. Doyle. *Modern British and Irish Drama,* pp. 63-71. Hymarx Outline Series, No. 123. Boston, Student Outlines, 1961.

Canby, Henry Seidel. [Review article of J. W. Luce and Co. edition, *The Works;* Francis Bickley, *J. M. Synge and the Irish Dramatic Movement;* P. P. Howe, *J. M. Synge: A Critical Study;* William Butler Yeats, *The Cutting of an Agate*], *Yale Review* (New Haven), n.s. II (July 1913), 767-772.

Cazamian, Louis. "Modern Times (1660-1950): The New Romanticism", in *A History of English Literature,* translated by W. D. MacInnes, and Louis Cazamian. Revised edition, London, Macmillan, 1954; revised edition, London and New York, 1957; revised edition, London, 1960.

Cazamian, Madeleine L. "Le Théâtre de J. M. Synge", *La Revue du Mois* (Paris), XII (10 October 1911), 456-468.

Chandler, Frank Wadleigh. *Aspects of Modern Drama.* New York, Macmillan, 1914.

Chew, Samuel C., and Richard D. Altick. "Synge", *A Literary History of England,* edited by Albert C. Baugh, pp. 1513-1514. New York, Appleton-Century-Crofts, 1948.

Chica Salas, Susana. "Synge y García Lorca: Approximación de dos mundos poéticos", *Revista hispánica moderna* (New York), XXVII:2 (April 1961), 128-137.

Clark, Barrett Harper, and George Freedley, eds. *A History of Modern Drama.* New York and London, D. Appleton-Century, 1947.

Clark, James M. "The Irish Literary Movement", *Englische Studien* (Leipzig), XLIX (July 1915), 50-98. [See pp. 69-80]

Clark, William Smith, ed. "Introduction to *The Playboy of the Western World.* The Rise of the Irish Theater and Drama: Synge and Folk-Comedy", in *Chief Patterns of World Drama: Aeschylus to Anderson,* pp. 887-891. Boston, Houghton Mifflin, 1946.

Cohn, Ruby, and Bernard F. Dukore, eds. "John Millington Synge, 1871-1909", in *Twentieth Century Drama: England, Ireland, the United States,* pp. 91-94. New York, Random House, 1966.

Collins, Arthur S. *English Literature of the Twentieth Century,* pp. 290-294. London, University Tutorial Press, 1951.

Colum, Mary M. "Shaw and Synge", *Forum and Century* (New York), XCIV (December 1935), 357-358.

Colum, Padraic. *The Road Round Ireland*, pp. 352-373. New York, Macmillan, 1926.

Conacher, W. M. "The Irish Literary Movement", *Queen's Quarterly* (Kingston, Ontario), XLV (Spring 1938), 56-65.

Connell, F. Norreys. "John Millington Synge", *The English Review* (London), II (June 1909), 609-613.

Coxhead, Elizabeth. *J. M. Synge and Lady Gregory*. Writers and Their Work, No. 149. London, Longmans, Green, for the British Council and the National Book League, 1962.

Cunliffe, John William. "John Millington Synge (1871-1909)", in *English Literature During the Last Half Century*, pp. 231-237. New York, Macmillan, 1919.

————. "The Irish Drama and J. M. Synge (1871-1909)", in *Modern English Playwrights: A Short History of the English Drama from 1825*, pp. 131-142. New York and London, Harper, 1927.

Dickinson, Page L. *The Dublin of Yesterday*. London, Methuen, 1929.

Dickinson, Thomas Herbert. *An Outline of Contemporary Drama*, pp. 227-228. Boston and New York, Houghton Mifflin, 1927.

Dietrich, Margaret [Margarete]. *Das moderne Drama: Strömungen, Gestalten, Motive*, pp. 366-367. Stuttgart, Alfred Kröner, 1961.

Dooley, Roger B. *Modern British and Irish Drama*, pp. 92-95. Monarch Review Notes and Study Guide, No. 624. New York, Thor Publications, 1964.

"Drama", *The Nation* (New York), XCIII (30 November 1911), 528-529. [A critique of the Irish plays presented in America, largely devoted to Synge's works and, in particular, *Well* and *Playboy*]

Dukes, Ashley. "J. M. Synge", in *The Youngest Drama: Studies of Fifty Dramatists*, pp. 50-51. London, Ernest Benn, 1923.

Dyboski, Roman. "Dramat: John Millington Synge (1871-1909)", in *Sto Lat Literatury Angielskiej*, pp. 825-836. Warsaw, "Pax", 1957.

Eaton, Walter Prichard. *The Drama in English*, pp. 288-290. New York, Scribner's, 1930. [A short discussion of Synge's dramatic dialogue and the influence it had on Eugene O'Neill]

————. "Some Plays Worth While", *The American Magazine* (New York), LXXIII (February 1912), 487-496. [See p. 492]

Edwards, Philip. [Review of Alan Price, *Synge and Anglo-Irish Drama*], *Review of English Studies* (Oxford), n.s. XIII (August 1962), 320-322.

Ellehauge, Martin. "J. M. Synge", in *Striking Figures Among Modern English Dramatists*, pp. 16-29. Copenhagen, Levin and Munksgaard, 1931.

Ellis-Fermor, Una Mary. "John Millington Synge", in *The Irish Dramatic Movement*. London, Methuen, 1939.

——————. "Synge, (Edmund) John Millington (1871-1909)", in *The Oxford Companion to the Theatre*, edited by Phyllis Hartnoll, p. 931. Third edition, London, Oxford University Press, 1967. [With the exception of a few minor differences, this is the same article as appears in the second edition (see below, next entry), and exactly the same as in the first edition]

——————. "Synge, John Millington (1871-1909)", in *The Oxford Companion to the Theatre*, edited by Phyllis Hartnoll, pp. 780-781. London, Oxford University Press, 1951; second edition, London, 1957.

Elton, Oliver. *Modern Studies*, pp. 308-312. London, Edward Arnold, 1907.

Enright, Dennis Joseph. "A Note on Irish Literature and the Irish Tradition", *Scrutiny* (Cambridge, England), X (January 1942), 247-255. [See pp. 252-254]

Erskine, John. *The Delight of Great Books*, pp. 310-313. New York, Columbia University Press, 1916.

Ervine, St. John Greer. *How to Write a Play*, pp. 20-22. London, G. Allen and Unwin; New York, Macmillan, 1928.

——————. *Some Impressions of My Elders*, pp. 116-118, 129-132, 198-202. New York, Macmillan, 1922. [Most of this material was reprinted from *The North American Review* (see below, next two entries, for cross references)]

——————. "Some Impressions of My Elders: Bernard Shaw and J. M. Synge", *The North American Review* (New York), CCXI (May 1920), 669-681. [See pp. 673-675; reprinted in *Some Impressions of My Elders*, pp. 198-202]

——————. "Some Impressions of My Elders: John Galsworthy", *The North American Review* (New York), CCXIII (March 1921), 371-384. [See pp. 372-374; reprinted in *Some Impressions of My Elders*, pp. 116-118]

Evans, Sir Benjamin Ifor. *A Short History of English Drama*, pp. 179-180. Pelican Books No. 172. Harmondsworth, Middlesex, Penguin,

1948; revised library edition, London and New York, Staples Press, 1950; second edition, revised and enlarged, Riverside Studies in Literature, Boston, Houghton Mifflin, 1965.

Farmer, A. J. [Review of Jan Setterquist, *Ibsen and the Beginnings of Anglo-Irish Drama, I. John Millington Synge*], *Revue de Littérature Comparée* (Paris), XXVII (July-September 1953), 369-370.

Fausset, Hugh L'A. "Synge and Tragedy", *The Fortnightly Review* (London), CXXI, n.s. CXV (1 February 1924), 258-273. [See pp. 266-271]

Fay, Gerard. *The Abbey Theatre: Cradle of Genius.* Dublin, Clonmore and Reynolds; London, Hollis and Carter; New York, Macmillan, 1958.

Fay, William George, and Catherine Carswell. *The Fays of the Abbey Theatre: An Autobiographical Record.* London, Rich and Cowan; New York, Harcourt, Brace, 1935.

Fay, William P. "Le Théâtre National Irlandais ou les débuts de l'Abbey Theatre", *La Revue [des Deux Mondes]* (Paris), No. 17 (1 September 1959), 93-103. [See pp. 98-100]

Fehr, Bernhard. "Das Drama der keltischen Renaissance: Synge und Colum", in *Die englische Literatur des 19. und 20. Jahrhunderts,* pp. 503-504. Berlin-Neubabelsberg, Akademische Verlagsgesellschaft Athenaion, 1923.

Figgis, Darrell. "The Art of J. M. Synge", *The Fortnightly Review* (London), XCVI, n.s. CX (1 December 1911), 1056-1068. [See pp. 1060-1068. Virtually the same article appears in *The Forum* (see below, next entry)]

—————. "The Art of J. M. Synge", *The Forum* (New York), XLVII (January 1912), 55-70. [See pp. 60-70. Reprinted in *Studies and Appreciations* (see below, next entry)]

—————. "J. M. Synge" and "The Art of J. M. Synge", in *Studies and Appreciations,* pp. 23-33, 34-59. London, J. M. Dent, 1912.

Fletcher, Rev. D. "The Plays of Synge", *Transactions of the Rochdale Literary and Scientific Society* (Rochdale, England), XI (1912-1913), 99-104.

Flood, Jeanne. [Review of J. M. Synge, *Collected Works, Vols. III and IV,* edited by Ann Saddlemyer], *Eire-Ireland* (St. Paul, Minnesota), III: 4 (Winter 1968), 143-144.

Fraser, George Sutherland. *The Modern Writer and His World,* pp. 157-159. London, Derek Verschoyle, 1953.

Fréchet, René. [Review article of J. M. Synge, *Collected Works:* Vol. I, *Poems,* edited by Robin Skelton; Vol. II, *Prose,* edited by Alan

Price; Vols. III and IV, *Plays,* edited by Ann Saddlemyer], *Etudes Anglaises* (Paris), Année XXI, No. 3 (July-September 1968), 320-323.

──────. [Review of Alan Price, *Synge and Anglo-Irish Drama*], *Etudes Anglaises* (Paris), Annee XXI, No. 3 (July-September 1968), 319.

──────. [Review of Jan Setterquist, *Ibsen and the Beginnings of Anglo-Irish Drama, I. John Millington Synge*], *Etudes Anglaises* (Paris), VII (January 1954), 132-133.

──────. "Le Thème de la parole dans le théâtre de J. M. Synge", *Etudes Anglaises* (Paris), Année XXI, No. 3 (July-September 1968), 243-256.

Freyer, Grattan. "The Irish Contribution", in *The Pelican Guide to English Literature: The Modern Age,* Vol. 7, edited by Boris Ford. Baltimore, Penguin, 1961; reprinted with revisions, 1964.

──────. "The Little World of J. M. Synge", *Politics and Letters* (London), 1:4 (Summer 1948), 5-12.

Fricker, Robert. "Synge, O'Casey und Johnston", in *Das moderne englische Drama,* pp. 45-68. Göttingen, Vandenhoeck and Ruprecht, 1964. [See pp. 45-52]

Ganz, Arthur. "J. M. Synge and the Drama of Art", *Modern Drama* (Lawrence, Kansas), X (May 1967), 57-68.

Gaskell, Ronald. "The Realism of J. M. Synge", *Critical Quarterly* (London), V (Autumn 1963), 242-248.

Gassner, John W., ed. "John Millington Synge (1871-1909)", in *A Treasury of the Theatre: From Henrik Ibsen to Arthur Miller,* pp. 626-627. Revised edition for colleges, New York, Simon and Schuster, 1950. [See below, next two entries, for same essay]

──────. *A Treasury of the Theatre,* III, 626-627. Revised edition, New York, Simon and Schuster, 1951.

──────. *A Treasury of the Theatre: From Henrik Ibsen to Eugene Ionesco,* pp. 626-627. Third College edition, Simon and Schuster, 1960.

──────. "John Millington Synge and the Irish Muse", in *Masters of the Drama,* pp. 553-562. New York, Random House, [1940]; Third revised and enlarged edition, New York, 1945.

──────. "John Millington Synge: Synthesis in Folk Drama", in *The Theatre In Our Times: A Survey of the Men, Materials and*

Movements in the Modern Theatre, pp. 216-224. New York, Crown Publishers, 1954.

Gill, Michael J. "Neo-Paganism and the Stage", *The New Ireland Review* (Dublin), n.s. XXVII: 3 (May 1907), 179-187. [See pp. 184-186]

Grebanier, Bernard D. N., Samuel Middlebrook, Stith Thompson, and William Watt, eds. "John Millington Synge (1871-1909)", in *English Literature and Its Backgrounds: From the Forerunners of Romanticism to the Present*, II, 1056-1057. Revised edition, New York, Dryden Press, 1949.

Greene, David H., and Edward M. Stephens. *J. M. Synge: 1871-1909*. New York, Macmillan, 1959.

Gregory, Lady Isabella Augusta. "The Coming of the Irish Players", *Collier's* (New York), XLVIII (21 October 1911), 15, 24.

Guerrero Zamora, Juan. "John Millington Synge", in *Historia del teatro contemporaneo*, III, 28-33. Barcelona, Juan Flors, 1962.

Gwynn, Stephen Lucius. *Irish Literature and Drama in the English Language: A Short History*, pp. 161-180. London and New York, Thomas Nelson, 1936.

Habart, Michel. "Le Théâtre irlandais", *Théâtre Populaire* (Paris), No. 9 (September-October 1954), 24-43.

Hamilton, Clayton Meeker. "The Irish National Theatre, V. [John M. Synge]", *The Bookman* (New York), XXXIV (January 1912), 508-516. [See pp. 513-516]

——————. *Studies in Stagecraft*, pp. 138-144. New York, Henry Holt; London, Grant Richards, 1914.

Hatcher, Harlan, ed. "J. M. Synge", in *Modern British Dramas*, pp. 211-216. New York, Harcourt, Brace, 1941.

Henn, Thomas Rice. "The Irish Tragedy (Synge, Yeats, O'Casey)", in *The Harvest of Tragedy*, pp. 197-216. London, Methuen, 1956. [See pp. 201-205]

Hensel, Georg. "Synge: die irische Realität, fröhlich", in *Spielplan: Schauspielführer, von der Antike bis zur Gegenwart*, II, 792-796. Berlin, Propyläen, 1966.

Hoare, Dorothy Mackenzie. *The Works of Morris and of Yeats in Relation to Early Saga Literature*, pp. 105-110. Cambridge (England), Cambridge University Press, 1937.

Hoare, John Edward. "Ireland's National Drama", *North American Review* (New York), CXCIV (October 1911), 566-575. [See pp. 570-573]

Hoare, John Edward. "John Synge", *The University Magazine* (Toronto), X (February 1911), 91-109.

Hogan, John Joseph. [Review of Jan Setterquist, *Ibsen and the Beginnings of Anglo-Irish Drama, I. John Millington Synge*], *Studia Neophilologica* (Upsala), XXIV: 3 (1952), 209-211.

Holloway, Joseph. *Joseph Holloway's Abbey Theatre: A Selection from His Unpublished Journal, "Impressions of a Dublin Playgoer"*, edited by Robert Hogan and Michael J. O'Neill. Carbondale and Edwardsville, Southern Illinois University Press; London and Amsterdam, Feffer and Simons, 1967.

Hortmann, Wilhelm. *Englische Literatur im 20. Jahrhundert*, pp. 30-33. Berne, A. Francke, 1965.

Howarth, Herbert. "Edmund John Millington Synge, 1871-1909", in *The Irish Writers: 1880-1940; Literature Under Parnell's Star*, pp. 212-244. London, Rockliff, 1958; New York, Hill and Wang, 1959.

Howe, Percival Presland. *J. M. Synge: A Critical Study*. London, Martin Secker, 1912.

——————. *The Repertory Theatre: A Record and a Criticism*. London, Martin Secker, 1910; New York, Mitchell Kennerley, 1911.

Hudson, Lynton. *The Twentieth Century Drama*, pp. 41-44. London, G. G. Harrap, 1946.

Huneker, James. "John M. Synge", in *The Pathos of Distance: A Book of a Thousand and One Moments*, pp. 228-235. New York, Scribner's, 1913.

Huscher, Herbert. [Review article of Alan Price, *Synge and Anglo-Irish Drama*], *Anglia: Zeitschrift für englische Philologie* (Tübingen), LXXX (1962), 226-231. [See pp. 229-231]

"Immortalizing Synge", *Current Literature* (New York), LIII (December 1912), 695. [A review of P. P. Howe, *J. M. Synge: A Critical Study;* J. W. Luce and Co. edition, *The Works*]

Irish Plays, pp. 8-10. Toured under the direction of Alfred Wareing, summer 1906. Dublin, n.p., 1906. [A pamphlet of 12 pages found, as far as I know, only at the New York Public Library. Contains plot outlines of *Riders* (p. 8) and *Shadow* (pp. 9-10)]

"The Irish Theatre as an Exponent of the Irish People", *The American Review of Reviews* (New York), XLV (March 1912), 356-357.

Jackson, Holbrook. "John M. Synge", in *All Manner of Folk: Interpretations and Studies*, pp. 61-77. London, Grant Richards; New York, Mitchell Kennerley, 1912.

Jameson, Storm. *Modern Drama in Europe,* pp. 212-216. New York, Harcourt; London, W. Collins, 1920.

Jeffares, A. Norman. [Review of Jan Setterquist, *Ibsen and the Beginnings of Anglo-Irish Drama, I. John Millington Synge*], *Neuphilologische Mitteilungen* (Helsinki) LIV: 7-8 (1953), 371-373.

"John Synge and His Critics", *The Independent* (New York), LXXIII (7 November 1912), 1071-1073. [A review article of Francis Bickley, *J. M. Synge and the Irish Dramatic Movement;* P. P. Howe, *J. M. Synge: A Critical Study;* W. B. Yeats, *J. M. Synge and the Ireland of His Time*]

Johnston, Denis. *John Millington Synge.* Columbia Essays on Modern Writers, No. 12. New York and London, Columbia University Press, 1965.

Kaul, R. K. "Synge as a Dramatist: An Evaluation", *An English Miscellany* (St. Stephen's College, Delhi), III (1965), 37-51.

Kavanagh, Peter. *The Story of The Abbey Theatre: From Its Origins in 1899 to the Present.* New York, Devin-Adair, 1950.

Kelly, Blanche Mary. *The Voice of the Irish,* pp. 264-268. New York, Sheed and Ward, 1952.

Kenny, M. "The Plays of the 'Irish' Players", *America* (New York), VI (4 November 1911), 78-79.

Kernan, Alvin B. [Introductory Essay to *Riders to the Sea*], in *Character and Conflict: An Introduction to Drama,* pp. 557-558. Second edition, New York, Harcourt, Brace and World, 1969.

Kleinstück, Johannes Walter. *W. B. Yeats oder: Der Dichter in der modernen Welt,* pp. 54-56. Hamburg, Leibniz-Verlag, 1963.

Knight, George Wilson. *The Golden Labyrinth: A Study of British Drama,* pp. 323-325. New York, Norton; London, Phoenix House, 1962.

Kraft, Irma. *Plays, Players, Playhouses: International Drama of Today,* pp. 147-148. New York, George Dobsevage, 1928.

Krause, David. " 'The Rageous Ossean': Patron-Hero of Synge and O'Casey", *Modern Drama* (Lawrence, Kansas), IV (December 1961), 268-291.

—————. *Sean O'Casey: The Man and His Work.* London, MacGibbon and Kee, 1960.

—————. "Synge und das irische Melodrama", *Theater heute* (Hanover), V: 3 (March 1964), 62-63.

Krieger, Hans. "J. M. Synge", *Die neueren Sprachen* (Marburg), XXIV

(1916), 602-605. [Reprinted in *John Millington Synge* (see below, next entry)]

Krieger, Hans. *John Millington Synge, ein Dichter der "keltischen Renaissance"*, pp. 9-16, 110-147. Inaugural Dissertation. Marburg, N. G. Elwert'sche, 1916.

Kronenberger, Louis. "Synge", in *The Thread of Laughter: Chapters on English stage Comedy from Jonson to Maugham*, pp. 279-288. New York, Knopf, 1952.

Lalou, René. "Synge et le théâtre", in *Panorama de la littérature anglaise contemporaine*, pp. 189-195. Paris, Editions KRA, 1926.

Lamm, Martin. *Det moderna dramat*, pp. 308-319. Stockholm, A. Bonniers, 1948.

—————. *Modern Drama*, translated by Karin Elliott. Oxford, Basil Blackwell, 1952. [See pp. 302-314]

Leyburn, Ellen Douglass. "The Theme of Loneliness in the Plays of Synge", *Modern Drama* (Lawrence, Kansas), I (September 1958), 84-90.

Lieder, Paul Robert, Robert Morss Lovett, and Robert Kilburn Root, eds. "John Millington Synge, 1871-1909", in *British Poetry and Prose*, II, 908-909. Revised edition, Boston and New York, Houghton Mifflin, 1938.

Liljegren, S. B. [Review of Just Thorning, *J. M. Synge: En moderne irsk Dramatiker*], *Englische Studien* (Leipzig), LVIII (1924), 294-296.

Love, Henry Melville. "John Millington Synge", *The Colonnade* (New York), VII (April 1914), 224-229.

Lowther, George. "J. M. Synge and the Irish Revival", *The Oxford and Cambridge Review* (London), No. 25 (November 1912), 43-59.

Lynd, Robert. "The Fame of J. M. Synge", in *Old and New Masters*, pp. 94-97. London, T. F. Unwin, 1919; reissued Freeport, New York, Books for Libraries Press, 1970.

—————. *Home Life in Ireland*, pp. 311-312. London, Mills and Boon, 1909.

—————. *Ireland a Nation*, pp. 171, 174-176. London, Grant Richards, 1919. [American edition, New York, Dodd, Mead, 1920; see pp. 192, 205, 208-211]

—————. "The Nation and the Man of Letters", *Dana* (Dublin), I (April 1905), 371-376. [See pp. 373-376]

MacCarthy, B. G. [Review of Jan Setterquist, *Ibsen and the Beginnings of Anglo-Irish Drama, I. John Millington Synge*], *Modern Language Review* (Cambridge, England), XLIX (January 1954), 73-75.

MacCarthy, Sir Desmond. *Theatre,* pp. 41-44. London, MacGibbon and Kee, 1954.

McHugh, Roger. "Yeats, Synge and the Abbey Theatre", *Studies* (Dublin), XLI (September and December 1952), 333-340. [A review of Jan Setterquist, *Ibsen and the Beginnings of Anglo-Irish Drama, I. John Millington Synge;* see pp. 335-337]

McMahon, Seán. "Clay and Worms", *Eire-Ireland* (St. Paul, Minnesota), V: 4 (Winter 1970), 116-134. [See pp. 123-133]

MacSiubhlaigh, Máire [Mary Walker], and Edward Kenny. *The Splendid Years: Recollections of M. Nic Shiubhlaigh,* as told to Edward Kenny, pp. 39-48, 53-56, 59, 62-63, 79-88, 106-107, 112. Dublin, James Duffy, 1955.

Maguire, Mary C. "John Synge", *The Irish Review* (Dublin), I (March 1911), 39-43. [A review article of Maunsel and Co. edition, *The Works*]

Mair, George Herbert. *English Literature: Modern,* pp. 246-248. Home University Library of Modern Knowledge. New York, Henry Holt; London, Williams and Norgate, [1911]. [See below, next two entries, for same essay]

――――――――. *English Literature, Modern: 1450-1939,* pp. 207-209. Home University Library of Modern Knowledge. Second edition, revised and enlarged, London and New York, Oxford University Press, 1944.

――――――――, and Alfred Charles Wood. *Modern English Literature: 1450-1959,* pp. 207-209. Third revised edition, London, Oxford University Press, 1960.

Malone, Andrew E. *The Irish Drama.* London, Constable; New York, Scribner's, 1929.

Marriott, James William. *Modern Drama,* pp. 194-197. London, Thomas Nelson, [1934]

Melchinger, Siegfried. *Drama zwischen Shaw und Brecht,* pp. 388-389. Bremen, Carl Schünemann, 1957.

――――――――, and Henning Rischbieter, eds. "John Millington Synge (1871-1909)", in *Welttheater: Bühnen, Autoren, Inszenierungen,* pp. 429-430. Wien, Buchgemeinschaft Donauland, 1962.

Mencken, H. L. "The New Dramatic Literature", *The Smart Set* (New York), XXXIV: 4 (August 1911), 151-158. [A review of J. W. Luce and Co. editions, *Riders to the Sea* and *The Tinker's Wedding;* see pp. 152-153]

Mercier, Vivian. "Irish Comedy: The Probable and the Wonderful", *University Review* (Dublin), VIII (1956), 45-53.

—————. *The Irish Comic Tradition*. Oxford, The Clarendon Press, 1962.

Miller, Anna Irene. "The National Theatre of Ireland", in *The Independent Theatre in Europe: 1887 to the Present*. New York, Ray Long and R. R. Smith, 1931; reissued New York, Benjamin Blom, 1966.

Miller, Nellie Burget. "Synge: The Drama of Contemporary Peasant Life", in *The Living Drama*, pp. 337-340. New York and London, Century, 1924.

Montague, Charles Edward. "The Plays of J. M. Synge", in *Dramatic Values*, pp. 1-15. London, Methuen, 1911; Third edition, revised, London, Methuen, 1925.

Morris, Lloyd R. *The Celtic Dawn: A Survey of the Renascence in Ireland, 1889-1916*, pp. 124-134. New York, Macmillan, 1917.

Moses, Montrose J. "W. B. Yeats and the Irish Players", *The Metropolitan Magazine* (New York), XXXV (January 1912), 23-25, 61-62.

—————, ed. "John Millington Synge (1871-1909)", in *Representative British Dramas: Victorian and Modern*, pp. 787-789. Boston, Little, Brown, 1918; revised edition, Boston, 1931.

"New Poems and Plays", *The American Review of Reviews* (New York), XLVI (December 1912), 750-752. [A review of P. P. Howe, *J. M. Synge: A Critical Study*, see pp. 750-751]

"A New Thing in the Theater: Some Impressions of the Much-Discussed 'Irish Players' ", *Harper's Weekly* (New York), LV (9 December 1911), 19.

Nicoll, Allardyce. *British Drama: An Historical Survey from the Beginnings to the Present Time*, pp. 404-410, 449-451. New York, T. Y. Crowell; London, G. G. Harrap, 1925; third revised edition, London, 1932; fourth revised edition, London, 1947.

—————. *World Drama: From Aeschylus to Anouilh*, pp. 690-695. London, G. G. Harrap, [1949].

Nordman, C. A. "J. M. Synge, Dramatikern", *Finsk Tidskrift för Vitterhet, Vetenskap, Konst Och Politik* (Helsinki), LXXIX (July-December 1915), 26-70.

O'Brien, Maurice N. *Some Irish Plays: A Selection*. Play Bureau Publacation, No. 10. New York, National Play Bureau, Federal Theatre Project, 1937.

O'Connor, Brother Anthony Cyril. "Synge and National Drama",

Unitas: Revista de cultura y vida universitaria (Manila), XXVII: 2 (April 1954), 294-346. See pp. 318-346]

—————. "Synge and National Drama", *Unitas: Revista de cultura y vida universitaria* (Manila), XXVII: 3 (July 1954), 430-464. [See pp. 444-463]

O'Connor, Frank [Michael Francis O'Donovan]. *The Backward Look: A Survey of Irish Literature*. London, Macmillan, 1967. [The American edition has a different title: *A Short History of Irish Literature: A Backward Look*. New York, G. P. Putnam, (1967)]

—————. "All the Olympians", *Saturday Review* (New York), XLIX (10 December 1966), 30-32, 99. [Reprinted in *The Backward Look: A Survey of Irish Literature*, London, 1967, pp. 183-189]

—————."Synge", in *The Irish Theatre*. Lectures delivered during the Abbey Theatre Festival held in Dublin in August 1938, edited by Lennox Robinson, pp. 41-52. London, Macmillan, 1939.

O'Hagan, Thomas. "The Irish Dramatic Movement", in *Essays on Catholic Life*, pp. 57-73. Baltimore, John Murphy, 1916; reissued by Books for Libraries Press, Freeport, New York, 1965, 1969.

O'Hegarty, P. S. "Book Reviews: Synge and Irish Literature", *The Dublin Magazine*, n.s. VII: 1 (January-March 1932), 51-56. [A review article of Daniel Corkery, *Synge and Anglo-Irish Literature*, see pp. 51-53]

O'Mahony, Mathew. *Play Guide for Irish Amateurs*, pp. 23, 28, 61, 70, 77, 88. Dublin, James Duffy, 1946.

—————. *Progress Guide to Anglo-Irish Plays*, pp. xi, 17, 54, 73, 102, 116, 122, 182. Dublin, Progress House, 1960.

Onofrio, Lilia d'. "John M. Synge, dramaturgo irlandes contemporaneo (A propósito de su drama *Jinetes hacia el mar*)", in *Nueve ensayos de critica literaria*, pp. 69-79. Buenos Aires, "El Ateneo", 1942.

O'Ryan, Agnes. "The Drama of the Abbey Theatre", *The Irish Educational Review* (Dublin), VI: 3 (December 1912), 154-163. [See pp. 156-158]

Paul-Dubois, M. Louis. "Le Théâtre irlandais: Synge", *Revue des Deux Mondes* (Paris), XXVII (1 June 1935), 631-657. [See pp. 637-644]

Peacock, Ronald. "Synge", in *The Poet in the Theatre*. London, Routledge and Kegan Paul; New York, Harcourt, Brace, 1946.

Pellizzi, Camillo. *Il teatro inglese*. Il teatro del novecento, collezione critica di "Scenario" diretta da Silvio d'Amico, III, 278-286. Milan, Fratelli Treves, 1934.

—————. *English Drama: The Last Great Phase*, translated by Rowan Williams, pp. 212-218, 256. London, Macmillan, 1935.

Perry, Henry Ten Eyck. *Masters of Dramatic Comedy and Their Social Themes*, pp. 364-366. Cambridge (Massachusetts), Harvard University Press, 1939.

Pittwood, Ernest H. "John Millington Synge", *Holborn Review* (London), LV; n.s. IV (July 1913), 488-501. [A review article of Maunsel and Co. edition, *The Works;* Francis Bickley, *J. M. Synge and the Irish Dramatic Movement;* Darrell Figgis, *Studies and Appreciations*]

"The Players", *Everybody's Magazine* (New York), XXVI (February 1912), 231-242. [See pp. 238 and 240]

"The Poetry of Ireland", *The Living Age* (Boston), CCLXXI (7 October 1911), 15-24. [A review of Maunsel and Co. edition, *The Works,* see pp. 15-19]

"The Poetry of Ireland: I", *The Church Quarterly Review* (London), LXXII (July 1911), 406-421. [A review article of Maunsel and Co. edition, *The Works;* in particular, see part I, pp. 406-413]

Popkin, Henry. "Introduction", in John Millington Synge, *The Playboy of the Western World and Riders to the Sea*. New York, Avon Books, 1967.

Price, Alan F. "Introduction and Notes", in *Emerald Apex: A Selection from J. M. Synge's Studies of Irish People and Places*, pp. vii-xx, 119-128. London and Glasgow, Blackie, 1966.

——. *Synge and Anglo-Irish Drama*. London, Methuen, 1961.

Quinn, Owen. "No Garland for John Synge", *Envoy* (Dublin), III: 11 (October 1950), 44-51.

Rabuse, Georg. "J. M. Synges Verhältnis zur französischen Literatur und besonders zu Maeterlinck", *Archiv für das Studium der neueren Sprachen* (Brunswick, Germany), CLXXIV (1938), 36-53.

——. [Review of Annemarie Aufhauser, *Sind die Dramen von John Millington Synge durch französische Vorbilder beeinflust?*], *Archiv für das Studium der neueren Sprachen* (Brunswick, Germany), CLXXIII (1938), 268-269.

Reade, Arthur Robert. *Main Currents in Modern Literature*, pp. 50-55. London, I. Nicholson and Watson, 1935.

Reeves, Geoffrey. [Review of J. M. Synge, *Four Plays and the Aran Isles*, edited by Robin Skelton], *New Theatre Magazine* (Bristol), III: 4 (July-September 1962), 37-38.

[Review and Appreciation of the Edition de luxe of J. M. Synge, *The Playboy of the Western World*, with ten illustrations in colour by John Keating, R.H.A. Edition de luxe, published by George Allen and Unwin, Ltd.], *Creative Art* (New York), II: 4 (April 1928), 302-303.

[Review of P. P. Howe, *J. M. Synge: A Critical Study*], *The English Review* (London), XII (September 1912), 326-327.

Reynolds, Ernest Randolph, *Modern English Drama: A Survey of the Theatre from 1900*. London, G. G. Harrap, 1949; revised edition, London, 1950.

Rivoallan, Anatole. "J. M. Synge", in *Littérature irlandaise contemporaine*, pp. 21-31. Paris, Hachette, 1939.

Roberts, George. "A National Dramatist", *The Shanachie* (Dublin), II: 3 (March 1907), 57-60.

Robinson, Lennox. *Ireland's Abbey Theatre: A History, 1899-1951*, pp. 36-37, 65-66. London, Sidgwick and Jackson, 1951.

Robinson, Norman L. "J. M. Synge", *The Central Literary Magazine*, (Birmingham, England), XXVIII (April 1927), 53-63.

Roy, James A. "J. M. Synge and the Irish Literary Movement", *Anglia: Zeitschrift für englische Philologie* (Tübingen), XXXVII (1913), 129-145. [A review article of Maunsel and Co. edition, *The Works;* P. P. Howe, *The Repertory Theatre;* P. P. Howe, *J. M. Synge: A Critical Study*, see pp. 139-145]

Ruberti, Guido. *Storia del teatro contemporaneo: L'evoluzione del teatro europeo dalle origini ai tempi nostri*, III, 892-894. Bologne, Licinio Cappelli, 1928.

Rynne, Catherine. "The Playwrights", in *The Story of the Abbey Theatre*, edited by Sean McCann. A Four Square Book. London, The New English Library, 1967. [See pp. 69-70, 73-74, 76-77]

Saddlemyer, Ann. *J. M. Synge and Modern Comedy*. New Dolmen Chapbooks, II. Dublin, Dolmen Press; London, Oxford University Press, 1968. [A lecture given at the Eighth International Yeats Summer School, Sligo, Ireland, 18 August 1967]

——————. "Rabelais *versus* à Kempis: The Art of J. M. Synge", *Komos* (Clayton, Victoria, Australia), 1: 3 (October 1967), 85-96.

——————, ed. "Synge to MacKenna: The Mature Years", *The Massachusetts Review* (Amherst), V (Winter 1964), 279-296.

Salvat, Ricard. *Teatre contemporani*, I, 281-283. Barcelona, Ediciones 62, 1966.

Schubel, Fr. [Review of Jan Setterquist, *Ibsen and the Beginnings of Anglo-Irish Drama, I. John Millington Synge*], *Archiv für das Studium der neueren Sprachen* (Brunswick, Germany), CLXXXXIII (1957), 60-61.

Scott-James, Rolfe Arnold. *Fifty Years of English Literature: 1900-1950*, pp. 91-93. London, Longmans, Green, 1951.

──────. "J. M. Synge", in *Personality in Literature*, pp. 135-139. London, Martin Secker, 1913. [Reprinted from "A Book of the Day: The Dramatist of Ireland", *Daily News* (London), 1 February 1911, p. 3]

──────. "J. M. Synge", in *Personality in Literature: 1913-1931*, pp. 135-139. New York, Henry Holt, 1932. [Same article as above]

Sear, H. G. "John Millington Synge and Music", *The Sackbut* (London), III (November 1922), 119-123. [See pp. 122-123]

Setterquist, Jan. "Ibsen and Synge", *Studia Neophilologica* (Upsala), XXIV (1951/52), 69-75; 136-145; 146-149; 150-151. [Reprinted in *Ibsen and the Beginnings of Anglo-Irish Drama* (see below, next entry)]

──────. *Ibsen and the Beginnings of Anglo-Irish Drama: I. John Millington Synge*. Upsala Irish Studies, Vol. 2, edited by S. B. Liljegren. Upsala, A.-B. Lundequistka; Dublin, Hodges, Figgis; Copenhagen, Munksgaard; Cambridge (Massachusetts), Harvard University Press, 1951.

Sherman, Stuart P. "The Exoticism of John Synge", in *On Contemporary Literature*, pp. 190-210. New York, Henry Holt, 1917.

Short, Ernest Henry. *Sixty Years of Theatre*, pp. 374-376. London, Eyre and Spottiswoode, 1951. [Same article appears in *Theatrical Cavalcade* (see below, next entry)]

──────. *Theatrical Cavalcade*, pp. 206-208. London, Eyre and Spottiswoode, 1942.

Simons, Leo. *Het Drama en Het Tooneel in Hun Ontwikkeling*, V, 552-556. Nederlandsche Bibliotheek. Encyclopaedie in Monografieën. Amsterdam, 1932.

Skelton, Robin. *J. M. Synge and His World*. London, Thames and Hudson, 1971.

──────. *The Writings of J. M. Synge*. London, Thames and Hudson, 1971.

──────, and David R. Clark. *Irish Renaissance:* A Gathering of Essays, Memoirs, Letters, and Dramatic Poetry from *The Massachusetts Review*, pp. 16, 18, 20, 65-79. Dublin, Dolmen; London, Oxford University Press, 1965. [Reprinted from *The Massachusetts Review* (Amherst), V, Winter 1964]

Sobel, Bernard, ed. *The New Theatre Handbook and Digest of Plays*,

p. 632. Eighth edition, completely revised, New York, Crown Publishers, 1959. [For brief plot summaries of plays, see alphabetical listing]

Sobel, Bernard, ed. *The Theatre Handbook and Digest of Plays.* New York, Crown Publishers, 1935; second revised edition, 1940; revised edition, 1948.

Storer, Edward. "Dramatists of To-Day: J. M. Synge", *The British Review* (London), V (January 1914), 73-80. [Reprinted in *The Living Age* (see below, next entry)]

——. "Dramatists of To-Day: V—J. M. Synge", *The Living Age* (Boston), CCLXXX (28 March 1914), 777-781.

Strong, Leonard Alfred George. "J. M. Synge", *Beacon* (London), II (July 1922), 695-701. [See pp. 698-701. Reprinted in *The Living Age* (see below, next entry)]

——. "J. M. Synge", *The Living Age* (Boston), CCCXIV (9 September 1922), 656-660. [See pp. 658-660]

——. "John Millington Synge", *The Bookman* (New York), LXXIII (April 1931), 125-136. [See pp. 130-136. Reprinted in *The Dublin Magazine* (see below, next entry)]

——. "John Millington Synge", *The Dublin Magazine*, n.s. VII: 2 (April-June 1932), 12-32. [See pp. 21-31]

——. *John Millington Synge.* P. E. N. Books. London, Allen and Unwin, 1941.

——. "John Millington Synge" in *Personal Remarks*, pp. 46-62. London, P. Nevill, 1953. [Reprinted from *The Bookman* and *The Dublin Magazine* (see above)]

Styan, John Louis. "Synge and O'Casey", in *The Dark Comedy: The Development of Modern Comic Tragedy*, pp. 146-148. Cambridge (England), Cambridge University Press, 1962. [Second edition, 1968, pp. 130-132]

Synge, (Rev.) Samuel. *Letters to My Daughter: Memories of John Millington Synge*, pp. 286-287. Dublin and Cork, Talbot Press, 1931.

Taylor, Herbert. "The Plays of J. M. Synge", *Papers of the Manchester Literary Club* (Manchester), XXXVI (1910), 160-169. [Published also with *The Manchester Quarterly*]

Tennyson, Charles. "Irish Plays and Playwrights", *The Quarterly Review* (London), CCXV (July 1911), 219-243. [A review of Maunsel and Co. edition, *The Works*, see pp. 231-234]

——. "The Rise of the Irish Theatre", *The Contemporary Review* (London), C (August 1911), 240-247. [See pp. 244-245]

Téry, Simone. "J. M. Synge", in *L'Ile des Bardes: "Notes sur la littérature irlandaise contemporaine"*, pp. 140-166. Paris, Ernest Flammarion, 1925.

—————. "J. M. Synge et son oeuvre", *Revue Anglo-Américaine* (Paris), II (1924), 204-216.

Tilgher, Adriano. "Il teatro di John Millington Synge", in *Studi sul teatro contemporaneo*, pp. 225-228. Rome, Libreria di Scienze e Lettere, 1923.

Tindall, William York. *Forces in Modern British Literature: 1885-1956*, pp. 68-69. New York, Knopf, 1947.

Tobin, Michael. "The Ponderings of a Playgoer", *Iris Hibernia* (Fribourg, Switzerland), IV: 3 (1960), 27-39. [See pp. 33-34]

Townshend, George. "The Irish Drama", *The Drama* (Chicago), I (August 1911), 93-104. [In particular, see pp. 99-104]

Trewin, John Courtenay. *The Theatre Since 1900*. Twentieth Century Histories. London, Andrew Dakers, 1951.

Triyidic, C. "John Millington Synge devant l'opinion irlandaise", *Études Anglaises* (Paris), VII (April 1954), 185-189.

Tupper, James W. "J. M. Synge and His Work", *The Dial* (Chicago), LIV (16 March 1913), 233-235. [A review article of Francis Bickley, *J. M. Synge and the Irish Dramatic Movement;* P. P. Howe, *J. M. Synge: A Critical Study*]

—————. "Synge and the Irish Theatre", *The Dial* (Chicago), LVI (1 March 1914), 177-179. [A review of Maurice Bourgeois, *John Millington Synge and the Irish Theatre*]

Ua Fuaráin, Eoghan. "The Anglo-Irish Dramatic Movement", *Irisleabhar Muighe Nuadhad* (Maynooth), I: 4 (An Cháisg [Easter] 1910), 6-16.

Ulanov, Barry, ed. "John Millington Synge, 1871-1909", in *Makers of the Modern Theater*, pp. 235-237. New York, McGraw-Hill, 1961.

Van Doren, Carl Clinton, and Mark Van Doren. *American and British Literature Since 1890*, pp. 291-297. New York and London, Century, 1925; revised and enlarged edition, New York, Appleton-Century, 1939.

Völker, Klaus. *Irisches Theater I: William Butler Yeats* [und] *John Millington Synge*. Friedrichs Dramatiker des Welttheaters, Band 29. Velber bei Hannover, Friedrich, 1967.

Ward, Alfred Charles. *Twentieth Century Literature: 1901-1940*, pp. 109-111. London, Methuen, 1928; fifth edition, revised, London, 1933; seventh edition, revised and enlarged, London, 1940.

Warnock, Robert, ed. "John Millington Synge (1871-1909)", in *Representative Modern Plays: British,* pp. 338-341. Chicago, Scott, Foresman, 1953.

Watkins, Ann. "The Irish Players in America: Their Purpose and Their Art", *The Craftsman* (New York), XXI (January 1912), 352-363. [See pp. 361-363]

Watson, Ernest Bradlee, and Benfield Pressey, eds. [Introductory Essay to J. M. Synge, *Riders to the Sea*], in *Contemporary Drama: English and Irish Plays,* I, pp. 5-10. New York, Scribner's, 1931. [Reprinted in Ernest Bradlee Watson and Benfield Pressey, eds., *Contemporary Drama: Fifteen Plays, American, English and Irish, European,* pp. 240-242. New York, Scribner's, 1959]

Wauchope, George Armstrong. "The New Irish Drama", *Bulletin of the University of South Carolina* (Columbia), No. 168 (1 October 1925), 1-11. [Extension Division, University of South Carolina, 1925. Reprint from Division for Women Series No. 1, October 1919, see pp. 6-7]

Webb, Geoffrey. "The Best and Worst of Synge", *The Dublin Review* (London), No. 516 (Summer 1968), 165-166. [A review of J. M. Synge, *Collected Works, Vols. III* and *IV, Plays,* edited by Ann Saddlemyer]

Weiss, Samuel A. "The Poet and Dramatist John Millington Synge", in *Drama in the Modern World: Plays and Essays,* p. 175. Boston, D. C. Heath, 1964.

Weygandt, Cornelius. "John Millington Synge", in *Irish Plays and Playwrights,* pp. 160-197. London, Constable; Boston and New York, Houghton Mifflin, 1913.

White, Herbert Oliver. "John Millington Synge", *Irish Writing* (Cork), No. 9 (October 1949), 57-61. [A talk broadcast by the B.B.C. on the Northern Ireland Home Service and later rebroadcast on the Third Programme]

Whiting, Frank M. *An Introduction to the Theatre,* pp. 78-80. New York, Harper and Row, 1954; revised edition, New York, 1961. [New York, 1961 edition, see pp. 83-84]

Whitman, Charles Huntington, ed. "John Millington Synge", in *Representative Modern Dramas,* pp. 771-773. New York, Macmillan, 1936.

Williams, Harold. *Modern English Writers: Being a Study of Imaginative Literature, 1890-1914,* pp. 206-216. New York, Knopf, 1919.

Williams, Raymond. "J. M. Synge", in *Drama: From Ibsen to Eliot,* pp. 154-174. London, Chatto and Windus, 1952.

Wyatt, Euphemia van Rennselaer. "Three Plays", *The Catholic World* (New York), CLXXXV (May 1957), 148. [A review of *Riders, Shadow,* and *Tinker's*]

Yeats, John Butler. "Synge and the Irish", in *Essays Irish and American,* pp. 51-61. Dublin, Talbot Press; London, T. F. Unwin; New York, Macmillan, 1918.

Yeats, William Butler. *Autobiographies.* London, Macmillan, 1955. [Consisting of "Reveries over Childhood and Youth", "The Trembling of the Veil", "Dramatis Personae", "Estrangement", "The Death of Synge" and "The Bounty of Sweden".]

──────. *The Autobiography of William Butler Yeats. Consisting of Reveries over Childhood and Youth, The Trembling of the Veil and Dramatis Personae,* pp. 185, 266, 292-295, 322, 323, 356, 374, 375, 376, 385, 403-404, 412, 416, 417, 421, 422, 431, 432-436, 437-438, 441, 442-444, 446-448, 451, 470. New York, Macmillan, 1938.

──────. *The Cutting of an Agate,* pp. 114-122, 126-129, 152-154, 168-169, 170, 171. New York, Macmillan, 1912. [London edition of 1919 is the same as the New York 1912 edition. Both editions include the following essays: "The Tragic Theatre" (pp. 25-35), "Preface to the First Edition of *The Well of The Saints*" (pp. 111-122), "Preface to the First Edition of John M. Synge's Poems and Translations" (pp. 123-129), "J. M. Synge and the Ireland of His Time", (pp. 130-176)]

──────. *The Death of Synge, and Other Passages from an Old Diary,* pp. 10, 11-12, 12-13, 14-15, 15-16, 17, 18-19, 23-24, 26-28, 30-32, 33-34. Dublin, Cuala Press, 1928.

──────. *Dramatis Personae, 1896-1902, Estrangement, The Death of Synge, The Bounty of Sweden,* pp. 34, 56, 57, 59, 69, 75, 90-91, 100, 101, 105, 106, 111, 112, 124-129, 130, 131-132, 135-136, 137-138, 141-143, 149, 171, 182, 184, 185-186, 187-188, 189. London, Macmillan, 1936. [New York, Macmillan, 1936 edition: pp. 36, 60, 61, 62-63, 74, 80, 97-98, 108, 109, 113, 114, 120, 121, 133-137, 139, 140-141, 144-145, 146-147, 150-152, 157, 181, 192, 194-195, 196-198, 199]

──────. *Essays,* pp. 294-296, 369-378, 379-384, 385-424, 488-489. London and New York, Macmillan, 1924. [Includes the following essays: "The Tragic Theatre" (pp. 294-296), "Preface to the First Edition of *The Well of the Saints*" (pp. 369-378), "Preface to the First Edition of John M. Synge's Poems and Translations" (pp. 379-384), "J. M. Synge and the Ireland of His Time" (pp. 385-424)]

──────. *Essays and Introductions,* pp. 238-239, 298-305, 306-310, 311-342, 515, 527, 528, 529. New York and London, Macmillan, 1961. [Includes the following essays: "Preface to the First Edition of

The Well of the Saints" (pp. 298-305), "Preface to the First Edition of John M. Synge's *Poems and Translations*" (pp. 306-310), "J. M. Synge and the Ireland of His Time" (pp. 311-342)]

—————. *Explorations*. Selected by Mrs. W. B. Yeats, pp. 106, 114, 137, 138, 143-144, 157, 182, 183, 184, 188, 192, 225-226, 226-228, 229-230, 234, 248, 249, 252, 253-254, 254-255. London and New York, Macmillan, 1962.

—————. *The Hour Glass, Cathleen Ni Houlihan, The Golden Helmet, The Irish Dramatic Movement*, pp. 112, 120, 142, 147-148, 186, 187, 188, 191-192, 196, 227-228, 228-230, 231-232. Being the Fourth Volume of the Collected Works in Verse and Prose of William Butler Yeats. Stratford-on-Avon, Shakespeare Head Press, 1908. [Includes the following essays: "The Controversy over *The Playboy of the Western World*" (pp. 227-228), "From Mr. Yeats' Opening Speech in the Debate on February 4, 1907, at the Abbey Theatre" (pp. 228-230), and "On Taking *The Playboy* to London" (pp. 231-232)]

—————. "Introduction: Mr. Synge and His Plays", in *The Well of the Saints* by J. M. Synge. Being Volume Four of Plays for an Irish Theatre. London, A. H. Bullen, 1905.

—————. "J. M. Synge and the Ireland of His Time", *The Forum* (New York), XLVI (August 1911), 179-200.

—————. *The Letters of W. B. Yeats*, edited by Allan Wade. New York, Macmillan, 1955.

—————. *Plays and Controversies*, pp. 44, 54, 83, 84, 90-91, 120, 139-140, 141, 142, 146-147, 152, 192-193, 194-196, 197-198, 205, 209, 210-211, 212. London, Macmillan, 1923. [The contents of the American edition, published in New York, 1924, are the same as those of the English edition]

—————. *Synge and the Ireland of His Time by William Butler Yeats with a Note Concerning a Walk through Connemara with Him by Jack Butler Yeats*. Churchtown, Dundrum, Cuala Press, 1911.

—————. *W. B. Yeats: Selected Criticism*, edited by A. Norman Jeffares. London, Macmillan, 1964. [See pp. 132, 144, 167, 185, 188, 189-190, 199, 201-205, 260]

GENERAL LITERARY CRITICISM

Allen, Beverly S. "John Synge: A problem of His Genius", *The Colonnade* (New York), XI (January 1916) 5-15.

Andrews, Irene Dwen. "The Irish Literary Theatre", *Poet-Lore* (Boston), XXXIX (Spring 1928), 94-100.

Barnes, T. R. "Yeats, Synge, Ibsen and Strindberg", *Scrutiny* (Cambridge, England), V:3 (December 1936), 257-262. [See pp. 259-260]

Barnett, Pat. "The Nature of Synge's Dialogue", *English Literature in Transition* (West Lafayette, Indiana), X:3 (1967), 119-129.

Bauman, Richard. "John Millington Synge and Irish Folklore", *Southern Folklore Quarterly* (Jacksonville, Florida), XXVII (December 1963), 267-279.

Bentley, Eric Russell. *In Search of Theater.* New York, Knopf, 1947; Vintage Books, 1953.

Bewley, Charles. "The Irish National Theatre", *The Dublin Review* (London), CLII (January 1913), 132-144.

Bickley, Francis Lawrance. *J. M. Synge and the Irish Dramatic Movement*, pp. 9-31. London, Constable; Boston and New York, Houghton Mifflin, 1912.

————. "Synge and the Drama", *The New Quarterly* (London), III (February 1910), 73-84.

Birmingham, George A. "The Literary Movement in Ireland", *The Fortnightly Review* (London) LXXXVIII, n.s. LXXXII (2 December 1907), 947-957. [See pp. 954-955]

Blake, Warren Barton. "Irish Plays and Players", *The Independent* (New York), LXXIV (6 March 1913), 515-519. [A review of Cornelius Weygandt, *Irish Plays and Playwrights*]

Bourgeois, Maurice. *John Millington Synge and the Irish Theatre.* London, Constable, 1913; reissued by Benjamin Blom, Bronx, New York, 1965.

————. "Synge and Loti", *The Westminster Review* (London), CLXXIX (May 1913), 532-536.

Boyd, Ernest Augustus. "J. M. Synge", in *Ireland's Literary Renais-*

sance, pp. 316-335. Dublin, Maunsel; London and New York, Knopf, 1916; revised edition, New York, 1922.

Brann, Henry A. "The Modern Literary Conscience", *America* (New York), VI (21 October 1911), 30-31.

Brawley, Benjamin. "John Millington Synge", in *A Short History of the English Drama,* pp. 233-234. New York, Harcourt, Brace, 1921.

Brophy, G. M. "J. M. Synge and the Revival of the Irish Drama", *Everyman* (London), I (18 October 1912), 8.

Brophy, Liam. "The 'Shocking' Synge", *The Word* (Donamon, Co. Roscommon), (March 1959), 6-8.

C., G. [Review of Francis Bickley, *J. M. Synge and the Irish Dramatic Movement*], *Rhythm* (London), II (March 1913), 486.

Casey, Helen. "Synge's Use of the Anglo-Irish Idiom", *The English Journal* (Chicago), XXVII (November 1938), 773-776.

Chandler, Frank Wadleigh. *Aspects of Modern Drama.* New York, Macmillan, 1914.

Chica Salas, Susana. "Synge y García Lorca: Approximación de dos mundos poéticos", *Revista hispánica moderna* (New York), XXVII: 2 (April 1961), 128-137.

Clark, Barrett Harper. "Riders to the Sea", in *Representative One-Act Plays by British and Irish Authors,* pp. 391-393. Boston, Little, Brown, 1921.

Colum, Padraic. "The Irish Literary Movement", *The Forum* (New York), LIII (January-June 1915), 133-148. [See p. 145]

——————. *My Irish Year,* pp. 93-94. London, Mills and Boon; New York, James Pott, 1912. [A brief discussion of Synge's dialogue]

——————. *The Road Round Ireland,* pp. 352-373. New York, Macmillan, 1926.

Corkery, Daniel. *Synge and Anglo-Irish Literature: A Study,* pp. 65-109, 233-243. Dublin and Cork, Cork University Press; London, Longmans, Green, 1931.

Coxhead, Elizabeth. " 'Collaboration'—Hyde and Synge", in *Lady Gregory: A Literary Portrait,* pp. 108-126. London, Macmillan, 1961; second edition, revised and enlarged, London, Secker and Warburg, 1966. [See pp. 108-121]

Cunliffe, John William. "John Millington Synge (1871-1909)", in *English Literature in the Twentieth Century,* pp. 105-110. New York, Macmillan, 1933.

Day-Lewis, Sean. "Synge's Song", *Drama: The Quarterly Theatre*

Review (London), No. 90 (Autumn 1968), 35-38. [A review article of J. M. Synge, *Collected Works, Vols. III and IV, Plays*, edited by Ann Saddlemyer]

Downer, Alan S. "John Millington Synge and the Irish National Theatre", in *Twenty-Five Modern Plays*, edited by S. Marion Tucker; revised edition by Alan S. Downer. New York, Harper and Row, 1948. [An introductory essay to *Riders*, see p. 295]

"Drama", *The Nation* (New York), XCIII (12 October 1911), 346-347. [A review of J. W. Luce and Co. edition, *The Aran Islands, Riders to the Sea*, and *The Tinker's Wedding*]

Dunsany, Lord. "Irish Writers I Have Known", *The Atlantic Monthly* (Boston), CXCII (September 1953), 66-68.

Durham, Willard Higley, and John W. Dodds, eds. "John Millington Synge, 1871-1909", in *British and American Plays: 1830-1945*, pp. 229, 780. New York, Oxford University Press, 1947.

Ellis-Fermor, Una Mary. *The Frontiers of Drama*, pp. 80, 82-83. London, Methuen, 1945.

—————. "John Millington Synge", in *The Irish Dramatic Movement*. London, Methuen, 1939.

Ervine, St. John Greer. *The Organised Theatre: A Plea in Civics*, pp. 27, 82-83, 84-86, 118. London, Allen and Unwin, 1924.

Everson, Ida G. "Lennox Robinson and Synge's *Playboy* (1911-1930): Two Decades of American Cultural Growth", *The New England Quarterly* (Brunswick, Maine), XLIV (March 1971), 3-21.

Fausset, Hugh L'A. "Synge and Tragedy", *The Fortnightly Review* (London), CXXI, n.s. CXV (1 February 1924), 258-273. [See pp. 258-273]

Fay, Gerard. *The Abbey Theatre: Cradle of Genius*. Dublin, Clonmore and Reynolds; London, Hollis and Carter; New York, Macmillan, 1958.

Fay, William George, and Catherine Carswell. *The Fays of the Abbey Theatre: An Autobiographical Record*. London, Rich and Cowan; New York, Harcourt, Brace, 1935.

Figgis, Darrell. "The Art of J. M. Synge", *The Fortnightly Review* (London), XCVI, n.s. CX (1 December 1911), 1056-1068. [See pp. 1056-1060. Virtually the same article appears in *The Forum* (see below, next entry)]

—————. "The Art of J. M. Synge", *The Forum* (New York), XLVII (January 1912), 55-70. [See pp. 55-60. Reprinted in *Studies and Appreciations* (see below)]

Figgis, Darrell. "J. M. Synge", *The Bookman* (London), XL (April 1911), 30-33. [Review article of Maunsel and Co. edition, *The Works*]

——————. "J. M. Synge" and "The Art of J. M. Synge", in *Studies and Appreciations,* pp. 23-33; 34-59. London, J. M. Dent, 1912.

Flood, Jeanne. "The Pre-Aran Writing of J. M. Synge", *Eire-Ireland* (St. Paul, Minnesota), V : 3 (Autumn 1970), 63-80.

"Foreword", in *John Millington Synge: Some Unpublished Letters and Documents of J. M. Synge Formerly in the Possession of Mr. Lawrence Wilson of Montreal and Now for the First Time Published for Him by The Redpath Press,* pp. 5-6. Montreal, Redpath Press, 1959.

Fréchet, René. "Sean O'Casey", in *Le Théâtre moderne: hommes et tendances,* edited by Jean Jacquot. Paris, Editions du Centre National de la Recherche Scientifique, 1958. [See pp. 325-330]

——————. [Review article of J. M. Synge, *Collected Works:* Vol. I, *Poems,* edited by Robin Skelton; Vol. II, *Prose,* edited by Alan Price; Vols. III and IV, *Plays,* edited by Ann Saddlemyer], *Etudes Anglaises* (Paris) Année XXI, No. 3 (July-September 1968), 320-323.

——————. [Review of *The Autobiography of J. M. Synge,* constructed from the Manuscripts by Alan Price], *Etudes Anglaises* (Paris), Année XXI, No. 3 (July-September 1968), 319-320.

Frenzel, Herbert. *John Millington Synge's Work as a Contribution to Irish Folk-Lore and to the Psychology of Primitive Tribes.* Inaugural Dissertation. Düren-Rhld, Max Danielewski, 1932.

"Further Opinion of the Irish Players", *America* (New York), VI (14 October 1911), 11-12.

Gaskell, Ronald. [Review of J. M. Synge, *The Plays and Poems of J. M. Synge,* edited by T. R. Henn], *Critical Quarterly* (London), VI (Winter 1964), 381-382.

Gerstenberger, Donna Lorine. *John Millington Synge.* Twayne's English Authors Series, 12. New York, Twayne, 1964.

——————. [Review of David H. Greene and Edward M. Stephens, *J. M. Synge: 1871-1909*], *The Western Humanities Review* (Salt Lake City), XVII (Spring 1963), 193.

——————. "Yeats and Synge: 'A Young Man's Ghost' ", in *W. B. Yeats, 1865-1965: Centenary Essays on the Art of W. B. Yeats,* edited by Desmond Ernest Stewart Maxwell and S. B. Bushrui. Ibadan, Nigeria, Ibadan University Press, 1965.

Gibbon, Monk. [Review article of David H. Greene and Edward M. Stephens, *J. M. Synge: 1871-1909*], *Studies* (Dublin), XLVIII (Autumn 1959), 359-361.

Gordon, Donald James. "Lionel Johnson, J. M. Synge and George Pollexfen", in *W. B. Yeats: Images of a Poet*. Manchester, Exhibition Catalogue, 3 May to 3 June 1961. Victoria University of Manchester. Whitworth Art Gallery, [1961]. [See pp. 35-37]

"Gossip", *The Irish Book Lover* (Dublin), III (March 1912), 132-133.

Graves, Alfred Perceval. "Anglo-Irish Literature: Synge", in *The Cambridge History of English Literature*, edited by Sir A. W. Ward and A. R. Waller, XIV, 363-365. Cambridge, Cambridge University Press; New York, G. P. Putnam's, 1917.

Greene, David H. "Synge and the Celtic Revival", *Modern Drama* (Lawrence, Kansas), IV (December 1961), 292-299.

——————. "Synge and the Irish", *Colby Library Quarterly* (Waterville, Maine), Ser. 4, No. 9 (February 1957), 158-166.

——————, and Edward M. Stephens. *J. M. Synge: 1871-1909*. New York, Macmillan, 1959.

Gregory, Lady Isabella Augusta. *Our Irish Theatre: A Chapter of Autobiography*, pp. 33, 34, 35, 42, 43, 76, 93-94, 99, 104, 108, 109-118, 119-139, 147-148, 149, 156-157, 169-252, 280-309, 316. New York and London, G. P. Putnam's, 1913.

Guerrero Zamora, Juan. "John Millington Synge", in *Historia del teatro contemporáneo*, III, 23-24. Barcelona, Juan Flors, 1962.

Gwynn, Stephen Lucius, ed. *Scattering Branches: Tributes to the Memory of W. B. Yeats*, pp. 9-11, 127, 200. New York and London, Macmillan, 1940. [Includes material from Stephen Gwynn, W. G. Fay and L. A. G. Strong]

Hackett, Francis. "John Synge", in *Horizons: A Book of Criticism*, pp. 189-197. New York, B. W. Huebsch, 1918.

Henn, Thomas Rice. "Yeats and Synge", in *The Lonely Tower: Studies in the Poetry of W. B. Yeats*, pp. 72-86. London, Methuen, 1950.

Hind, Charles Lewis. *More Authors and I*, pp. 279-284. London, John Lane; New York, Dodd, Mead, 1922.

Holloway, Joseph. *Joseph Holloway's Abbey Theatre: A Selection from His Unpublished Journal, "Impressions of a Dublin Playgoer"*, edited by Robert Hogan and Michael J. O'Neill. Carbondale and Edwardsville, Southern Illinois University Press; London and Amsterdam, Feffer and Simons, 1967.

Honig, Edwin. *Garcia Lorca*, pp. 214-215. Norfolk, Connecticut, New Directions, 1944.

Howarth, Herbert. "Edmund John Millington Synge, 1871-1909", in *The Irish Writers: 1880-1940; Literature Under Parnell's Star*, pp. 212-244. London, Rockliff, 1958; New York, Hill and Wang, 1959.

Howe, Percival Presland. *J. M. Synge: A Critical Study*. London, Martin Secker, 1912.

Huneker, James. "John M. Synge", in *The Pathos of Distance: A Book of a Thousand and One Moments*, pp. 228-235. New York, Scribner's, 1913.

Huscher, Herbert. [Review article of Alan Price, *Synge and Anglo-Irish Drama*], *Anglia: Zeitschrift für englische Philologie* (Tübingen), LXXX (1962), 226-231. [See pp. 226-229]

[Introductory Essay to John Millington Synge, *Riders to the Sea* and *In the Shadow of the Glen*], *The Bibelot* (Portland, Maine), XIX (1913), 239-245.

"Ireland's Greatest Dramatist", *The Literary Digest* (New York), XXXVIII (17 April 1909), 652. [An obituary article]

"Irish Opinion on 'The Irish Players' ", *America* (New York), V (7 October 1911), 614-615.

"The Irish Theatre", *Literary World* (London), n.s. LXXIX (5 June 1913), 182-183. [A review of Cornelius Weygandt, *Irish Plays and Playwrights*]

Jacobs, Willis D. "A Silent Sinner", *The American Mercury* (New York), LXXXI (August 1955), 159-160.

Johnston, Denis. *John Millington Synge*. Columbia Essays on Modern Writers, No. 12. New York and London, Columbia University Press, 1965.

Jordan, John. "The Irish Theatre—Retrospect and Premonition", in *Contemporary Theatre,* edited by John Russell Brown and Bernard Harris, pp. 166-167. Stratford-Upon-Avon Studies, 4. London, Edward Arnold; New York, St. Martin's, 1962.

Kain, Richard Morgan. *Dublin: In the Age of William Butler Yeats and James Joyce*. Norman, University of Oklahoma Press, 1962.

K[avanagh], P[atrick]. "Paris in Aran", *Kavanagh's Weekly* (Dublin), I: 9 (7 June 1952), 7. [A review article of John M. Synge, *Collected Plays,* with an Introduction by William Robert Rodgers]

Kenny, M. "The Irish Pagans", *America* (New York), VI (21 October 1911), 31-32.

——————."The 'Irish' Players and Playwrights", *America* (New York), V (30 September 1911), 581-582.

Krause, David. " 'The Rageous Ossean': Patron-Hero of Synge and O'Casey", *Modern Drama* (Lawrence, Kansas), IV (December 1961), 268-291.

Krause, David. *Sean O'Casey: The Man and His Work*. London, MacGibbon and Kee, 1960.

Kronenberger, Louis. "Synge", in *The Thread of Laughter: Chapters on English Stage Comedy from Jonson to Maugham*, pp. 279-288. New York, Knopf, 1952.

Krutch, Joseph Wood. "Synge and the Irish Protest", in *"Modernism" in Modern Drama: A Definition and an Estimate*. Ithaca, New York, Cornell University Press, 1953.

Lennartz, Franz. *Auslandische Dichter und Schriftsteller*, pp. 737-745. Stuttgart, Alfred Kröner, [1955]. [Includes a discussion of the Irish literary movement, the Abbey Theatre, and Synge]

Levin, Harry. *James Joyce: A Critical Introduction*. Norfolk, Connecticut, New Directions, 1941; revised and augmented edition (New Directions Paperback No. 87), Norfolk, Connecticut; New Directions, 1960.

Lucas, Frank Laurence. *The Drama of Chekhov, Synge, Yeats, and Pirandello*, pp. 150-166. London, Cassell, 1963.

Lunari, Gigi. "Lady Gregory e Synge", in *Il movimento drammatico irlandese (1899-1922)*, pp. 85-107. Documenti di teatro 13. Bologne, Cappelli, 1960.

Lynd, Robert. *Ireland a Nation*, pp. 171, 174-176. London, Grant Richards, 1919. [American edition, New York, Dodd, Mead, 1920; see pp. 192, 205, 208-211]

McMahon, Seán. "Clay and Worms", *Eire-Ireland* (St. Paul, Minnesota), V:4 (Winter 1970), 116-134.

MacNeice, Frederick Louis. *The Poetry of W. B. Yeats*. New York, Oxford University Press, 1941.

M[antle]., B[urns]. "John Millington Synge (1871-1909)", in *A Treasury of the Theatre: An Anthology of Great Plays from Aeschylus to Eugene O'Neill*, edited by Burns Mantle and John Gassner, pp. 441-443. New York, Simon and Schuster, 1935.

Mennloch, Walter. "Dramatic Values", *The Irish Review* (Dublin), I (September 1911), 325-329. [A review of W. B. Yeats, *Synge and the Ireland of His Time;* C. E. Montague, *Dramatic Values*]

Mercer, Caroline G. "Stephen Dedalus's Vision and Synge's Peasant Girls", *Notes and Queries* (London), CCV, n.s. VII (December 1960), 473-474.

Mercier, Vivian. "Irish Comedy: The Probable and the Wonderful", *University Review* (Dublin), VIII (1956), 45-53.

Mikhail, E. H. "French Influences on Synge", *Revue de Littérature*

Comparée (Paris), Année 42, No. 3 (July-September 1968), 429-431.

Monahan, Michael. "Yeats and Synge", in *Nova Hibernia: Irish Poets and Dramatists of Today and Yesterday*, pp. 13-37. New York, Mitchell Kennerley, 1914.

Moore, George. *Hail and Farewell: A Trilogy: Vale*, pp. 194-219. New York, Appleton; London, Heinemann, 1914. [Most of this material was reprinted from *The English Review* (see below next entry)]

——————. "Yeats, Lady Gregory, and Synge: II", *The English Review* (London), XVI (February 1914), 350-364.

Morris, Alton Chester, Biron Walker, and Philip Bradshaw, eds. "John Millington Synge, *The Playboy of the Western World*", in *Imaginative Literature*, p. 247. New York, Harcourt, Brace and World, 1968.

Morris, Lloyd R. "Four Irish Poets", *Columbia University Quarterly* (New York), XVIII (September 1916), 332-344. [See section II, pp. 336-339]

Mušek, Karel. "Irské Literární Divadlo", *Máj* (Prague), III:2 (2 November 1906), 17-19, [Divadelní List Máje]

——————. [Review of Maunsel and Co. edition, *The Aran Islands*], *Lumir* (Prague), XXXV (15 June 1907), 383-384.

Nagarkar, Kiran. "Synge", *Quest: A Quarterly of Inquiry, Criticism and Ideas* (Bombay), No. 56 (1968), 46-48.

O'Brien, Conor Cruise. *Writers and Politics*, pp. 110, 121-122. Pantheon Books. New York, Random House, 1965.

O'Connor, Frank [Michael Francis O'Donovan]. *The Backward Look: A Survey of Irish Literature*. London, Macmillan, 1967. [The American edition has a different title: *A Short History of Irish Literature: A Backward Look*. New York, G. P. Putnam, 1967]

——————. "Synge", in *The Irish Theatre*. Lectures delivered during the Abbey Theatre Festival held in Dublin in August 1938, edited by Lennox Robinson, pp. 31-40. London, Macmillan, 1939.

O'Conor, Norreys Jephson. *Changing Ireland: Literary Backgrounds of the Irish Free State, 1889-1922*. Cambridge (Massachusetts), Harvard University Press, 1924.

O Faolain, Sean. [Review of Daniel Corkery, *Synge and Anglo-Irish Literature*], *The Criterion* (London) XI (October 1931), 140-142.

O'Hagan, Thomas. "The Irish Dramatic Movement", in *Essays on Catholic Life*, pp. 57-73. Baltimore, John Murphy, 1916; reissued by Books for Libraries Press, Freeport, New York, 1965, 1969.

O'Neill, George. "Irish Drama and Irish Views", *The American Catholic Quarterly Review* (Philadelphia), XXXVII (April 1912), 322-332. [Argues that Synge's plays are not Irish, and that they slander Ireland]

O Síocháin, P. A. [Sheehan, Patrick Augustine]. "Synge and the Aran Islands", and "Synge's Life on the Islands", in *Aran: Islands of Legend,* pp. 159-166; 167-176. Dublin, Foilsiúcháin Eireann; New York, Devin-Adair, 1962.

Owen, Alice G. [Review of J. M. Synge, *The Autobiography of J. M. Synge,* Constructed from the Manuscripts by Alan Price], *Library Journal* (New York), XCII (1 June 1967), 2151.

Phelps, William Lyon. *The Advance of English Poetry in the Twentieth Century,* pp. 171-177. New York, Dodd, Mead, 1918.

Price, Alan F. "Introduction", in J. M. Synge, *The Autobiography of J. M. Synge,* Constructed from the Manuscripts by Alan Price with Fourteen Photographs by J. M. Synge and an Essay on Synge and the Photography of His Time by P. J. Pocock. Dublin, The Dolmen Press; London, Oxford University Press, 1965.

————. "Introduction and Notes", in *Emerald Apex: A Selection from J. M. Synge's Studies of Irish People and Places,* pp. vii-xx, 119-128. London and Glasgow, Blackie, 1966.

————. *Synge and Anglo-Irish Drama.* London, Methuen, 1961.

————. "Synge's Prose Writings: A First View of the Whole", *Modern Drama* (Lawrence, Kansas), XI (December 1968), 221-226.

Pritchett, Victor Sawdon. "The End of the Gael", in *In My Good Books,* pp. 155-160. London, Chatto and Windus, 1942.

Portyanskaya, N. A. "Dzh. Sing i B. Shou" [J. Synge and B. Shaw], *Irkutskii pedagogicheskii institut* (Irkutsk), XXVI (1967), 198-216.

Quinn, Owen. "No Garland for John Synge", *Envoy* (Dublin), III: 11 (October 1950), 44-51.

R. "Synge a Yeats", *Jeviště* (Prague), II: 43 (27 October 1921), 638-640.

Reid, Benjamin L. *The Man from New York: John Quinn and His Friends.* New York, Oxford University Press, 1968.

————. *William Butler Yeats: The Lyric of Tragedy.* Norman, Oklahoma, University of Oklahoma Press, 1961.

[Review of P. P. Howe, *J. M. Synge: A Critical Study*], *North American Review* (New York), CXCVI (October 1912), 571-572.

"Reviews", *Inis Fáil* (London), No. 29 (February 1907), 5. [A brief discussion of Synge in relation to an article he contributed to the *Shanachie* magazine]

Riva, Serafino. *La tradizione celtica e la moderna letteratura irlandese, I. John Millington Synge,* pp. 148-162. Rome, Religio, 1937.

Robinson, Lennox. *Curtain Up: An Autobiography,* pp. 40-41, 140. London, Michael Joseph, 1942.

Ronsley, Joseph. *Yeats's Autobiography: Life as Symbolic Pattern.* Cambridge (Massachusetts), Harvard University Press, 1968.

Roy, James A. "J. M. Synge and the Irish Literary Movement", *Anglia: Zeitschrift für englische Philologie (Tübingen),* XXXVII (1913), 129-145. [A review article of Maunsel and Co. edition, *The Works;* P. P. Howe, *The Repertory Theatre;* P. P. Howe, *J. M. Synge: A Critical Study,* see pp. 129-139]

Rusk, W. S. [Review of John Masefield, *John M. Synge: A Few Personal Recollections with Biographical Notes*], *The Sewanee Review* (Sewanee, Tenn.), XXIV (January 1916), 120-123. [See pp. 120-121]

Rust, Adolf. *Beiträge zu einer Geschichte der neu-keltischen Renaissance,* pp. 27-31; 81-87. Bückeburg, Grimme'sche Hofbuchdruckerei, 1922.

Saddlemyer, Ann. "Rabelais *versus* à Kempis: The Art of J. M. Synge", *Komos* (Clayton, Victoria, Australia), I:3 (October 1967), 85-96.

—————. " 'A Share in the Dignity of the World': J. M. Synge's Aesthetic Theory", in *The World of W. B. Yeats: Essays in Perspective,* edited by Robin Skelton and Ann Saddlemyer. Seattle, University of Washington Press, 1965.

—————. " 'Worn Out with Dreams': Dublin's Abbey Theatre", in *The World of W. B. Yeats: Essays in Perspective,* edited by Robin Skelton and Ann Saddlemyer. Seattle, University of Washington Press, 1965.

Saul, George Brandon. [Review of David H. Greene and Edward M. Stephens, *J. M. Synge: 1871-1909*], *The Arizona Quarterly* (Tucson), XV (Winter 1959), 373-374.

Sear, H. G. "John Millington Synge and Music", *The Sackbut* (London), III (November 1922), 119-123.

Sherman, Stuart P. "The Exoticism of John Synge", in *On Contemporary Literature,* pp. 190-210. New York, Henry Holt, 1917.

—————. "John Synge", *The Nation* (New York), XCV (26 December 1912), 608-611. [A review article of J. W. Luce and Co.

edition, *The Works;* W. B. Yeats, *The Cutting of an Agate;* P. P. Howe, *J. M. Synge: A Critical Study*]

Siebels, Eva. "Die Frau in dem Drama des John Synge—ein Spiegel der irischen Seele", *Die Frau* (Berlin), XLVIII (March 1941), 178-182.

Skelton, Robin. *J. M. Synge and His World.* London, Thames and Hudson, 1971.

————. *The Writings of J. M. Synge.* London, Thames and Hudson, 1971.

Stamm, Rudolf. *Geschichte des englischen Theaters,* p. 407. Berne, A. Francke, 1951.

————. *Three Anglo-Irish Plays,* pp. 3-6. Bibliotheca Anglicana (Texts and Studies), v. 5. Berne, A. Francke, 1943.

Starkie, Enid. *From Gautier to Eliot: The Influence of France on English Literature, 1851-1939,* pp. 125-126. London, Hutchinson, 1960.

Starkie, Walter. "Everything Irish Was Sacred", *Saturday Review* (New York), XLII (18 April 1959), 19-20. [A review of David H. Greene and Edward M. Stephens, *J. M. Synge: 1871-1909*]

Stockwell, La Tourette. [Review of Adelaide Duncan Estill, *The Sources of Synge*], *Journal of English and Germanic Philology* (Urbana, Illinois), XXXIX (July 1940), 436-437.

Strong, Leonard Alfred George. "J. M. Synge", *Beacon* (London), II (July 1922), 695-701. [See pp. 695-698. Reprinted in *The Living Age* (see below, next entry)]

————. "J. M. Synge", *The Living Age* (Boston), CCCXIV (9 September 1922), 656-660. [See pp. 656-658]

————. "John Millington Synge", *The Bookman* (New York), LXXIII (April 1931), 125-136. [See pp. 125-127. Reprinted in *The Dublin Magazine* (see below, next entry)]

————. "John Millington Synge", *The Dublin Magazine,* n.s. VII: 2 (April-June 1932), 12-32. [See pp. 12-16]

————. *John Millington Synge.* P. E. N. Books. London, Allen and Unwin, 1941.

————. "John Millington Synge" in *Personal Remarks,* pp. 34-37. London, P. Nevill, 1953. [Reprinted from *The Bookman* and *The Dublin Magazine* (see above)]

Sutton, Graham. "John Millington Synge", *The Bookman* (London), LXIX (March 1926), 299-301.

Synge, (Rev.) Samuel. *Letters to My Daughter: Memories of John Millington Synge.* Dublin and Cork, Talbot Press, 1931.

"Synge and His Critics", *The New Witness* (London), I (2 January 1913), 282-283. [A review of Francis Bickley, *J. M. Synge and the Irish Dramatic Movement;* P. P. Howe, *J. M. Synge: A Critical Study*]

Taniguchi, Jiro. *A Grammatical Analysis of Artistic Representation of Irish English, with a Brief Discussion of Sounds and Spelling.* Tokyo, Shinozaki Shorin, [1955].

Taylor, Estella Ruth. *The Modern Irish Writers: Cross Currents of Criticism.* Lawrence, Kansas, University of Kansas Press, 1954.

Tennyson, Charles. "Irish Plays and Playwrights", *The Quarterly Review* (London), CCXV (July 1911), 219-243. [A review of Maunsel and Co. edition, *The Works,* see pp. 227-231]

Téry, Simone. "J. M. Synge", in *L'Ile des Bardes: "Notes sur la Littérature irlandaise contemporaine",* pp. 140-166. Paris, Ernest Flammarion, 1925.

"Tinkers and Bully Boys", *Newsweek* (New York), LIII (20 April 1959), 119. [A review of David H. Greene and Edward M. Stephens, *J. M. Synge: 1871-1909*]

Ua F., R. "J. M. Synge", *Inis Fáil* (London) No. 53 (April 1909), 12. [A short obituary article that briefly touches on Synge's work]

Ua Fuaráin, Eoghan. "National Drama in Ireland", *Irisleabhar Muighe Nuadhad* (Maynooth), I : 3 (An Cháisg [Easter] 1909), 22-29.

Ussher, Arland. "Irish Literature", *Zeitschrift für Anglistik und Amerikanistik* (Leipzig), XIV : 1 (1966), 30-55. [See p. 52]

van Hamel, A. G. "On Anglo-Irish Syntax", *Englische Studien* (Leipzig), XLV (September 1912), 272-292.

————. [A review of Maurice Bourgeois, *John Millington Synge and the Irish Theatre*], *Englische Studien* (Leipzig), XLIX (January 1916), 318-322.

Warner, Alan. "The Poet as Watcher", *Threshold* (Belfast), No. 22 (Summer 1969), 64-70. [See pp. 66-68]

Watkins, Ann. "The Irish Players in America : Their Purpose and Their Art", *The Craftsman* (New York), XXI (January 1912), 352-363. [See pp. 352-359]

Weygandt, Cornelius. "John Millington Synge", in *Irish Plays and Playwrights,* pp. 160-197. London, Constable; Boston and New York, Houghton Mifflin, 1913.

Williams, Harold. *Modern English Writers: Being a Study of Imaginative Literature, 1890-1914*, pp. 206-216. New York, Knopf, 1919.

Williams, Raymond. "J. M. Synge", in *Drama: From Ibsen to Eliot*, pp. 154-174. London, Chatto and Windus, 1952.

Woods, Anthony S. "Synge Stayed Home by the Fireside", *The Catholic World* (New York), CXLI (April 1935), 46-52. [Concludes that Synge "had his fingers upon the life-pulse of Ireland"]

"The Works of J. M. Synge", *The Living Age* (Boston), CCLXIX (15 April 1911), 163-166. [A review article of Maunsel and Co. edition, *The Works*]

Yeats, John Butler. "Synge and the Irish", in *Essays Irish and American*, pp. 51-61. Dublin, Talbot Press; London, T. F. Unwin; New York, Macmillan, 1918.

—————. "Synge and the Irish: Random Reflections on a Much-Discussed Dramatist from the Standpoint of a Fellow-Countryman", *Harper's Weekly* (New York), LV (25 November 1911), 17.

Yeats, William Butler. *Autobiographies*. London, Macmillan, 1955. [Consisting of "Reveries over Childhood and Youth", "The Trembling of the Veil", "Dramatis Personae", "Estrangement", "The Death of Synge" and "The Bounty of Sweden".]

—————. *Autobiographies: Reveries over Childhood and Youth and the Trembling of the Veil*, pp. 254, 266, 385, 423-427, 467, 468. London, Macmillan, 1926. [The contents of the American edition, published in New York, Macmillan, 1927, are the same as those of the English edition]

—————. *The Autobiography of William Butler Yeats. Consisting of Reveries over Childhood and Youth, The Trembling of the Veil and Dramatis Personae*, pp. 185, 266, 292-295, 322, 323, 356, 374, 375, 376, 385, 403-404, 412, 416, 417, 421, 422, 431, 432-436, 437-438, 441, 442-444, 446-448, 451, 470. New York, Macmillan, 1938.

—————. *The Bounty of Sweden: A Meditation, and a Lecture Delivered Before the Royal Swedish Academy and Certain Notes*, pp. 1, 28, 40, 43-47, 48-49. Dublin, Cuala Press, 1925.

—————. *The Cutting of an Agate*, pp. 142-143, 144, 148-149, 156, 157-158, 165, 166-167, 175. New York, Macmillan, 1912. [London edition of 1919 is the same as the New York 1912 edition. Both editions include the following essays: "The Tragic Theatre" (pp. 25-35), "Preface to the First Edition of *The Well of The Saints*" (pp. 111-122), "Preface to the First Edition of John M. Synge's Poems and Translations" (pp. 123-129), "J. M. Synge and the Ireland of His Time" (pp. 130-176)]

Yeats, William Butler. *The Death of Synge, and Other Passages from an Old Diary,* pp. 10, 11-12, 12-13, 14-15, 15-16, 17, 18-19, 23-24, 26-28, 30-32, 33-34. Dublin, Cuala Press, 1928.

——————. "J. M. Synge and the Ireland of His Time", *The Forum* (New York), XLVI (August 1911), 179-200.

——————. *Dramatis Personae, 1896-1902, Estrangement, The Death of Synge, The Bounty of Sweden,* pp. 34, 56, 57, 59, 69, 75, 90-91, 100, 101, 105, 106, 111, 112, 124-129, 130, 131-132, 135-136, 137-138, 141-143, 149, 171, 182, 184, 185-186, 187-188, 189. London, Macmillan, 1936. [New York, Macmillan, 1936 edition: pp. 36, 60, 61, 62-63, 74, 80, 97-98, 108, 109, 113, 114, 120, 121, 133-137, 139, 140-141, 144-145, 146-147, 150-152, 157, 181, 192, 194-195, 196-198, 199]

——————. *Essays,* pp. 294-296, 369-378, 379-384, 385-424, 488-489. London and New York, Macmillan, 1924. [Includes the following essays: "The Tragic Theatre" (pp. 294-296), "Preface to the First Edition of *The Well of the Saints*" (pp. 360-378), "Preface to the First Edition of John M. Synge's Poems and Translations" (pp. 379-384), "J. M. Synge and the Ireland of His Time" (pp. 385-424)]

——————. *Essays and Introductions,* pp. 238-239, 298-305, 306-310, 311-342, 515, 527, 528, 529. New York and London, Macmillan, 1961. [Includes the following essays: "Preface to the First Edition of *The Well of The Saints*" (pp. 298-305), "Preface to the First Edition of John M. Synge's *Poems and Translations*" (pp. 306-310), "J. M. Synge and the Ireland of His Time" (pp. 311-342)]

——————. *Explorations.* Selected by Mrs W. B. Yeats, pp. 106, 114, 137, 138, 143-144, 157, 182, 183, 184, 188, 192, 225-226, 226-228, 229-230, 234, 248, 249, 252, 253-254, 254-255. London and New York, Macmillan, 1962.

——————. "Introduction: Mr Synge and His Plays", in *The Well of the Saints* by J. M. Synge. Being Volume Four of Plays for an Irish Theatre. London, A. H. Bullen, 1905.

——————. *The Irish National Theatre,* pp. 5-11. Estratto dagli Atti del IV convegno della "Fondazione Alessandro Volta", Roma 8-14 Ottobre, 1934. Rome, Reale Accademia d'Italia, 1935. [With résumés in Italian and French]

——————. *The Letters of W. B. Yeats,* edited by Allan Wade. New York, Macmillan, 1955.

——————. "More Memories", *The Dial* (Chicago), LXXIII (September 1922), 283-302. [Includes Synge's famous remark: "There are three things any two of which have often come together, but never all three: ecstasy, asceticism, austerity; I wish to bring all three together", see pp. 300-301. Reprinted in *The Trembling of the Veil.* 1922; and in *Autobiographies,* 1926]

Yeats, William Butler. *Plays and Controversies*, pp. 44, 54, 83, 84, 90-91, 120, 139-140, 141, 142, 146-147, 152, 192-193, 194-196, 197-198, 205, 209, 210-211, 212. London, Macmillan, 1923. [The contents of the American edition, published in New York, 1924, are the same as those of the English edition]

——————. *Les Prix Nobel en 1923*, pp. 4, 6-8, 9. Stockholm, P. A. Nordstedt and Söner, 1924. [Yeats's lecture "The Irish Dramatic Movement" is the last in the volume, and is paged separately, pp. 1-11; it was also issued separately in 1924. Yeats delivered his lecture in Stockholm to the Swedish Royal Academy on 13 December 1923. In his preface to *The Bounty of Sweden*, dated 15 June 1924, he wrote that "a couple of months ago" he had dictated as many of his words as he could remember and added thereto "certain explanatory notes". The lecture and preface have been reprinted in *The Bounty of Sweden: A Meditation, and a Lecture Delivered Before the Royal Swedish Academy and Certain Notes*. Dublin, Cuala Press, 1925]

——————. *Synge and the Ireland of His Time by William Butler Yeats with a Note Concerning a Walk through Connemara with Him by Jack Butler Yeats*. Churchtown, Dundrum, Cuala Press, 1911.

——————. *A Vision*, pp. 163-169. Revised edition, London, Macmillan, 1937, and New York, 1938; reissued with the author's final revisions, New York, 1956, and London, 1961; second edition, reissued with corrections, London, 1962. [The first version of this book was privately printed for subscribers only in London, 1925, under the title: *A Vision; an Explanation of Life Founded upon the Writings of Giraldus and upon Certain Doctrines Attributed to Kusta ben Luka*]

Z[abel], M[orton] D. "Synge and the Irish" *Poetry* (Chicago), XLII (May 1933), 101-106.

DEIRDRE OF THE SORROWS

Barnet, Slyvan, Morton Berman, and William Burto, eds. "J. M. Synge: *Deirdre of The Sorrows*", in *The Genius of the Irish Theater*, pp. 151-154. Mentor Books. New York, The New American Library, 1960.

Bickley, Francis. "Deirdre", *Irish Review* (Dublin), II (July 1912), 252-255.

Bourgeois, Maurice. *John Millington Synge and the Irish Theatre*, pp. 212-217. London, Constable, 1913; reissued by Benjamin Blom, Bronx, New York, 1965.

Boyd, Ernest Augustus. "J. M. Synge", in *Ireland's Literary Renaissance*, pp. 330-332. Dublin, Maunsel; London and New York, Knopf, 1916; revised edition, New York, 1922.

Corkery, Daniel. *Synge and Anglo-Irish Literature: A Study*, pp. 205-227. Dublin and Cork, Cork University Press; London, Longmans, Green, 1931.

Empson, William. *Seven Types of Ambiguity*, pp. 38-42. Second revised edition, London, Chatto and Windus; Norfolk, Connecticut, New Directions, 1947; third revised edition, London, 1963.

Estill, Adelaide Duncan. *The Sources of Synge*, pp. 34-41. Philadelphia, University of Pennsylvania, 1939.

Fackler, Herbert V. "J. M. Synge's *Deirdre of the Sorrows:* Beauty Only", *Modern Drama* (Lawrence, Kansas), XI (February 1969), 404-409.

Figgis, Darrell. "J. M. Synge" and "The Art of J. M. Synge", in *Studies and Appreciations*, pp. 56-58. London, J. M. Dent, 1912. ["Art of J. M. Synge" originally appeared in the *Fortnightly Review* and in the *Forum*]

Firkins, O. W. "Synge at the Bramhall Playhouse", *Weekly Review* (New York), III (6 October 1920), 297-299. [Review].

Fricker, Robert. *Das historische Drama in England von der Romantik bis zur Gegenwart*, pp.199, 247-248. A Dissertation. Berne, A. Francke, 1940. [Also appears as No. 8 in the series "Schweizer Anglistische Arbeiten"]

Gassner, John. [Introductory Essay to John Millington Synge, *Deirdre*
57

of the Sorrows], *Theatre Arts* (New York), XXXIV (August 1950), 68-69.

————. "The Theater Arts", *Forum* (New York), CXIII (January 1950), 24-27. [Review; see p. 27]

Gerstenberger, Donna Lorine. *John Millington Synge,* pp. 94-108. Twayne's English Authors Series, 12. New York, Twayne, 1964.

Greene, David H. "Synge's Unfinished Deirdre", *PMLA* (New York), LXIII (December 1948), 1314-1321.

Gregory, Lady Isabella Augusta. *Our Irish Theatre: A Chapter of Autobiography,* pp. 137-139. New York and London, G. P. Putnam's, 1913.

Guerrero Zamora, Juan. "John Millington Synge", in *Historia del teatro contemporáneo,* III, 25-26. Barcelona, Juan Flors, 1962.

Gunnell, Doris. "Le Nouveau théâtre irlandais", *La Revue* [late *Revue des Revues*] (Paris), XCIV : 1 (1 January 1912), 91-106. [See pp. 102-104]

Hoare, Dorothy Mackenzie. *The Works of Morris and of Yeats in Relation to Early Saga Literature,* pp. 130-132. Cambridge, Cambridge University Press, 1937.

Holloway, Joseph. *Joseph Holloway's Abbey Theatre: A Selection from His Unpublished Journal, "Impressions of a Dublin Playgoer",* edited by Robert Hogan and Michael J. O'Neill. Carbondale and Edwardsville, Southern Illinois University Press; London and Amsterdam, Feffer and Simons, 1967.

Howe, Percival Presland. *J. M. Synge: A Critical Study,* pp. 84-99. London, Martin Secker, 1912.

Krieger, Hans. "J. M. Synge", *Die neueren Sprachen* (Marburg), XXIV (1916), 542-552. [Reprinted in *John Millington Synge* (see below, next entry)]

————. *John Millington Synge, ein Dichter der "keltischen Renaissance",* pp. 91-100. Inaugural Dissertation. Marburg, N. G. Elwert'sche, 1916.

Lewis, Theophilus. " 'Deirdre of the Sorrows' ", *America* (New York), CII (14 November 1959), 217. [Review]

Lowther, George. "J. M. Synge and the Irish Revival", *The Oxford and Cambridge Review* (London), No. 25 (November 1912), 43-59. [See pp. 55-57]

Lucas, Frank Laurence. *The Drama of Chekhov, Synge, Yeats, and Pirandello*, pp. 225-237. London, Cassell, 1963.

M., M. "Irish Plays and Players", *Inis Fáil* (London), No. 67 (June 1910), 9. [Review]

McArthur, Herbert. "Tragic and Comic Modes", *Criticism* (Detroit), III (Winter 1961), 36-45. [See pp. 39-43]

McHugh, Roger. "Literary Treatment of the Deirdre Legend", *Threshold* (Belfast), I (February 1957), 36-49.

Malcolm, Donald. "Near Myth", *The New Yorker*, XXXV (24 October 1959), 91-92. [Review]

"New Synge Play Badly Put On by Celtic Players", *The New York Clipper*, LXVIII (29 September 1920), 19. [Review]

Nordman, C. A. "J. M. Synge, Dramatikern", *Finsk Tidskrift för Vitterhet, Vetenskap, Konst och Politik* (Helsinki), LXXIX (July-December 1915), 26-70. [See pp. 57-62]

O'Connor, Brother Anthony Cyril. "Synge and National Drama", *Unitas: Revista de cultura y vida universitaria* (Manila), XXVII: 3 (July 1954), 430-464. [See pp. 430-444]

Orel, Harold. "Synge's Last Play: 'And a Story Will Be Told For Ever' ", *Modern Drama* (Lawrence, Kansas), IV (December 1961), 306-313.

Peacock, Ronald. "Synge", in *The Poet in the Theatre*, pp. 108-109. London, Routledge and Kegan Paul; New York, Harcourt, Brace, 1946.

Price, Alan F. *Synge and Anglo-Irish Drama*, pp. 191-215. London, Methuen, 1961.

Riva, Serafino. *La tradizione celtica e la moderna letteratura irlandese, I. John Millington Synge*, pp. 234-252. Rome, Religio, 1937.

Rivoallan, Anatole. "J. M. Synge", in *Littérature irlandaise contemporaine*, pp. 25-29. Paris, Hachette, 1939.

Rust, Adolf. *Beiträge zu einer Geschichte der neu-keltischen Renaissance*, pp. 77-80. Bückeburg, Grimme'sche Hofbuchdruckerei, 1922.

Setterquist, Jan. "Ibsen and Synge", *Studia Neophilologica* (Upsala), XXIV (1951/52), 131-135. [Reprinted in *Ibsen and the Beginnings of Anglo-Irish Drama* (see below, next entry)]

——. *Ibsen and the Beginnings of Anglo-Irish Drama: I. John Millington Synge*, pp. 71-75. Upsala Irish Studies, Vol. 2, edited by S. B. Liljegren, Upsala, A.-B. Lundequistka; Dublin, Hodges, Figgis; Copenhagen, Munksgaard; Cambridge, Massachusetts, Harvard University Press, 1951.

Shipley, Joseph T. *Guide to Great Plays,* pp. 763-764. Washington, D. C., Public Affairs Press, 1956.

Skelton, Robin. *The Writings of J. M. Synge,* pp. 132-152. London, Thames and Hudson, 1971.

Starkie, Walter. *Scholars and Gypsies: An Autobiography,* pp. 82-84. London, John Murray, 1963.

Stephens, Edward M. "Synge's Last Play", *Contemporary Review* (London), CLXXXVI (November 1954), 288-293.

Styan, John Louis. *The Elements of Drama,* pp. 126-128, 257-260. Cambridge, Cambridge University Press, 1960.

Thorning, Just. *J. M. Synge: En moderne irsk Dramatiker,* pp. 46-55. Studier fra Sprog- og Oldtidsforskning, No. 121. London and Copenhagen, V. Pios, 1921.

Völker, Klaus. *Irisches Theater I: William Butler Yeats* [*und*] *John Millington Synge,* pp. 74-77. Friedrichs Dramatiker des Welttheaters, Band 29. Velber bei Hannover, Friedrich, 1967.

Yeats, William Butler. *Autobiographies.* London, Macmillan, 1955. [Consisting of "Reveries over Childhood and Youth", "The Trembling of the Veil", "Dramatis Personae", "Estrangement", "The Death of Synge" and "The Bounty of Sweden".]

——————. *The Cutting of an Agate,* pp. 25-27. New York, 1912. [London edition of 1919 is the same as the New York 1912 edition. Both editions include the following essays: "The Tragic Theatre" (pp. 25-35), "Preface to the First Edition of *The Well of The Saints*" (pp. 111-122), "Preface to the First Edition of John M. Synge's Poems and Translations" (pp. 123-129), "J. M. Synge and the Ireland of His Time" (pp. 130-176)]

——————. "The Death of Synge, and Other Pages from an Old Diary", *The Dial* (Chicago), LXXXIV April 1928), 271-288. [For a discussion of *Deirdre,* see pp. 286-287. The same article appears in *The London Mercury* (see below, next entry) with the title word "Pages" altered to "Passages"]

——————. "The Death of Synge, and Other Passages from an Old Diary", *The London Mercury,* XVII (April 1928), 637-651. [See pp. 649-650]

——————. *The Death of Synge, and Other Passages from an Old Diary,* pp. 30-32. Dublin, Cuala Press, 1928.

——————. *Essays and Introductions,* pp. 238-239, 309-310. New York and London, Macmillan, 1961.

——————. "The Tragic Theatre", *The Mask* (Florence), III (October 1910), 77-81. [For a discussion of *Deirdre,* see p. 77. Reprinted, in part, as the Preface to *Plays for an Irish Theatre,* 1911; and in *The Cutting of an Agate,* 1919]

THE PLAYBOY OF THE WESTERN WORLD

Adams, J. Donald. "The Irish Dramatic Movement", *The Harvard Monthly* (Cambridge, Mass.), LIII (November 1911), 44-48. [See p. 47]

Agate, Captain James E. *The Amazing Theatre*, pp. 218-219. London, G. G. Harrap, 1939.

——————. *Buzz, Buzz! Essays of the Theatre*, pp. 150-153. London, W. Collins, [1918].

"The Aldrich Playboy", *Newsweek* (Dayton), XXVIII (4 November 1946), 85. [Review]

"Aping Ibsen at 'The Abbey' ", *The Lepracaun* (Dublin), II: 22 (February 1907), 419. [Review. Cartoon entitled "The Playboy and the Tomboy" appears on p. 422]

"Applause in December", *Harper's Bazaar* (New York), LXXX (December 1946), 220. [Review]

Bessai, Diane E. "Little Hound in Mayo: Synge's Playboy and the Comic Tradition in Irish Literature", *Dalhousie Review* (Halifax, Nova Scotia), XLVIII (Autumn 1968), 372-383.

Blissett, William. "Synge's Playboy", *Adam International Review* (London), Nos. 239-240 (1954), 17-20. [Also appears under *Colonnade* II: 5 (Winter 1954), 17-20, which is included in this issue of the *Adam International Review*]

Borel, Jacques. "Sur 'Le Baladin du monde occidental' ", *Critique* (Paris), XXII (January 1966), 54-59. [Review article of J. M. Synge, *The Playboy of the Western World* (London, Methuen, 1961); *Four Plays and the Aran Islands*, edited by Robin Skelton (London and New York, Oxford University Press, 1962); *Le Baladin du monde occidental* (Cahiers de documentation de la Comedie de l'Est, No. 8, 1962); J. M. Synge, *Théâtre*, translated by Maurice Bourgeois (Paris, Gallimard, 1942)]

Bourgeois, Maurice. *John Millington Synge and the Irish Theatre*, pp. 193-212. London, Constable, 1913; reissued by Benjamin Blom, Bronx, New York, 1965.

Boyd, Ernest Augustus. "J. M. Synge", in *Ireland's Literary Renaissance*, pp. 326-329. Dublin, Maunsel; London and New York, Knopf, 1916; revised edition, New York, 1922.

Brooks, Sydney. "The Irish Peasant as a Dramatic Issue", *Harper's Weekly* (New York), LI (9 March 1907), 344. [Article dated London, 2 February 1907]

Byrne, Dawson. *The Story of Ireland's National Theatre: The Abbey Theatre, Dublin*, pp. 56-64. Dublin, Talbot Press, 1929.

Carroll, Sydney Wentworth. " 'The Playboy of the Western World' ", in *Some Dramatic Opinions*, pp. 69-73. London, F. V. White, [1923].

Clark, Barrett Harper. *The British and American Drama of To-Day: Outlines for Their Study*, pp. 194-197. New York, Henry Holt, 1915.

——————. "John M. Synge", in *A Study of the Modern Drama*, pp. 342-344. New York and London, Appleton, 1925; revised edition, New York, Appleton-Century, 1938.

——————. " 'The Playboy' in Paris", *The Colonnade* (New York), XI (January 1916), 23-26.

Clark, James M. "The Irish Literary Movement", *Englische Studien* (Leipzig), XLIX (July 1915), 50-98. [See pp. 73-79]

Clark, William Smith, ed. "Introduction to *The Playboy of the Western World*. The Rise of the Irish Theater and Drama: Synge and Folk-Comedy", in *Chief Patterns of World Drama: Aeschylus to Anderson*, pp. 890-891. Boston, Houghton Mifflin, 1946.

Cohn, Ruby, and Bernard F. Dukore, eds. "John Millington Synge, 1871-1909", in *Twentieth Century Drama: England, Ireland, the United States*, pp. 92-94. New York, Random House, 1966.

Colligan, Francis J. "The Playboy of the Abbey Theatre Players", *San Francisco Quarterly*, I (May 1935), 81-88.

Colum, Mary Maguire. *Life and the Dream*, pp. 136-139, 140. London, Macmillan; Garden City, New York, Doubleday, 1947. [Concerns Yeats and the *Playboy* riots]

——————. "Memories of Yeats", *The Saturday Review of Literature* (New York), XIX (25 February 1939), 3-4, 14. [See p. 4]

Corkery, Daniel. *Synge and Anglo-Irish Literature: A Study*, pp. 179-204. Dublin and Cork, Cork University Press; London, Longmans, Green, 1931.

Cowell, Raymond. "John Millington Synge, *The Playboy of the Western World*", in *Twelve Modern Dramatists*, pp. 57-65. Pergamon Oxford English Series. Oxford and London, Pergamon Press, 1967.

Coxhead, Elizabeth. " 'Collaboration'—Hyde and Synge", in *Lady Gregory: A Literary Portrait*, pp. 108-126. London, Macmillan, 1961; second edition, revised and enlarged, London, Secker and Warburg, 1966. [See pp. 115-120]

——————. *J. M. Synge and Lady Gregory*, pp. 18-21. Writers and Their Work, No. 149. London, Longmans, Green, for the British Council and the National Book League, 1962.

Cusack, Cyril. "A Player's Reflections on *Playboy*", *Modern Drama* (Lawrence, Kansas), IV (December 1961), 300-305.

D'Amico, Silvio. *Storia del teatro drammatico*, II, 266. Milan, Garzanti, 1960.

Davie, Donald. "The Young Yeats", in *The Shaping of Modern Ireland*, edited by Conor Cruise O'Brien. Toronto, University of Toronto Press; London, Routledge and Kegan Paul, 1960. [See pp. 146-147]

Dickinson, Page L. *The Dublin of Yesterday*, pp. 85-87. London, Methuen, 1929.

[Dickinson, Page L., Frank Sparrow, and Joseph M. Hone]. *The Abbey Row. Not Edited by W. B. Yeats*. Dublin, Maunsel, [1907]. ["That night Joe Hone, Sparrow and I adjourned after the play, and somebody suggested writing an account of the evening. We did so, and a pamphlet was produced and finished next day which took the form of a parody on the *Arrow*, the journal of the theatre edited by W. B. Yeats. It was illustrated by Richard and William Orpen, and the original cover represented Erin leading an Irish wolfhound: our cover, Mrs. Grundy restraining Synge". P. L. Dickinson, *The Dublin of Yesterday*, p. 87. (London, Methuen, 1929)]

"Drama", *The Nation* (New York), XCIII (30 November 1911), 528-529. [A critique of the Irish plays presented in America, largely devoted to Synge's works and, in particular, *Well* and *Playboy*, see p. 529]

Dukes, Ashley. "Fashions in Comedy: Notes on London Summer Season", *Theatre Arts* (New York), XXVII (October 1943), 584-590. [Review]

"Editorial Notes: 'The Playboy of the Western World' ", *The Forum* (New York), XLVII (March 1912), 380-381.

Ellis-Fermor, Una Mary. "John Millington Synge", in *The Irish Dramatic Movement*, pp. 175-179. London, Methuen, 1939.

Erzgräber, Willi. "John Millington Synge: *The Playboy of the Western World*", in *Das moderne englische Drama: Interpretationen*, edited by Horst Oppel, pp. 87-108. Berlin, Erich Schmidt, 1963.

Estill, Adelaide Duncan. *The Sources of Synge*, pp. 29-33. Philadelphia, University of Pennsylvania, 1939.

Everson, Ida G. "Lennox Robinson and Synge's *Playboy* (1911-1930): Two Decades of American Cultural Growth", *The New England Quarterly* (Brunswick, Maine), XLIV (March 1971), 3-21.

—————. "Young Lennox Robinson and the Abbey Theatre's First American Tour (1911-1912)", *Modern Drama* (Lawrence, Kansas), IX (May 1966), 74-89. [See pp. 82-84]

Farjeon, Herbert. "The Birth of the Playboy", *Theatre Arts* (New York), XVI (March 1932), 228-236.

Fay, William George, and Catherine Carswell. *The Fays of the Abbey Theatre: An Autobiographical Record*, pp. 211-219. London, Rich and Cowan; New York, Harcourt, Brace, 1935.

Fechter, Paul. *Das europäische Drama. Geist und Kultur im Spiegel des Theaters. II. Vom Naturalismus zum Expressionismus*, pp. 257-259. Mannheim, Bibliographisches Institut, 1957.

Figgis, Darrell. "J. M. Synge" and "The Art of J. M. Synge", in *Studies and Appreciations*, pp. 53-56. London, J. M. Dent, 1912. ["Art of J. M. Synge" originally appeared in the *Fortnightly Review* and in the *Forum*]

Gassner, John W. "*The Playboy of the Western World*", in *The Theatre In Our Times: A Survey of the Men, Materials and Movements in the Modern Theatre*, pp. 537-542. New York, Crown Publishers, 1954.

Gerstenberger, Donna Lorine. *John Millington Synge*, pp. 75-93. Twayne's English Authors Series, 12. New York, Twayne, 1964.

Gibbs, Wolcott. "Gaels and Gagmen", *The New Yorker*, XXII (2 November 1946), 51-52. [Review]

Gilder, Rosamond. "New Year, New Plays: Broadway in Review, *The Playboy of the Western World*", *Theatre Arts* (New York), XXXI (January 1947), 21-22. [Review]

Grande, Julian. " 'The Playboy of the Western World': 'Much Ado about Nothing' ", *Ireland* (Dublin), VI: 8 (March 1907), 385-387. [This issue was printed in January-February, but not released until March; hence the title page is dated March, although the date January-February appears at the top of each page]

Greene, David H. "The Playboy and Irish Nationalism", *The Journal of English and Germanic Philology* (Urbana, Illinois), XLVI (April 1947), 199-204.

—————, and Edward M. Stephens. *J. M. Synge: 1871-1909*, pp. 234-271. New York, Macmillan, 1959.

Gregory, Lady Isabella Augusta. "An Explanation", *The Arrow* (Dublin), I: 4 (1 June 1907), [Lady Gregory explains why *Playboy* is being brought to England]

——————. "The Fight Over 'The Playboy' ", and " 'The Playboy' in America", in *Our Irish Theatre: A Chapter of Autobiography*, pp. 109-118, 130-134, 169-252, 280-309. New York and London, G.P. Putnam's, 1913.

Gunnell, Doris. "Le Nouveau théâtre irlandais", *La Revue* [late *Revue des Revues*] (Paris), XCIV: 1 (1 January 1912), 91-106. [See pp. 100-102]

Gvozdev, Aleksei Aleksandrovich. *Khrestomatīa po istorii zapadnogo teatra na rubezhe XIX-XX vekov* [Reader on the History of the Western Theatre at the Turn of the Twentieth Century], pp. 337-338. Moscow, Iskusstvo, 1939.

Hamilton, Clayton. "Significant Plays of the Recent London Season: 'The Play-Boy of the Western World' ", *The Bookman* (New York), XXXII (October 1910), 136-147. [See pp. 145-146]

Hart, William E., ed. "Introduction", in J. M. Synge, *The Playboy of the Western World and Riders to the Sea*. New York, Appleton-Century-Crofts, 1966.

Hayes, Richard. "The Road to the Isles", *The Commonweal* (New York), LXVIII (20 June 1958), 303-304. [Review]

Henry, P. L. "The Playboy of the Western World", *Philologica Pragensia: Časopis pro moderní filologii* (Prague), n.s. VIII (1965), 189-204.

Hensel, Georg. "Synge: die irische Realität, fröhlich", in *Spielplan: Schauspielführer, von der Antike bis zur Gegenwart*, II, 793-796. Berlin, Propyläen, 1966.

Holloway, Joseph. *Joseph Holloway's Abbey Theatre: A Selection from His Unpublished Journal, "Impressions of a Dublin Playgoer"*, edited by Robert Hogan and Michael J. O'Neill. Carbondale and Edwardsville, Southern Illinois University Press; London and Amsterdam, Feffer and Simons, 1967.

Hone, Joseph Maunsell. *William Butler Yeats: The Poet in Contemporary Ireland*, pp. 85-89. Irishmen of To-day Series. Dublin and London, Maunsel, [1916]

Hornblow, Arthur. "Mr Hornblow Goes to the Play", *Theatre Magazine* (New York), XXXIV (July 1921), 14, 60. [Photograph of Gladys Hurbut as Pegeen Mike, p. 14; review p. 60]

Howe, Percival Presland. *J. M. Synge: A Critical Study*, pp. 61-76. London, Martin Secker, 1912.

Howe, Percival Presland. "The *Playboy* in the Theatre", *The Oxford and Cambridge Review* (London), No. 21 (July 1912), 37-51.

Hueffer [Ford], Ford Madox. *The Critical Attitude*, pp. 82-83. London, Duckworth, 1911.

"Irish Home Rule in the Drama", *Current Literature* (New York), L (January 1911), 81-84.

Johnson, Wallace H. "The Pagan Setting of Synge's *Playboy*", *Renascence* (Milwaukee), XIX (Spring 1967), 119-121.

Johnston, Denis. *John Millington Synge*, pp. 29-39. Columbia Essays on Modern Writers, No. 12. New York and London, Columbia University Press, 1965.

Kain, Richard M. "A Scrapbook of The '*Playboy* Riot' ", *The Emory University Quarterly* (Atlanta), XXII (Spring 1966), 5-17.

Kilroy, James F. "The Playboy as Poet", *PMLA* (New York), LXXXIII (May 1968), 439-442.

Krieger, Hans. "J. M. Synge", *Die neueren Sprachen* (Marburg), XXIV (1916), 467-478, 533-538. [Reprinted in *John Millington Synge* (see below, next entry)]

───────. *John Millington Synge, ein Dichter der "keltischen Renaissance"*, pp. 71-87. Inaugural Dissertation. Marburg, N. G. Elwert'sche, 1916.

Kronenberger, Louis. "Synge", in *The Thread of Laughter: Chapters on English Stage Comedy from Jonson to Maugham*, pp. 284-288. New York, Knopf, 1952.

───────, ed. [Introductory Essay to *The Playboy of the Western World*], in *Cavalcade of Comedy: 21 Brilliant Comedies from Jonson and Wycherley to Thurber and Coward*, p. 438. New York, Simon and Schuster, 1953.

Krutch, Joseph Wood. "Drama", *The Nation* (New York), CLXIII (9 November 1946), 536. [Krutch argues that Synge wrote *Playboy* "in accordance with a theory and as a sort of protest against what he regarded as the essential wrongness of the modern drama"]

Lamm, Martin. "Um John M. Synge", *Birtingur* (Reykavik), XI, Parts 3-4 (1965), 56-58. [Reprinted from the Swedish edition of Martin Lamm's *Det moderna dramat*. In the English edition, entitled *Modern Drama*, this article is a translation of pages 302-304, 310-311]

Lengeler, Rainer. "Phantasie und Komik in Synges *The Playboy of the Western World*", *Germanisch-Romanische Monatsschrift* (Heidelberg), n.s. XIX:3 (July 1969), 291-304.

Leventhal, A. J. "Dramatic Commentary", *The Dublin Magazine,* n.s. XXIII (October-December 1948), 48-49. [Review]

——————. "Dramatic Commentary", *The Dublin Magazine,* n.s. XXIX (October-December 1953), 40. [Review]

Lucas, Frank Laurence. *The Drama of Chekhov, Synge, Yeats, and Pirandello,* pp. 201-224. London, Cassell, 1963.

Lunari, Gigi. "Lady Gregory e Synge", in *Il movimento drammatico irlandese (1899-1922),* pp. 140-144. Documenti di teatro 13. Bologne, Cappelli, 1960.

M., H. G. " 'Playboy of the Western World' ", *Theatre World* (London), XLIV (April 1948), 10. [Review]

MacLean, Hugh H. "The Hero as Playboy", *The University of Kansas City Review,* XXI (Autumn 1954), 9-19.

MacSiubhlaigh, Máire [Mary Walker], and Edward Kenny. *The Splendid Years: Recollections of M. Nic Shiubhlaigh,* as told to Edward Kenny, pp. 79-88. Dublin, James Duffy, 1955.

"Manuscripts of John M. Synge", *Amherst Graduates' Quarterly* (Amherst, Massachusetts), XIX (August 1930), 259-261. [Concerns a typewritten manuscript of *Playboy* and a letter on permanent loan to Amherst College]

Metcalfe. "Drama: A Whole Lot of Different Things", *Life* (New York), LVIII (14 December 1911), 1090-1091.

Monahan, Michael. "The Matter With the 'Playboy' ", in *Nova Hibernia: Irish Poets and Dramatists of Today and Yesterday,* pp. 30-37. New York, Mitchell Kennerley, 1914. [An historical explanation of why the Catholic Church opposed *Playboy.* Reprinted from the *Papyrus* (see below, next entry)]

——————. "The Matter with the 'Playboy' ", *Papyrus* (Mount Vernon, N.Y.), III:4 (February 1912), 18-21, 300.

Moore, George. *Hail and Farewell: A Trilogy: Vale,* pp. 205-207, 213-216. New York, Appleton; London, Heinemann, 1914. [Most of this material was reprinted from *The English Review* (see below, next entry)]

——————. "Yeats, Lady Gregory, and Synge: II", *The English Review* (London), XVI (February 1914), 350-364. [See pp. 359-361]

Morgan, Arthur Eustace. *Tendencies of Modern English Drama,* pp. 205-207. London, Constable, 1924.

Moses, Montrose J. "W. B. Yeats and the Irish Players", *The Metropolitan Magazine* (New York), XXXV (January 1912), 23-25, 61-62. [See p. 23]

Murphy, Daniel J. "The Reception of Synge's *Playboy* in Ireland and America: 1907-1912", *Bulletin of the New York Public Library*, LXIV (October 1960), 515-533.

Nathan, George Jean. "The Playboy of the Western World: October 26, 1946", in *The Theatre Book of the Year: 1946-1947*, pp. 136-139. New York, Knopf, 1947. [Review]

" 'National' Plays", *The Nation* (New York), XCIII (19 October 1911), 376-378. [Review]

Nordman, C. A. "J. M. Synge, Dramatikern", *Finsk Tidskrift för Vitterhet, Vetenskap, Konst och Politik* (Helsinki), LXXIX (July-December 1915), 26-70. [See pp. 48-57]

"Notes and News", *The Oxford Magazine*, XXVIII (2 June 1910), 354. [Review]

O'Casey, Sean. "Song of a Shift", in *Drums Under the Windows*, pp. 168-190. London, Macmillan, 1945; New York, Macmillan, 1946. [A parody of the *Playboy* rioters]

O'Connor, Brother Anthony Cyril. "Synge and National Drama", *Unitas: Revista de cultura y vida universitaria* (Manila), XXVII: 2 (April 1954), 294-346. [See pp. 322-324, 338-345]

O'Connor, Frank [Michael Francis O'Donovan]. *The Art of the Theatre*, pp. 19-22. Dublin and London, Maurice Fridberg, 1947.

————. "Synge", in *The Irish Theatre*. Lectures delivered during the Abbey Theatre Festival held in Dublin in August 1938, edited by Lennox Robinson, pp. 44-49. London, Macmillan, 1939.

O'D, D. J. "John M. Synge", *The Irish Book Lover* (Dublin), III (September 1911), 31. [A reply to Maurice Bourgeois's request for information on Synge. The original request appeared in *The Irish Book Lover*, III (August 1911), 14]

"Old Play in Manhattan: The Playboy of the Western World", *Time* (Chicago), XLVIII (4 November 1946), 55-56. [Atlantic Overseas edition, p. 32]

Peacock, Ronald. "Synge", in *The Poet in the Theatre*, pp. 112-114. London, Routledge and Kegan Paul; New York, Harcourt, Brace, 1946.

Pearce, Howard D. "Synge's Playboy as Mock-Christ", *Modern Drama* (Lawrence, Kansas), VIII (December 1965), 303-310.

Phelan, Kappo. " 'The Playboy of the Western World' ", *The Common-*

weal (New York), XLV (8 November 1946), 95. [Review]

" 'The Playboy' ", *Inis Fáil* (London), No. 31 (April 1907), 3-4.

" 'The Playboy of the Western World' ", *The Bookman* (London), XXXII (August 1907), 181. [A review of Maunsel and Co. edition, *The Playboy*]

" 'The Playboy of the Western World' at the Mercury Theatre", *Theatre World* (London), XLIV (May 1948), 27-28. [Review]

"The Playboy of the Western World: Confounding Drama with Pastoral Poetry", *The Dramatist* (Easton, Pa.), III (January 1912), 224-225.

Podhoretz, Norman. "Synge's *Playboy:* Morality and the Hero", *Essays in Criticism* (Oxford), III (July 1953), 337-344.

Price, Alan Frederick. *Riders to the Sea, The Playboy of the Western World (J. M. Synge).* Notes on English Literature Series. Oxford, Blackwell, 1969.

——————. *Synge and Anglo-Irish Drama*, pp. 24-28, 161-180. London, Methuen, 1961.

Reid, Benjamin L. *The Man from New York: John Quinn and His Friends*, pp. 46-49, 115-117. New York, Oxford University Press, 1968.

Reinert, Otto, ed. "Comment", in *Drama: An Introductory Anthology* (Alternate Edition), pp. 696-701. Boston, Little, Brown, 1964.

Riva, Serafino. *La tradizione celtica e la moderna letteratura irlandese, I. John Millington Synge*, pp. 213-225. Rome, Religio, 1937.

Robinson, Lennox. *Curtain Up: An Autobiography*, pp. 40-41. London, Michael Joseph, 1942.

Rollins, Ronald G. "Huckleberry Finn and Christy Mahon: The Playboy of the Western World", *Mark Twain Journal* (Kirkwood, Missouri), XIII (Summer 1966), 16-19.

——————. "O'Casey and Synge: The Irish Hero as Playboy and Gunman", *Arizona Quarterly* (Tucson), XXII (Autumn 1966), 217-222.

Roosevelt, Theodore, and George Bernard Shaw. *A Note on the Irish Theatre by Theodore Roosevelt and An "Interview" on the Irish Players in America by George Bernard Shaw*, pp. 5, 16-18. New York, Mitchell Kennerly, 1912. [In every copy of this pamphlet the name John Quinn, which appears in the table of contents after the title "Note", and in the text after the "Note", has been inked over. The

Shaw "Interview" has been reprinted in *The Matter with Ireland*, pp. 61-68]

Rust, Adolf. *Beiträge zu einer Geschichte der neu-keltischen Renaissance*, pp. 66-77. Bückenburg, Grimme'sche Hofbuchdruckerei, 1922.

Ruyssen, Henri. "Le Théâtre irlandais", *Revue Germanique* (Paris), V (January-February 1909), 123-125. [See pp. 124-125]

Salerno, Henry F., ed. "John Millington Synge (1871-1909)", in *English Drama in Transition: 1880-1920*, pp. 415-419. New York, Pegasus, 1968.

Salmon, Eric. "J. M. Synge's *Playboy:* A Necessary Reassessment", *Modern Drama* (Lawrence, Kansas), XIII (September 1970), 111-128.

Sanderlin, R. Reed. "Synge's *Playboy* and the Ironic Hero", *The Southern Quarterly* (Hattiesburg, Miss.), VI (April 1968), 289-301.

Sarsfield. " 'The Playboy' Again", *Inis Fáil* (London), No. 33 (June 1907), 8-9.

Setterquist, Jan. "Ibsen and Synge", *Studia Neophilologica* (Upsala), XXIV (1951/52), 112-130. [Reprinted in *Ibsen and the Beginnings of Anglo-Irish Drama* (see below, next entry)]

——————. *Ibsen and the Beginnings of Anglo-Irish Drama: I. John Millington Synge*, pp. 52-70. Upsala Irish Studies, Vol. 2, edited by S. B. Liljegren. Upsala, A-B. Lundequistka; Dublin, Hodges, Figgis; Copenhagen, Munksgaard; Cambridge, Massachusetts, Harvard University Press, 1951.

Shaw, George Bernard. *The Matter with Ireland*, pp. 63-64, 84. Hitherto uncollected writings, edited by Dan H. Laurence and David H. Greene. New York, Hill and Wang, 1962.

Shipley, Joseph T. *Guide to Great Plays*, pp. 761-763. Washington, D.C., Public Affairs Press, 1956.

Shipp, Horace. "Plays with Ideas", *The English Review* (London), LI (December 1930), 782-784. [Review]

Sidnell, M. J. "Synge's Playboy and the Champion of Ulster", *Dalhousie Review* (Halifax, Nova Scotia), XLV (Spring 1965), 51-59.

Simons, L[eo]. "Tooneel-Bepeinzingen", *De Ploeg* (The Hague), II: 2 (August 1909), 56-63. [Review]

Skelton, Robin. *J. M. Synge and His World*, pp. 106-116. London, Thames and Hudson, 1971.

——————. *The Writings of J. M. Synge*, pp. 114-131. London, Thames and Hudson, 1971.

Smith, Harry W. "Synge's *Playboy* and the Proximity of Violence", *The Quarterly Journal of Speech* (New York), LV: 4 (December 1969), 381-387.

Solomont, Susan. *The Comic Effect of The Playboy of the Western World by John Millington Synge*. Bangor, Maine, Signalman Press, 1962.

"Some Plays of the Season Technically Considered", *The American Playwright* (New York), I (January 1912), 20-28. [See pp. 24-25]

Spacks, Patricia Meyer. "The Making of the Playboy", *Modern Drama* (Lawrence, Kansas), IV (December 1961), 314-323.

Spencer, T. J. B. [Review of J. M. Synge, *The Playboy of the Western World*, with introduction and notes by T. R. Henn], *Modern Language Review* (Cambridge, England), LVI (October 1961), 635.

Starkie, Walter. *Scholars and Gypsies: An Autobiography*, pp. 37-39, 84-85. London, John Murray, 1963.

"The Stormy Debut of the Irish Players", *Current Literature* (New York), LI (December 1911), 675-676.

Strong, Leonard Alfred George. "John Millington Synge", *The Bookman* (New York), LXXIII (April 1931), 125-136. [See pp. 134-136. Reprinted in *The Dublin Magazine* (see below, next entry)]

——————. "John Millington Synge", *The Dublin Magazine*, n.s. VII: 2 (April-June 1932), 12-32. [See pp. 27-30]

——————. *John Millington Synge*, pp. 34-41. P. E. N. Books, London, Allen and Unwin, 1941.

——————. "John Millington Synge" in *Personal Remarks*, pp. 53-59. London, P. Nevill, 1953. [Reprinted from *The Bookman* and *The Dublin Magazine* (see above)]

Styan, John Louis. *The Elements of Drama*, pp. 57-63. Cambridge, Cambridge University Press, 1960.

Sullivan, Mary Rose. "Synge, Sophocles, and the Un-Making of Myth", *Modern Drama* (Lawrence, Kansas), XII: 3 (December 1969), 242-253.

Sultan, Stanley. "The Gospel According to Synge", *Papers on Language and Literature* (Edwardsville, Ill.), IV (Fall 1968), 428-441.

——————. "A Joycean Look at The Playboy of the Western World", in *The Celtic Master: Contributions to the First James Joyce Symposium* in Dublin, 1967, edited by Maurice Harmon. Dublin, Dolmen Press, 1969.

"Summer Theatre", *Life Magazine* (Chicago), XXI (5 August 1946), 81-89. [Review; see pp. 81-83]

Suss, Irving D. "The 'Playboy' Riots", *Irish Writing* (Cork), No. 18 (March 1952), 39-42.

"Synge's Irish Play at the Bramhall Well Received", *The New York Clipper*, LXIX (20 April 1921), 23. [Review]

Thorndike, Ashley. *English Comedy*, pp. 582-584. New York, Macmillan, 1929.

Thorning, Just. *J. M. Synge: En moderne irsk Dramatiker*, pp. 32-46. Studier fra Sprog- og Oldtidsforskning, No. 121. London and Copenhagen, V. Pios, 1921.

Tilgher, Adriano. "Il teatro di John Millington Synge", in *Studi sul teatro contemporaneo*, pp. 219-225. Rome, Libreria di Scienze e Lettere, 1923.

Turner, W. J. " 'The Playboy of the Western World' ", *The London Mercury*, IV (September 1921), 537-539. [Review]

Untermeyer, Louis. "J. M. Synge and The Playboy of the Western World", *Poet-Lore* (Boston), XIX (Autumn 1908), 364-367. [A review of Maunsel and Co. edition, *The Playboy*]

Völker, Klaus. *Irisches Theater I: William Butler Yeats [und] John Millington Synge*, pp. 66-74. Friedrichs Dramatiker des Welttheaters, Band 29. Velber bei Hannover, Friedrich, 1967.

Walbrook, Henry MacKinnon. " 'The Playboy of the Western World' ", in *Nights at the Play*, pp. 107-110. London, W. J. Ham-Smith, 1911. [Review]

Walley, Harold Reinoehl. "Folk Drama", in *The Book of the Play: An Introduction to Drama*, pp. 443-447. New York, Scribner's, 1950. [See pp. 445-447]

Ward, Alfred Charles. *Specimens of English Dramatic Criticism XVII-XX Centuries*, pp. 248-259. London and New York, Oxford University Press, 1945. [Includes three articles from the *Irish Times* written at the time of the *Playboy* riots, the most famous being "That Dreadful Play" by Pat (P. D. Kenny)]

Whitaker, Thomas R., ed. "Introduction: On Playing with *The Playboy*", in *Twentieth Century Interpretations of The Playboy of the Western World*. Englewood Cliffs, New Jersey, Prentice-Hall, 1969.

Wieczorek, Hubert. *Irische Lebenshaltung im neuen irischen Drama*, pp. 44-46. Sprache und Kultur der Germanischen und Romanischen Völker. A. Anglistische Reihe, Band XXVI. Breslau, Priebatsch's Buchhandlung, 1937.

Williamson, Audrey. *Theatre of Two Decades*, pp. 185-186. London, Rockliff, 1951.

Wood, Edward Rudolf. "Introduction", in John M. Synge, *Riders to the Sea* and *The Playboy of the Western World*, pp. ix-xx. The Hereford Plays. London, Heinemann, 1961.

Wyatt, Euphemia van Rennselaer. "The Playboy of the Western World", *The Catholic World* (New York), CLXIV (December 1946), 262-263. [Review]

——————. "The Playboy of the Western World", *The Catholic World* (New York), CLXXXVII (July 1958), 312-313. [Review]

Yeats, John Butler."Synge and the Irish", in *Essays Irish and American* pp. 58-60. Dublin, Talbot Press, London, T. F. Unwin; New York, Macmillan, 1918.

——————. "Synge and the Irish: Random Reflections on a Much-Discussed Dramatist from the Standpoint of a Fellow-Countryman", *Harper's Weekly* (New York), LV (25 November 1911), 17, col. 3.

"Yeats, Synge and 'The Playboy' ", *The Irish Book Lover* (Dublin), IV (August 1912), 7-8. [An extract from J. M. Hone, "A Memory of 'The Playboy' ", *The Saturday Review* (London), 22 June 1912, pp. 776-777]

Yeats, William Butler. *Autobiographies*. London, Macmillan, 1955. [Consisting of "Reveries over Childhood and Youth", "The Trembling of the Veil", "Dramatis Personae", "Estrangement", "The Death of Synge" and "The Bounty of Sweden".]

——————. *The Bounty of Sweden: A Meditation, and a Lecture Delivered Before the Royal Swedish Academy and Certain Notes*, pp. 45-47. Dublin, Cuala Press, 1925.

——————. "The Controversy over 'The Playboy' ", *The Arrow* (Dublin), I:3 (23 February 1907), [1-2]. [Reprinted, in part, in "The Irish Dramatic Movement", in the *Collected Works*, Vol. IV, 1908; in *Plays and Controversies*, 1923; and in *Explorations*, 1962]

——————. *The Cutting of an Agate*, pp. 130-132. New York, 1912. [London edition of 1919 is the same as the New York 1912 edition. Both editions include the following essays: "The Tragic Theatre" (pp. 25-35), "Preface to the First Edition of *The Well of the Saints*" (pp. 111-122), "Preface to the First Edition of John M. Synge's Poems and Translations" (pp. 123-129), "J. M. Synge and the Ireland of His Time" (pp. 130-176)]

——————. *Dramatis Personae, 1896-1902, Estrangement, The Death of Synge, The Bounty of Sweden*, pp. 187-188. London, Macmillan, 1936. [New York, Macmillan, 1936 edition: pp. 196-198]

——————. *Explorations*. Selected by Mrs W. B. Yeats, pp. 225-230, 234, 253. London and New York, Macmillan, 1962.

Yeats, William Butler. *The Hour Glass, Cathleen Ni Houlihan, The Golden Helmet, The Irish Dramatic Movement*, pp. 227-232. Being the Fourth Volume of the Collected Works in Verse and Prose of William Butler Yeats. Stratford-on-Avon, Shakespeare Head Press, 1908. [Includes the following essays: "The Controversy over *The Playboy of the Western World*" (pp. 227-228), "From Mr Yeats' Opening Speech in the Debate on February 4, 1907, at the Abbey Theatre" (pp. 228-230), and "On Taking *The Playboy* to London" (pp. 231-232)]

——————. "Mr Yeats' Opening Speech at the Debate of February 4th at the Abbey Theatre", *The Arrow* (Dublin), I: 3 (23 February 1907), [6-9]. [Reprinted in part, in "The Irish Dramatic Movement", in the *Collected Works*, Vol. IV, 1908; in *Plays and Controversies*, 1923; and in *Explorations*, 1962]

——————. [On Taking "The Playboy" to London], *The Arrow* (Dublin), I: 4 (1 June 1907), [1-2]. [Reprinted in "The Irish Dramatic Movement", in the *Collected Works*, Vol. IV, 1908; in *Plays and Controversies*, 1923; and in *Explorations*, 1962]

——————. *Plays and Controversies*, pp. 192-198, 211. London, Macmillan, 1923. [The contents of the American edition, published in New York, 1924, are the same as those of the English edition]

——————. *Les Prix Nobel en 1923*, pp. 7-8. Stockholm, P. A. Nordstedt and Söner, 1924. [Yeats's lecture "The Irish Dramatic Movement" is the last in the volume, and is paged separately, pp. 1-11; was also issued separately in 1924. Yeats delivered his lecture in Stockholm to the Swedish Royal Academy on 13 December 1923. In his preface to *The Bounty of Sweden*, dated 15 June 1924, he wrote that " a couple of months ago" he had dictated as many of his words as he could remember and added thereto "certain explanatory notes". The lecture and preface have been reprinted in *The Bounty of Sweden: A Meditation, and a Lecture Delivered Before the Royal Swedish Academy and Certain Notes* (Dublin, Cuala Press, 1925)]

——————. *Synge and the Ireland of His Time by William Butler Yeats with a Note Concerning a Walk through Connemara with Him by Jack Butler Yeats*, pp. 1-3. Churchtown, Dundrum, Cuala Press, 1911.

Young, Ella. "The Playboy", in *Flowering Dusk: Things Remembered Accurately and Inaccurately*, pp. 95-96. New York, Longmans, Green, 1945.

Young, Stark. "After the Play", *The New Republic* (New York), XXVII (22 June 1921), 117. [Review]

——————. "Synge and Webb", *The New Republic* (New York), CXV (11 November 1946), 628. [Review]

RIDERS TO THE SEA

Aufhauser, Annemarie. *Sind die Dramen von John Millington Synge durch französische Vorbilder beeinflusst?*, pp. 33-45. Inaugural Dissertation. Würzburg, Richard Mayr, 1935.

Beerbohm, Max. "Some Irish Plays and Players", in *Around Theatres*, II, 402-407. New York, Knopf, 1930. [Review. Reprinted from *The Saturday Review* (London), 9 April 1904, pp. 455-457. Reprinted in *Around Theatres*, pp. 314-319. London, R. Hart-Davis, 1953]

Bourgeois, Maurice. *John Millington Synge and the Irish Theatre*, pp. 158-172. London, Constable, 1913; reissued by Benjamin Blom, Bronx, New York, 1965.

──────. "Synge and Loti", *The Westminster Review* (London), CLXXIX (May 1913), 532-536. [See pp. 534-535]

Boyd, Ernest Augustus. "J. M. Synge", in *Ireland's Literary Renaissance*, pp. 321-323. Dublin, Maunsel; London and New York, Knopf, 1916; revised edition, New York, 1922.

Brooks, Cleanth, and Robert B. Heilman. [Analysis and Questions: *Riders to the Sea*], in *Understanding Drama: Twelve Plays*, pp. 26-27, Appendix A. New York, Henry Holt, 1945.

Canfield, Curtis, ed. *Plays of the Irish Renaissance: 1880-1930*, pp. 155-156. New York, Ives Washburn, 1929.

Carpenter, Bruce. " 'Riders to the Sea' ", in *The Way of the Drama: A Study of Dramatic Forms and Moods*, pp. 64-65. New York, Prentice-Hall, 1929.

Clark, Barrett Harper. *The British and American Drama of To-Day: Outlines for Their Study*, pp. 191-193. New York, Henry Holt, 1915.

──────. "John M. Synge", in *A Study of the Modern Drama*, pp. 338-341. New York and London, Appleton, 1925; revised edition, New York, Appleton-Century, 1938.

Clark, David R., ed. "Introduction", in *John Millington Synge: Riders to the Sea*. The Charles E. Merrill Literary Casebook Series. Columbus, Ohio, Charles E. Merrill, 1970.

Cohen, Helen Louise, ed. [Introduction to J. M. Synge, *Riders to The Sea*], in *One-Act Plays by Modern Authors*, pp. 195-197. New York, Harcourt, Brace, 1921.

Collins, R. L. "The Distinction of *Riders to the Sea*", *The University of Kansas City Review*, XIII (Summer 1947), 278-284.

Combs, William W. "J. M. Synge's Riders to the Sea: A Reading and Some Generalizations", *Papers of the Michigan Academy of Science, Arts, and Letters* (Ann Arbor, Michigan), L (1965 [1964 Meeting]), 599-607.

Corkery, Daniel. *Synge and Anglo-Irish Literature: A Study*, pp. 135-146. Dublin and Cork, Cork University Press; London, Longmans, Green, 1931.

Currie, Ryder Hector, and Martin Bryan. "Riders to the Sea: Reappraised", *The Texas Quarterly* (Austin), XI (Winter 1968), 139-146.

Donoghue, Denis. "Synge: *Riders to the Sea;* A Study", *University Review* (Dublin), I (Summer 1955), 52-58.

"Drama", *The Nation* (New York), XCIII (7 December 1911), 559. [Review]

Eaton, Walter Prichard. *Plays and Players: Leaves from a Critic's Scrapbook*, pp. 297-298. Cincinnati, Stewart and Kidd, 1916.

Ellmann, Richard. *James Joyce*, pp. 128-129. New York, Oxford University Press, 1959.

Estill, Adelaide Duncan. *The Sources of Synge*, pp. 13-16. Philadelphia, University of Pennsylvania, 1939.

Fay, Gerard. "The Abbey Theatre and the One Act Play", *One Act Play Magazine* (New York), II:4 (August-September 1938), 323-326. [See pp. 324-326]

Figgis, Darrell. "J. M. Synge" and "The Art of J. M. Synge", in *Studies and Appreciations*, pp. 42-45. London, J. M. Dent, 1912. ["Art of J. M. Synge" originally appeared in the *Fortnightly Review* and in the *Forum*]

Firkins, O. W. "Rostand and Synge", *Weekly Review* (New York), III (18 August 1920), 155-156 [Review]

Gerstenberger, Donna Lorine. *John Millington Synge*, pp. 44-54. Twayne's English Authors Series, 12. New York, Twayne, 1964.

Greene, David H., and Edward M. Stephens. *J. M. Synge: 1871-1909*, pp. 143-159. New York, Macmillan, 1959.

Guerrero Zamora, Juan. "John Millington Synge", in *Historia del teatro contemporáneo*, III, 26-28. Barcelona, Juan Flors, 1962.

H., C. "J. M. Synge's 'The Shadow of the Glen' and 'Riders to the Sea' ", in *John Millington Synge: Some Unpublished Letters and*

Documents of J. M. Synge Formerly in the Possession Mr. Lawrence Wilson of Montreal and Now for the First Time Published for Him by The Redpath Press, pp. 28-33. Montreal, Redpath Press, 1959.

Harrison, Austin. "Strindberg's Plays", *English Review* (London), XIII (December 1912), 80-97. [A comparison between Strindberg's *The Crown Bride* and Synge's *Riders*]

Hoare, John Edward. "John Synge", *The University Magazine* (Toronto), X (February 1911), 91-109. [See pp. 96-98]

Howe, Percival Presland. *J. M. Synge: A Critical Study*, pp. 51-60. London, Martin Secker, 1912.

Johnston, Denis. *John Millington Synge*, pp. 18-23. Columbia Essays on Modern Writers, No. 12. New York and London, Columbia University Press, 1965.

Joyce, James. "*Riders to the Sea* by John M. Synge", in Herbert Gorman, *James Joyce*, p. 258. New York and Toronto, Farrar and Rinehart, 1939. [This is a programme note that Joyce wrote for a production in Zurich, 17 June 1918]

Krieger, Hans. "J. M. Synge", *Die neueren Sprachen* (Marburg), XXIV (1916), 408-415. [Reprinted in *John Millington Synge* (see below, next entry)]

—————. *John Millington Synge, ein Dichter der "keltischen Renaissance"*, pp. 52-59. Inaugural Dissertation. Marburg, N. G. Elwert'sche, 1916.

Krüger, Werner Adolf. "Synge, John M.", *Die neue Literatur* (Leipzig), XXXVI (April 1935), 229-230. [Review]

Lamm, Martin. *Det Moderna dramat*. Stockholm, A. Bonnier, 1948.

—————. *Modern Drama*, translated by Karin Elliott, pp. 306-309. Oxford, Basil Blackwell, 1952.

Levitt, Paul M. "The Structural Craftsmanship of J. M. Synge's *Riders to the Sea*", *Eire-Ireland* (St. Paul, Minn.), IV:1 (Spring 1969), 53-61.

Lucas, Frank Laurence. *The Drama of Chekhov, Synge, Yeats, and Pirandello*, pp. 181-188. London, Cassell, 1963.

MacSiubhlaigh, Máire. [Mary Walker], and Edward Kenny. *The Splendid Years: Recollections of M. Nic Shiubhlaigh*, as told to Edward Kenny, pp. 53-56. Dublin, James Duffy, 1955.

Millett, Fred B. *Reading Drama: A Method of Analysis with Selections for Study*. New York, Harper, 1950.

78   SYNGE: PUBLISHED CRITICISM

Nordman, C. A. "J. M. Synge, Dramatikern", *Finsk Tidskrift för Vetterhet, Vetenskap, Konst och Politik* (Helsinki), LXXIX (July-December 1915), 26-70. [See pp. 34-39]

O'Connor, Brother Anthony Cyril. "Synge and National Drama", *Unitas: Revista de cultura y vida universitaria* (Manila), XXVII: 2 (April 1954), 294-346. [See pp. 319-320; 328-337]

Onofrio, Lilia d'. "John M. Synge, dramaturgo irlandes contemporaneo (A propósito de su drama *Jinetes hacia el mar*)", in *Nueve ensayos de critica literaria*, pp. 69-79. Buenos Aires, "El Ateneo", 1942. [See pp. 73-78]

Ottaway, D. Hugh. " 'Riders to the Sea' ", *The Musical Times* (London), XCIII (August 1952), 358-360.

Ould, Hermon. *The Art of the Play*, pp. 148-150. London, Pitman, 1938.

Page, Curtis C., ed. *Drama: Synge's Riders to the Sea*. Casebooks for Objective Writing. Boston, Ginn, 1966.

Peacock, Ronald. "Synge", in *The Poet in the Theatre*, pp. 109-110. London, Routledge and Kegan Paul; New York, Harcourt, Brace, 1946.

Pittock, Malcolm. "Riders to the Sea", *English Studies* (Amsterdam), XLIX (October 1968), 445-449.

Price, Alan Frederick. *Riders to the Sea, The Playboy of the Western World* (*J. M. Synge*). Notes on English Literature Series. Oxford, Blackwell, 1969.

——————. *Synge and Anglo-Irish Drama*, pp. 181-191. London, Methuen, 1961.

Riva, Serafino. *La tradizione celtica e la moderna letteratura irlandese, I. John Millington Synge*, pp. 188-198. Rome, Religio, 1937.

Rowe, Kenneth Thorpe. "Analysis of a Great Play", in *Write That Play*, pp. 90-122. New York and London, Funk and Wagnalls, 1939.

Rust, Adolf. *Beiträge zu einer Geschichte der neu-keltischen Renaissance*, pp. 40-50. Bückeburg, Grimme'sche Hofbuchdruckerei, 1922.

Setterquist, Jan. "Ibsen and Synge", *Studia Neophilologica* (Upsala), XXIV (1951/52), 87-99. [Reprinted in *Ibsen and the Beginnings of Anglo-Irish Drama* (see below, next entry)]

——————. *Ibsen and the Beginnings of Anglo-Irish Drama; I. John Millington Synge*, pp. 27-39. Upsala Irish Studies, Vol. 2, edited by S. B. Liljegren. Upsala, A-B. Lundequistka; Dublin, Hodges, Figgis; Copenhagen, Munksgaard; Cambridge, Massachusetts, Harvard University Press, 1951.

Skelton, Robin. *The Writings of J. M. Synge,* pp. 41-52. London, Thames and Hudson, 1971.

Stamm, Rudolf. *Three Anglo-Irish Plays,* pp. 7-8. Bibliotheca Anglicana (Texts and Studies), v. 5. Berne, A. Francke, 1943.

Thorning, Just. *J. M. Synge: En moderne irsk Dramatiker,* pp. 16-21. Studier fra Sprog- og Oldtidsforskning, No. 121. London and Copenhagen, V. Pios, 1921.

Van Laan, Thomas F. "Form as Agent in Synge's *Riders to the Sea",* *Drama Survey* (Minneapolis), III (Winter 1964), 352-366.

Vernon, Frank. *The Twentieth-Century Theatre,* pp. 91-92. London, G. G. Harrap; Boston and New York, Houghton Mifflin, 1924.

Völker, Klaus. *Irisches Theater I: William Butler Yeats [und] John Millington Synge,* pp. 57-59. Friedrichs Dramatiker des Velttheaters, Band 29. Velber bei Hannover, Friedrich, 1967.

Warnock, Robert, ed. "Riders to the Sea", in *Representative Modern Plays: British,* pp. 341-345. Chicago, Scott, Foresman, 1953.

Watt, Homer A., and James B. Munn. [Introductory "Note" to J. M. Synge, *Riders to the Sea*], in *Ideas and Forms in English and American Literature,* p. 726. Chicago, Scott, Foresman, 1925.

Wood, Edward Rudolf. "Introduction", in John M. Synge, *Riders to the Sea* and *The Playboy of the Western World,* pp. xxi-xxiv. The Hereford Plays. London, Heinemann, 1961.

IN THE SHADOW OF THE GLEN

Aufhauser, Annemarie. *Sind die Dramen von John Millington Synge durch französische Vorbilder beeinflusst?*, pp. 21-33. Inaugural Dissertation. Würzburg, Richard Mayr, 1935.

Beerbohm, Max. "Some Irish Plays and Players", in *Around Theatres*, II, 402-407. New York, Knopf, 1930. [Review. Reprinted from *The Saturday Review* (London), 9 April 1904, pp. 455-457. Reprinted in *Around Theatres*, pp. 314-319. London, R. Hart-Davis, 1953]

Bourgeois, Maurice. *John Millington Synge and the Irish Theatre*, pp. 145-158. London, Constable, 1913; reissued by Benjamin Blom, Bronx, New York, 1965.

Colum, Padraic. "Early Days of the Irish Theatre", *The Dublin Magazine*, n.s. XXV (January-March 1950), 18-25. [See pp. 22-23]

Corkery, Daniel. *Synge and Anglo-Irish Literature: A Study*, pp. 123-134. Dublin and Cork, Cork University Press; London, Longmans, Green, 1931.

Estill, Adelaide Duncan. *The Sources of Synge*, pp. 3-12. Philadelphia, University of Pennsylvania, 1939.

Fay, Gerard. "The Abbey Theatre and the One Act Play", *One Act Play Magazine* (New York), II: 4 (August-September 1938), 323-326. [See pp. 324-326]

Figgis, Darrell. "J. M. Synge" and "The Art of J. M. Synge", in *Studies and Appreciations*, pp. 45-48. London, J. M. Dent, 1912. ["Art of J. M. Synge" originally appeared in the *Fortnightly Review* and in the *Forum*]

Gerstenberger, Donna Lorine. *John Millington Synge*, pp. 37-43. Twayne's English Authors Series, 12. New York, Twayne, 1964.

Greene, David H. "*The Shadow of the Glen* and *The Widow of Ephesus*", *PMLA* (New York), LXII (March 1947), 233-238.

——————, and Edward M. Stephens. *J. M. Synge: 1871-1909*, pp. 143-159. New York, Macmillan, 1959.

H., C. "J. M. Synge's 'The Shadow of the Glen' and 'Riders to the Sea' ", in *John Millington Synge: Some Unpublished Letters and Documents of J. M. Synge Formerly in the Possession of Mr. Lawrence Wilson of Montreal and Now for the First Time Published*

81

for Him by The Redpath Press, pp. 28-33. Montreal, Redpath Press, 1959.

Hoare, John Edward. "John Synge", *The University Magazine* (Toronto), X (February 1911), 91-109. [See pp. 92-96]

Howe, Percival Presland. *J. M. Synge: A Critical Study*, pp. 43-51. London, Martin Secker, 1912.

Krieger, Hans. "J. M. Synge", *Die neueren Sprachen* (Marburg), XXIV (1916), 359-362; 404-408. [Reprinted in *John Millington Synge* (see below, next entry)]

————. *John Millington Synge, ein Dichter der "keltischen Renaissance"*, pp. 44-52. Inaugural Dissertation. Marburg, N. G. Elwert'sche, 1916.

Krüger, Werner Adolf. "Synge, John M.", *Die neue Literatur* (Leipzig), XXXVI (April 1935), 229-230. [Review]

Lucas, Frank Laurence. *The Drama of Chekhov, Synge, Yeats, and Pirandello*, pp. 167-180. London, Cassell, 1963.

MacSiubhlaigh, Máire [Mary Walker], and Edward Kenny. *The Splendid Years: Recollections of M. Nic Shiubhlaigh*, as told to Edward Kenny, pp. 39-48. Dublin, James Duffy, 1955.

Nordman, C. A. "J. M. Synge, Dramatikern", *Finsk Tidskrift för Vitterhet, Vetenskap, Konst och Politik* (Helsinki), LXXIX (July-December 1915), 26-70. [See pp. 30-34]

"Notes and News", *The Oxford Magazine*, XXVIII (2 June 1910), 354. [Review]

Price, Alan F. "A Consideration of Synge's 'The Shadow of the Glen' ", *The Dublin Magazine*, n.s. XXVI (October-December 1951), 15-24.

————. *Synge and Anglo-Irish Drama*, pp. 118-126. London, Methuen, 1961.

Riva, Serafino. *La tradizione celtica e la moderna letteratura irlandese, I. John Millington Synge*, pp. 181-188. Rome, Religio, 1937.

Rust, Adolf. *Beiträge zu einer Geschichte der neu-keltischen Renaissance*, pp. 31-40. Bückeburg, Grimme'sche Hofbuchdruckerei, 1922.

Setterquist, Jan. "Ibsen and Synge", *Studia Neophilologica* (Upsala), XXIV (1951/52), 76-86. [Reprinted in *Ibsen and the Beginnings of Anglo-Irish Drama* (see below, next entry)]

————. *Ibsen and the Beginnings of Anglo-Irish Drama: I. John Millington Synge*, pp. 16-26. Upsala Irish Studies, Vol. 2, edited by S. B. Liljegren. Upsala, A.-B. Lundequistka; Dublin, Hodges,

Figgis; Copenhagen, Munksgaard; Cambridge, Massachusetts, Harvard University Press, 1951.

Skelton, Robin. "J. M. Synge and *The Shadow of the Glen*", *English* (London), XVIII (Autumn 1969), 91-97.

——. *The Writings of J. M. Synge*, pp. 53-63. London, Thames and Hudson, 1971.

Thorning, Just. *J. M. Synge: En moderne irsk Dramatiker*, pp. 9-16. Studier fra Sprog- og Oldtidsforskning, No. 121. London and Copenhagen, V. Pios, 1921.

Völker, Klaus. *Irisches Theater I: William Butler Yeats [und] John Millington Synge*, pp. 55-57. Friedrichs Dramatiker des Welttheaters, Band 29. Velber bei Hannover, Friedrich, 1967.

THE TINKER'S WEDDING

"The Bookman's Table: The Tinker's Wedding", *The Bookman* (London), XXXIII (March 1908), 260. [A review of Maunsel and Co. edition, *The Tinker's Wedding*]

Bourgeois, Maurice. *John Millington Synge and the Irish Theatre*, pp. 176-182. London, Constable, 1913; reissued by Benjamin Blom, Bronx, New York, 1965.

Corkery, Daniel. *Synge and Anglo-Irish Literature: A Study*, pp. 147-152. Dublin and Cork, Cork University Press; London, Longmans, Green, 1931.

Donoghue, Denis. " 'Too Immoral for Dublin': Synge's 'The Tinker's Wedding' ", *Irish Writing* (Cork), 30 (March 1955), 56-62.

Estill, Adelaide Duncan. *The Sources of Synge*, pp. 17-19. Philadelphia, University of Pennsylvania, 1939.

Gerstenberger, Donna Lorine. *John Millington Synge*, pp. 63-74. Twayne's English Authors Series, 12. New York, Twayne, 1964.

Greene, David H. *"The Tinker's Wedding*, A Revaluation", *PMLA* (New York), LXII (September 1947), 824-827.

Howe, Percival Presland. *J. M. Synge: A Critical Study*, pp. 76-84. London, Martin Secker, 1912.

"An Irish Playwright", *Independent* (New York), LXX (13 April 1911), 792-793. [A review of J. W. Luce and Co. edition, *The Tinker's Wedding*]

Krieger, Hans. "J. M. Synge", *Die neueren Sprachen* (Marburg), XXIV (1916), 538-541. [Reprinted in *John Millington Synge* (see below, next entry)]

—————. *John Millington Synge, ein Dichter der "keltischen Renaissance"*, pp. 87-91. Inaugural Dissertation. Marburg, N. G. Elwert'sche, 1916.

Leventhal, A. J. "Dramatic Commentary", *The Dublin Magazine*, n.s. XXVIII (January-March 1953), 37. [Review]

Lucas, Frank Laurence. *The Drama of Chekhov, Synge, Yeats, and Pirandello*, pp. 189-191. London, Cassell, 1963.

Nordman, C. A. "J. M. Synge, Dramatikern", *Finsk Tidskrift för Vitterhet, Vetenskap, Konst och Politik* (Helsinki), LXXIX (July-December 1915), 26-70. [See pp. 39-42]

Price, Alan F. *Synge and Anglo-Irish Drama,* pp. 127-137. London, Methuen, 1961.

Riva, Serafino. *La tradizione celtica e la moderna letteratura irlandese, I. John Millington Synge,* pp. 225-234. Rome, Religio, 1937.

Rust, Adolf. *Beiträge zu einer Geschichte der neu-keltischen Renaissance,* pp. 60-66. Bückeburg, Grimme'sche Hofbuchdruckerei, 1922.

Setterquist, Jan. "Ibsen and Synge", *Studia Neophilologica* (Upsala), XXIV (1951/52), 100-102. [Reprinted in *Ibsen and the Beginnings of Anglo-Irish Drama* (see below, next entry)]

———————. *Ibsen and the Beginnings of Anglo-Irish Drama: I. John Millington Synge,* pp. 40-42. Upsala Irish Studies, Vol. 2, edited by S. B. Liljegren. Upsala, A.-B. Lundequistka; Dublin, Hodges, Figgis; Copenhagen, Munksgaard; Cambridge, Massachusetts, Harvard University Press, 1951.

Skelton, Robin. *The Writings of J. M. Synge,* pp. 64-79. London, Thames and Hudson, 1971.

Thorning, Just. *J. M. Synge: En moderne irsk Dramatiker,* pp. 21-25. Studier fra Sprog- og Oldtidsforskning, No. 121. London and Copenhagen, V. Pios, 1921.

Völker, Klaus. *Irisches Theater I: William Butler Yeats [und] John Millington Synge,* pp. 59-63. Friedrichs Dramatiker des Welttheaters, Band 29. Velber bei Hannover, Friedrich, 1967.

THE WELL OF THE SAINTS

Agate, Captain James E. *Buzz, Buzz! Essays of the Theatre,* pp. 153-156. London, W. Collins, [1918]

Aufhauser, Annemarie. *Sind die Dramen von John Millington Synge durch französische Vorbilder beeinflusst?,* pp. 46-61. Inaugural Dissertation. Würzburg, Richard Mayr, 1935.

Bourgeois, Maurice. *John Millington Synge and the Irish Theatre,* pp. 182-193. London, Constable, 1913; reissued by Benjamin Blom, Bronx, New York, 1965.

Boyd, Ernest Augustus. "J. M. Synge", in *Ireland's Literary Renaissance,* pp. 324-325. Dublin, Maunsel; London and New York, Knopf, 1916; revised edition, New York, 1922.

Corkery, Daniel. *Synge and Anglo-Irish Literature: A Study,* pp. 153-178. Dublin and Cork, Cork University Press; London, Longmans, Green, 1931.

DeCasseres, Benjamin. "The Well of the Saints", *Arts and Decoration* (New York), XXXVI (March 1932), 42, 63-64.

"Drama", *The Nation* (New York), XCIII (30 November 1911), 528-529. [A critique of the Irish plays presented in America, largely devoted to Synge's works and, in particular, *Well* and *Playboy,* see p. 529]

Edwards, Philip. [Review of Alan Price, *Synge and Anglo-Irish Drama*], *Review of English Studies* (Oxford), n.s. XIII (August 1962), 320-322. [See pp. 320-321]

Ellehauge, Martin. "J. M. Synge", in *Striking Figures Among Modern English Dramatists,* pp. 20-23. Copenhagen, Levin and Munksgaard, 1931.

Estill, Adelaide Duncan. *The Sources of Synge,* pp. 20-28. Philadelphia, University of Pennsylvania, 1939.

Fay, William George, and Catherine Carswell. *The Fays of the Abbey Theatre: An Autobiographical Record,* pp. 166-169. London, Rich and Cowan; New York, Harcourt, Brace, 1935.

Gerstenberger, Donna Lorine. *John Millington Synge,* pp. 55-62. Twayne's English Authors Series, 12. New York, Twayne, 1964.

Greene, David H., and Edward M. Stephens. *J. M. Synge: 1871-1909*, pp. 170-180. New York, Macmillan, 1959.

Hoare, John Edward. "John Synge", *The University Magazine* (Toronto), X (February 1911), 91-109. [See pp. 99-102]

Holloway, Joseph. *Joseph Holloway's Abbey Theatre: A Selection from His Unpublished Journal, "Impressions of a Dublin Playgoer"*, edited by Robert Hogan and Michael J. O'Neill. Carbondale and Edwardsville, Southern Illinois University Press; London and Amsterdam, Feffer and Simons, 1967.

Howe, Percival Presland. *J. M. Synge: A Critical Study*, pp. 33-43. London, Martin Secker, 1912.

Keohler, Thomas. "The Irish National Theatre", *Dana* (Dublin), I : 11 (March 1905), 351-352. [Review]

Krieger, Hans. "J. M. Synge", *Die neueren Sprachen* (Marburg), XXIV (1916), 415-423; 462-467. [Reprinted in *John Millington Synge* (see below, next entry)]

——————. *John Millington Synge, ein Dichter der "keltischen Renaissance"*, pp. 59-71. Inaugural Dissertation. Marburg, N. G. Elwert'sche, 1916.

Lebeau, Henry. "Les Spectacles du Mois—Mars 1905—Étranger: Irlande, Dublin: *The Well of the Saints*", *La Revue d'Art Dramatique et Musical* (Paris), XX (15 April 1905), 56-60.

A Lover of the West [Henry Lebeau]. " 'The Well of the Saints' ", *Dana* (Dublin), I (April 1905), 364-368.

Lowther, George. "J. M. Synge and the Irish Revival", *The Oxford and Cambridge Review* (London), No. 25 (November 1912), 43-59. [See pp. 50-54]

Lucas, Frank Laurence. *The Drama of Chekhov, Synge, Yeats and Pirandello*, pp. 192-200. London, Cassell, 1963.

Malcolm, Donald. "Off Broadway: [*The Well of the Saints*]", *The New Yorker*. XXVX (18 April 1959), 80-81. [Review]

Meyerfeld, Max. "Letters of John Millington Synge: From Material Supplied by Max Meyerfeld", *Yale Review* (New Haven), n.s. XIII (July 1924), 690-709.

Nordman, C. A. "J. M. Synge, Dramatikern", *Finsk Tidskrift för Vetterhet, Vetenskap, Konst och Politik* (Helsinki), LXXIX (July-December 1915), 26-70. [See pp. 42-48]

"On Mr. Synge", *The Arrow* (Dublin), I : 3 (23 February 1907), [3]. [Reprinted from an editorial on *The Well of the Saints* in the *United Irishman* (Dublin), 11 February 1905, p. 1]

O'Riordan, Conal. "Synge in Dutch", *The Irish Review* (Dublin), II: 22 (December 1912), 557-558. [A review of J. M. Synge, *De Heiligenbron Tooneelspel in Drie Bedrijven* (*The Well of the Saints*), translated by Leo Simons]

Price, Alan F. *Synge and Anglo-Irish Drama*, pp. 138-161. London, Methuen, 1961.

Riva, Serafino. *La tradizione celtica e la moderna letteratura irlandese, I. John Millington Synge*, pp. 198-213. Rome, Religio, 1937.

Rust, Adolf. *Beiträge zu einer Geschichte der neu-keltischen Renaissance*, pp. 50-60. Bückeburg, Grimme'sche Hofbuchdruckerei, 1922.

Schoepperle, Gertrude. "John Synge and His Old French Farce", *North American Review* (New York), CCXIV (October 1921), 503-513.

Setterquist, Jan. "Ibsen and Synge", *Studia Neophilologica* (Upsala), XXIV (1951/52), 103-111. [Reprinted in *Ibsen and the Beginnings of Anglo-Irish Drama* (see below, next entry)]

—————. *Ibsen and the Beginnings of Anglo-Irish Drama: I. John Millington Synge*, pp. 43-51. Upsala Irish Studies, Vol. 2, edited by S. B. Liljegren. Upsala, A.-B. Lundequistka; Dublin, Hodges, Figgis; Copenhagen, Munksgaard; Cambridge, Massachusetts, Harvard University Press, 1951.

Skelton, Robin. *The Writings of J. M. Synge*, pp. 91-102. London, Thames and Hudson, 1971.

Thorning, Just. *J. M. Synge: En moderne irsk Dramatiker*, pp. 25-32. Studier fra Sprog-og Oldtidsforskning, No. 121. London and Copenhagen, V. Pios, 1921.

The Two Tigers. "Jack and Jill Attend the Theatre", *Rhythm* (London), II (August 1912), 120-121. [A parodic review, done in "Syngesong" fashion, of *Well*]

Völker, Klaus. *Irisches Theater I: William Butler Yeats [und] John Millington Synge*, pp. 63-66. Friedrichs Dramatiker des Welttheaters, Band 29. Velber bei Hannover, Friedrich, 1967.

Wyatt, Euphemia van Rennselaer. "Early Stages", *The Catholic World* (New York), CLXXXIX (June 1959), 243. [Review]

When The Moon Has Set

Metwally, Abdalla A. "Synge's *When the Moon Has Set*", *Studies in Modern Drama* (Beirut), I (1971), 38-59.

NON-DRAMATIC PROSE WORKS

The Aran Islands

"The Aran Islands", *Independent* (New York), LXXI (6 July 1911), 44. [A review of J. W. Luce and Co. edition, *The Aran Islands*]

"The Aran Islands", *The Literary World* (London), LXXIII (15 June 1907), 260. [A review of Maunsel and Co. edition, *The Aran Islands*]

Cazamian, Madeleine L. " 'The Aran Islands' ", *Revue Anglo-Américaine* (Paris), IV (June 1927), 458-459. [A review of the Tauchnitz edition, *The Aran Islands*]

Corkery, Daniel. *Synge and Anglo-Irish Literature: A Study*, pp. 110-122. Dublin and Cork, Cork University Press; London, Longmans, Green, 1931.

Gerstenberger, Donna Lorine. *John Millington Synge*, pp. 21-29. Twayne's English Authors Series, 12. New York, Twayne, 1964.

Glöde, O. [Review of John M. Synge, *The Aran Islands*, Tauchnitz edition, Leipzig, 1926], *Englische Studien* (Leipzig), LXI (May 1927), 301-302.

Howe, Percival Presland. *J. M. Synge: A Critical Study*, pp. 100-125. London, Martin Secker, 1912.

Krieger, Hans. "J. M. Synge", *Die neueren Sprachen* (Marburg), XXIV (1916), 294-301; 346-349. [Reprinted in *John Millington Synge* (see below, next entry)]

——————. *John Millington Synge, ein Dichter der "keltischen Renaissance"*, pp. 24-34. Inaugural Dissertation. Marburg, N. G. Elwert'sche, 1916.

Mušek, Karel. [Review of Maunsel and Co. edition, *The Aran Islands*], *Lumír* (Prague), XXXV (15 June 1907), 383-384.

O Síocháin, P. A. "Synge's Isles of Romance", *Irish Digest* (Dublin), LXXIX (2 December 1963), 37-40.

Price, Alan F. *Synge and Anglo-Irish Drama*, pp. 78-89. London, Methuen, 1961.

Skelton, Robin. *The Writings of J. M. Synge*, pp. 24-40. London, Thames and Hudson, 1971.

In Wicklow, West Kerry and Connemara

Corkery, Daniel. *Synge and Anglo-Irish Literature: A Study*, pp. 110-122. Dublin and Cork, Cork University Press; London, Longmans, Green, 1931.

Gerstenberger, Donna Lorine. *John Millington Synge,* pp. 29-32. Twayne's English Authors Series, 12. New York, Twayne, 1964.

Howe, Percival Presland. *J. M. Synge: A Critical Study*, pp. 100-125. London, Martin Secker, 1912.

Krieger, Hans. "J. M. Synge", *Die neueren Sprachen* (Marburg), XXIV (1916), 349-359. [Reprinted in *John Millington Synge* (see below, next entry)]

——————. *John Millington Synge, ein Dichter der "keltischen Renaissance"*, pp. 34-44. Inaugural Dissertation. Marburg, N. G. Elwert'sche, 1916.

Pope, T. Michael. "Poetry and the Peasant", *The New Witness* (London), I (20 February 1913), 504. [A review of Maunsel and Co. edition, *In Wicklow and West Kerry*]

Price, Alan F. *Synge and Anglo-Irish Drama*, pp. 89-106. London, Methuen, 1961.

[Review of J. W. Luce and Co. edition, *In Wicklow, West Kerry, The Congested Districts*], *The Nation* (New York), XCVI (3 April 1913), 337.

Skelton, Robin. *The Writings of J. M. Synge*, pp. 103-113. London, Thames and Hudson, 1971.

POETRY AND TRANSLATIONS

Bickley, Francis. "Earth to Earth", *Bookman* (London), XXXVI (August 1909), 224. [A review of Cuala Press edition, *Poems and Translations*]

——————. *J. M. Synge and the Irish Dramatic Movement*, pp. 92-96. London, Constable; Boston and New York, Houghton Mifflin, 1912.

Bourgeois, Maurice. *John Millington Synge and the Irish Theatre*, pp. 231-235. London, Constable, 1913; reissued by Benjamin Blom, Bronx, New York, 1965.

Chislett, William, Jr. "The Irish Note in J. M. Synge's Translations", in *Moderns and Near-Moderns: Essays on Henry James, Stockton, Shaw, and Others*, pp. 157-159. New York, The Grafton Press, 1928.

Corkery, Daniel. *Synge and Anglo-Irish Literature: A Study*, pp. 228-232. Dublin and Cork, Cork University Press; London, Longmans, Green, 1931.

Davie, Donald A. "The Poetic Diction of John M. Synge", *The Dublin Magazine* (Dublin), n.s. XXVII (January-March 1952), 32-38.

Donoghue, Denis. "Flowers and Timber—A Note on Synge's Poems", *Threshold* (Belfast), I (Autumn 1957), 40-47.

Farren, Robert [O Faracháin, Roibeárd], *The Course of Irish Verse in English*, pp. 123-128. New York, Sheed and Ward, 1947.

Gerstenberger, Donna Lorine. *John Millington Synge*, pp. 109-128. Twayne's English Authors Series, 12. New York, Twayne, 1964.

Henn, Thomas Rice. [Review of J. M. Synge, *Collected Works, Vol. I, Poems*, edited by Robin Skelton], *Modern Language Review*, (London), LVIII (July 1963), 420-421.

Krieger, Hans. "J. M. Synge", *Die neueren Sprachen* (Marburg), XXIV (1916), 594-602. [Reprinted in *John Millington Synge* (see below, next entry)]

——————. *John Millington Synge, ein Dichter der "keltischen Renaissance"*, pp. 102-110. Inaugural Dissertation. Marburg, N. G. Elwert'sche, 1916.

Morris, Lloyd R. *The Celtic Dawn: A Survey of the Renascence in Ireland, 1889-1916*, pp. 80-81. New York, Macmillan, 1917.

"Notes on Current Books: *Translations,* by J. M. Synge", *The Virginia Quarterly Review* (Charlottesville), XXXIX (Winter 1963), xxii. [A brief notice of J. M. Synge, *Translations,* edited by Robin Skelton]

Parker, Derek. "Rank on Rank", *The Poetry Review* (London), n.s. LIV (Summer 1963), 185-186. [A review of J. M. Synge, *Collected Works, Vol. I, Poems,* edited by Robin Skelton]

Phelps, William Lyon. "The Advance of English Poetry in the Twentieth Century: Part VI", The Bookman (New York), XLVII (March 1918), 58-72. [See pp. 63-66]

Pinto, Vivian de Sola. "Yeats and Synge", in *Crisis in English Poetry: 1880-1940,* pp. 75-98. London, Hutchinson University Library, 1951.

Price, Alan F. *Synge and Anglo-Irish Drama,* pp. 107-117. London, Methuen, 1961.

Riva, Serafino. *La tradizione celtica e la moderna letteratura irlandese, I. John Millington Synge,* pp. 253-316. Rome, Religio, 1937.

Skelton, Robin. "The Poetry of J. M. Synge", *Poetry Ireland* (Dublin), No. 1 (Autumn 1962), 32-44.

——————. *The Writings of J. M. Synge,* pp. 153-170. London, Thames and Hudson, 1971.

Strong, Leonard Alfred George. "John Millington Synge", *The Bookman* (New York), LXXIII (April 1931), 125-136. [See pp. 127-130. Reprinted in *The Dublin Magazine* (see below, next entry)]

——————. "John Millington Synge", *The Dublin Magazine,* n.s. VII: 2 (April-June 1932), 12-32. [See pp. 16-21]

——————. *John Millington Synge,* pp. 15-24. P. E. N. Books. London, Allen and Unwin, 1941.

——————. "John Millington Synge" in *Personal Remarks,* pp. 37-45. London, P. Nevill, 1953. [Reprinted from *The Bookman* and *The Dublin Magazine* (see above)]

Wild, Friedrich. *Die englische Literatur der Gegenwart seit 1870.* Versdichtungen (unter Ausschluss des Dramas), pp. 171-172. Leipzig, Dioskuren, 1931.

Wood, Frederick T. [Review of J. M. Synge, *Collected Works, Vol. I, Poems,* edited by Robin Skelton], *English Studies* (Amsterdam), XLIV (June 1963), 232.

PASSAGES REFERRING TO SYNGE
EN PASSANT

A., M. "After the Play", *The New Republic* (New York), XVIII (1 March, 1919), 153. [A brief comparison of Synge and Lord Dunsany]

Archer, William. *Play-Making: A Manual of Craftsmanship*, p. 396. Boston, Small, Maynard; London, Chapman and Hall, 1912.

Arnold, Sidney. *Irish Literature and Its Influence*, p. 8. A Lecture delivered on 20 September 1953 at the Irish Club, London. So. Chingford, Essex, The Candlelight Press, 1953. [Says Synge is responsible for doing away with the "stage Irishman"]

Bentley, Eric Russell. *The Playwright as Thinker: A Study of Drama in Modern Times*. New York, Harcourt, Brace, 1946.

Bergholz, Harry. *Die Neugestaltung des modernen englischen Theaters, 1870-1930*. Berlin, Karl Bergholz, 1933.

Bickley, Francis. [A review of John Masefield, *The Widow in the Bye-Street*], *Bookman* (London), XLII (August 1912), 211-212.

Blythe, Ernest [Blaghd, Earnán de]. *The Abbey Theatre*, pp. [6-7]. Dublin, National Theatre Society, [1963].

Bourgeois, Maurice. "Post Bag: Synge's Works", *The Irish Book Lover* (Dublin), III (August 1911), 14.

Boyd, Ernest Augustus. *Appreciations and Depreciations: Irish Literary Studies*, pp. 25-26. Dublin, Talbot Press; London, T. F. Unwin, 1917.

——————. *Portraits: Real and Imaginary*, p. 237. London, Jonathan Cape; New York, G. H. Doran, 1924. [Briefly mentions the *Playboy* riots]

Bradbrook, Muriel Clara. *Ibsen: The Norwegian, A Revaluation*. First Edition, London, Chatto and Windus, 1946; New edition, Hamden, Connecticut, Archon Books, 1966. [Has quotations from Synge, and a brief comparison (p. 54) of Peer Gynt and Christy Mahon]

Bromage, Mary Cogan. "Literature of Ireland Today", *The South Atlantic Quarterly* (Durham), XLII (January 1943), 27-37. [See pp. 33 and 35]

Colum, Mary Maguire. *From These Roots: The Ideas That Have Made Modern Literature*, pp. 266-267. New York and London, Scribner's, 1937. [A brief mention of French influences on Synge]

Corrigan, Robert Willoughby, ed. "The Irish Dramatic Flair", in *Masterpieces of the Modern Irish Theatre*, pp. 6-8. New York, Macmillan, 1967.

Crone, John S. *A Concise Dictionary of Irish Biography*, p. 243. New York, Longmans, Green, 1928.

De Blácam, Aodh. *A First Book of Irish Literature: From the Earliest Times to the Present Day*, p. 217. Dublin and Cork, Talbot Press, [1934]. [A thumbnail sketch of Synge and the plays, which he says "are freaks in theme and diction"]

De Selincourt, Ernest. *Wordsworthian and Other Studies*, pp. 199-201. Oxford, Clarendon Press, 1947. [A brief mention of Synge's dialogue in *Playboy*]

Donn, Brian. "The Dublin Actors in London", *Inis Fáil* (London), No. 34 (July 1907), 9. [A brief statement about the *Playboy*]

Duggan, G. C. *The Stage Irishman: A History of the Irish Play and Stage Characters from the Earliest Times*, p. 295. Dublin and Cork, Talbot Press, 1937.

Dukes, Ashley. *Modern Dramatists*, p. 95. London, Frank Palmer, [1911].

"Editor's Gossip", *The Irish Book Lover* (Dublin), V (March 1914), 144. [A quotation from George Moore concerning Synge's personal appearance]

Eglinton, John [William Kirkpatrick Magee]. *Irish Literary Portraits*, pp. 7, 29, 80. London, Macmillan, 1935.

Egri, Lajos. *The Art of Dramatic Writing: Its Basis in the Creative Interpretation of Human Motives*, p. 244. New York, Simon and Schuster, 1946; revised edition, London, Pitman, 1950. [A brief statement about *Riders*. Originally published by Simon and Schuster in 1942 as *How to Write a Play*]

Eliot, Thomas Stearns. *On Poetry and Poets*, p. 82. London, Faber and Faber; New York, Farrar, Strauss and Cudahy, 1957. [A brief discussion of Synge as a "poetic prose dramatist"]

——————. *Poetry and Drama*, pp. 21-22. The Theodore Spencer Memorial Lecture, Harvard University, 21 November 1950. London, Faber and Faber; Cambridge, Massachusetts, Harvard University Press, 1951. [A brief comment on Synge's language]

Ellehauge, Martin. "Nogle Hovedtyper indenfor det moderne irske Drama". *Edda* (Oslo). XXIX (1929), 456-464. [A brief discussion of *Deirdre*, see p. 459]

Ellmann, Richard. *Eminent Domain*, p. 41. New York, Oxford University Press, 1965. [Concerns Joyce's critical opinion of *Riders;* reprinted in *Yeats and Joyce* (see below, next entry)]

————. *Yeats and Joyce*, pp. 460-461. Being No. XI of the Dolmen Press Yeats Centenary Papers. Dublin, Dolmen; London, Oxford University Press, 1967.

Ervine, St. John Greer. *Some Impressions of My Elders*, pp. 296-297. New York, Macmillan, 1922. [Says that Synge was shy in company and garrulous on the road. Reprinted from *The North American Review* (see below, next entry)]

————. "Some Impressions of My Elders: II—W. B. Yeats", *The North American Review* (New York), CCXI (March 1920), 402-410. [See p. 409]

Fallon, Gabriel. "Dr. Kavanagh's 'Abbey Theatre' ", *The Irish Monthly* (Dublin), LXXIX (May 1950), 208-212, 240. [A review of Peter Kavanagh, *The Story of the Abbey Theatre*. See p. 209 for Fallon's correction of an error in names]

Fiocco, Achille. *Teatro universale: del naturalismo ai giorni nostri*, p. 84. [Bologna], Cappelli, 1963. [Devotes one paragraph to a general description of the plays]

Flanagan, Hallie. *Shifting Scenes of The Modern European Theatre*, p. 38. New York, Coward-McCann, 1928; London, G. G. Harrap, 1929. [Recalls Lady Gregory's description of Synge reading *Riders*]

"Forthcoming Works", *The Irish Book Lover* (Dublin), IV (February 1913), 128. [A bibliographical note about Maurice Bourgeois's thesis in English from Paris University on J. M. Synge and Bourgeois's plans to translate into French some of Synge's plays and non-dramatic writings]

"Forthcoming Works", *The Irish Book Lover* (Dublin), IV (June 1913), 198. [A bibliographical note about Maurice Bourgeois's book on Synge]

Fox, R. M. "Foundations of the Abbey", *Aryan Path* (Bombay), XXV (January 1964), 14-16. [An interesting comment on *Playboy*, see p. 15]

Galsworthy, John. "Meditation on Finality", *English Review* (London), XI (July 1912), 537-541. [A brief mention of Synge and *Playboy* on p. 539; reprinted in *The Inn of Tranquillity* (see below, next entry)]

————. *The Inn of Tranquillity: Studies and Essays*, p. 207. London, Heinemann, 1912.

Garrab, Arra M. "Times of Glory: Yeats's 'The Municipal Gallery Revisited' ", *Arizona Quarterly* (Tucson), XXI (Autumn 1965), 243-254. [See pp. 245, 246, 249, 250, 252, 253]

Gascoigne, Bamber. *Twentieth-Century Drama,* p. 69. London, Hutchinson, 1962. [A brief discussion of Synge's dramatic prose]

George, Walter Lionel. *Dramatic Actualities,* p. 83. London, Sidgwick and Jackson, 1914. [A brief consideration of the public attitude toward *Playboy*]

Gibbon, Monk. *The Masterpiece and the Man: Yeats as I Knew Him.* London, R. Hart-Davis, 1959.

Gogarty, Oliver St. John. *William Butler Yeats: A Memoir,* p. 7. Dublin, Dolmen, 1963. [Briefly relates story of first reading of *Riders* and "someone" (Yeats) exclaiming "Aeschylus"]

Gordon, Jan B. "The Imaginary Portrait: Fin-de-siècle Icon", *The University of Windsor Review* (Windsor, Ontario, Canada), V : 1 (Fall 1969), 81-104. [A brief paragraph on *Deirdre* and the relationship of life to art, see p. 100]

Gorki, Maxim. "Observations on the Theatre", *The English Review* (London), XXXVIII (April 1924), 494-498. [A brief comment on *Playboy,* see p. 495]

Greene, David H. "The Aran Islands: Last Fortress of the Celt", *The Commonweal* (New York), LXIV (21 September 1956), 609-610. [A general description of the Aran Islands]

——————. "John Millington Synge: MSS.", *Notes and Queries* (London), CLXXV (17 December 1938), 441. [A brief request for information about Synge manuscripts]

Greenwood, Ormerod. *The Playwright: A Study of Form, Method, and Tradition in the Theatre.* London, Pitman, [1950]. [Briefly analyses a speech in *Riders*]

Gregory, Lady Isabella Augusta. "The Irish Theatre and the People", *Yale Review* (New Haven), n.s. I (January 1912), 188-191. [A brief comment on Synge and *Riders*]

Gwynn, Stephen Lucius. *Dublin Old and New,* p. 50. Dublin, Browne and Nolan; London, G. G. Harrap; New York, Macmillan, 1938. [A sentence about Yeats's defence of *Playboy*]

——————. *The Masters of English Literature,* pp. 420-421. Revised edition, London, Macmillan, 1925.

Hackett, Francis. "A Fragment about Synge", *Theatre Arts* (New York), III (January 1919), 1. [A brief mention of *Shadow* reprinted from Francis Hackett, *Horizons* (see below, next entry)]

——————. *Horizons. A book of Criticism,* pp. 193-195. New York, B. W. Huebsch, 1919.

Hamilton, Clayton Meeker. *Conversations on Contemporary Drama,* p. 7. A Series of Nine Lectures, Delivered in Earl Hall, at Columbia

University, from 11 February to 7 April 1924. New York, Macmillan, 1924. [Speaks of Synge's "deathless eloquence"]

Henderson, Archibald. *The Changing Drama: Contributions and Tendencies*, p. 143. London, Grant Richards; New York, Henry Holt, 1914. [A very general, brief statement about Synge's drama being "novel in its elemental reversion to the type of dramatic art at the beginning of history"]

Hengist, Philip. "Inside Ireland", *Punch* (London), CCXLII (2 May 1962), 697. [A review of J. M. Synge, *Four Plays* and *The Aran Islands*, edited by Robin Skelton]

Hillebrand, Harold Newcomb. *Writing the One-Act Play: A Manual for Beginners*, pp. 134-135. New York, Knopf, 1925. [Analyses a passage from *Shadow*]

Hodgson, Geraldine E. "Some Irish Poetry", *The Contemporary Review* (London), XCVIII (September 1910), 323-340. [See p. 332]

Hone, Joseph Maunsell. *The Life of George Moore*. London and New York, Macmillan, 1936.

——————. *W. B. Yeats: 1865-1939*. London, Macmillan, 1943; second revised edition, London, Macmillan, 1962. [Interesting miscellany about Synge and about the *Playboy*]

Howe, P. P. "England's New Dramatists", *North American Review* (New York), CXCVIII (August 1913), 218-226. [See pp. 221, 225, 226]

Hunt, Hugh. *The Live Theatre*, p. 136. London, Oxford University Press, 1962. [A brief discussion of Synge, *Playboy* and *Riders*]

Inglis, Brian St. John. *The Story of Ireland*, pp. 28, 197. London, Faber and Faber, 1956. [A brief comment on *Playboy*]

"Irish Literary Society", *The Irish Book Lover* (Dublin), IV (May 1913), 169-170. [An interesting note about W. B. Yeats and Synge's *Deirdre*]

Jeffares, Alexander Norman. *W. B. Yeats: Man and Poet*. London, Routledge and Kegan Paul, 1949; second edition published with corrections, London, 1962. [Contains interesting miscellaneous information about Synge]

"John Synge's Future Fame", *The Irish Book Lover* (Dublin), I (October 1909), 33-34. [A review of Cuala Press edition, J. M. Synge, *Poems and Translations*]

Joyce, James. *The Critical Writings of James Joyce*, edited by Ellsworth Mason and Richard Ellmann. New York, Viking, 1959. [Includes Joyce's programme notes for *Riders*]

Kavanagh, Patrick. "Diary", *Envoy* (Dublin), IV: 16, (March 1951), 67-72. [See pp. 70-71. Argues that Synge's mind is coarse and that "the predominant note of Synge's writings is hate"]

Kavanagh, Peter. *The Irish Theatre: Being a History of the Drama in Ireland from the Earliest Period up to the Present Day*. Tralee, Kerryman, 1946.

Kiely, Benedict. "Joe the Post: Or a Portrait of the Irishman as a Mole", *Northwest Review* (Eugene, Oregon), IX: 2 (Fall-Winter 1967-1968), 110-116. [Review article of Robert Hogan and Michael J. O'Neill, eds. *Joseph Holloway's Abbey Theatre: A Selection from His Unpublished Journal, "Impressions of a Dublin Playgoer"*. Contains numerous quotations about Synge from Holloway's *Journal*]

Kitchin, Laurence. "Realism in the English Mid-Century Drama", *World Theatre* (Brussels), XIV (January-February 1965), 17-26. [See pp. 17, 20, 22]

Law, Hugh Alexander. *Anglo-Irish Literature*, pp. 258-259. Dublin and Cork, Talbot Press; London and New York, Longmans, Green, 1926.

Lewisohn, Ludwig. *The Modern Drama: An Essay in Interpretation*. New York, B. W. Huebsch, 1915. [A brief discussion of Synge and some of the plays]

Loftus, Richard J. *Nationalism in Modern Anglo-Irish Poetry*. Madison and Milwaukee, University of Wisconsin Press, 1964. [Interesting miscellany about *Playboy* riots and other subjects]

Lynd, Robert. *The Art of Letters*, pp. 225-226. London, T. F. Unwin, 1920. [Argues that people have praised Synge for the wrong reasons]

MacDonagh, Thomas. *Literature in Ireland: Studies Irish and Anglo-Irish*, pp. 16, 48, 49. Dublin, Talbot Press; London, T. F. Unwin, 1916.

McHugh, Roger. "James Joyce's Synge-Song", *Envoy* (Dublin), III: 12 (November 1950), 12-17. [See p. 14]

Mac Liammóir, Micheál. *All for Hecuba: An Irish Theatrical Autobiography*. London, Methuen, 1946.

——————. *Theatre in Ireland*, pp. 15-16. Dublin, Published for the Cultural Relations Committee of Ireland at The Three Candles, 1950.

McManus, L. *White Light and Flame: Memories of the Irish Literary Revival and the Anglo-Irish War*, pp. 68-69. Dublin and Cork, Talbot Press, 1929. [A personal remembrance]

Masefield, John Edward. *So Long to Learn: Chapters of an Autobiography*, pp. 154-155. London, Heinemann; New York, Macmillan,

1952. [Masefield describes his impressions at a reading of *Shadow* and *Riders*]

Montague, Charles Edward. "The Literary Play", in *Essays and Studies by Members of the English Association*, II, 85. Collected by H. C. Beeching. Oxford, Clarendon Press, 1911. [Reprinted in *A Writer's Notes on His Trade* (see below, next entry)]

——————. *A Writer's Notes on His Trade*, p. 125. London, Chatto and Windus, 1930.

Montgomery, K. L. [Kathleen and Letitia Montgomery]. "Some Writers of the Celtic Renaissance", *The Fortnightly Review* (London), XCVI, n.s. CX (1 September 1911), 545-561. [A brief mention of Synge as having a touch of "Swiftean truth", see p. 560]

Nathan, George Jean. "Foreword", in *Five Great Modern Irish Plays*. The Modern Library. New York, Random House, 1941. [A brief mention of *Playboy* and *Riders*]

Nevinson, Henry Woodd. *Books and Personalities*, pp. 248-249, 250. London and New York, John Lane, 1905. [Briefly discusses *Riders* and in a sentence *Shadow*]

[Note from *The Times* (London) on Synge's Realism], *The Irish Book Lover* (Dublin), IV (February 1913), 127.

O'Donnell, James Preston. *Sailing to Byzantium: A Study in the Development of the Later Style and Symbolism in the Poetry of William Butler Yeats*, pp. 27-28. Harvard Honors Theses in English, No. 11. Cambridge, Massachusetts, Harvard University Press, 1939. [A short discussion of Synge and *Playboy* riots and what both meant to Yeats]

"On Mr. Boyle and Mr. Synge, and Whether or Not the Liverpool Irish Would Hiss Them from the Stage", *The Arrow* (Dublin), I:3 (23 February 1907), [2-3]. [Reprinted from J. Bull, "As Others See Us", *The Leader* (Dublin), 15 December 1906, pp. 265-266]

O'Neill, Michael J. *Lennox Robinson*. New York, Twayne, 1964. [Touches upon various subjects of interest.]

O'Sullivan, Seamus. *The Rose and Bottle and Other Essays*, p. 123. Dublin, Talbot Press, 1946. [A short biographical passage about Synge in Dublin]

"Our Scrap Book", *The Irish Book Lover* (Dublin), II (May 1911), 155. [Extract from "Obituary: Mr. J. M. Synge", *The Times* (London), 25 March, 1909, p. 13]

"Our Scrap Book", *The Irish Book Lover* (Dublin), II (July 1911), 197. [Extract from "The Work of J. M. Synge", *The Spectator* (London), 1 April 1911, pp. 482-483]

"Our Scrap Book", *The Irish Book Lover* (Dublin), V (January 1914), 108. [A biographical note about Synge reprinted from *T. P.'s Weekly*]

Palmer, John. *The Future of the Theatre*, p. 168. London, G. Bell, 1913.

Peacock, Ronald. *The Art of Drama*, pp. 218-219. London, Routledge and Kegan Paul, 1957. [Says *Riders* achieves intensity of expression from the essentially symbolic nature of the subject]

Pearse, Pádraic H. *Collected Works of Pádraic H. Pearse: Political Writings and Speeches*, p. 145. Dublin, Cork and Belfast, Phoenix, 1924.

Pickering, Ernest Harold. *A Brief Survey of English Literature: From Its Beginnings to the Present Day, with Chapters on the Irish Literary Movement and American Literature*, pp. 224-225. London, G. G. Harrap, 1932 [1931]. [A paragraph on Synge, which includes mention of Synge's prose, *Riders* and *Playboy*]

"*Plays That May Not Be Patronized*", *America* (New York), VI (25 November 1911), 159-160. [Condemns *Well* as being "more immoral and far more blasphemous than 'The Playboy' "]

Poepping, Hilde. *James Stephens: Eine Untersuchung über die irische Erneuerungsbewegung in der Zeit von 1900-1930*. Schriftenreihe: Deutsche Gesellschaft für keltische Studien, No. 4. Inaugural Dissertation. Halle, Niemeyer, 1940.

Pollock, John Hackett. *William Butler Yeats*, pp. 49-51. Dublin, Talbot Press; London, Gerald Duckworth, 1935. [Briefly discusses the argument over *Playboy*]

"Post Bag: Synge's Works", *The Irish Book Lover* (Dublin), III (August 1911), 14. [An appeal by Maurice Bourgeois for information on Synge]

[A Reference to Darrell Figgis' article "The Art of J. M. Synge" in *The Fortnightly Review* (December 1911)], *The Irish Book Lover* (Dublin), III (January 1912), 97.

[A Reference to Maurice Bourgeois' thesis in *John Millington Synge and the Irish Theatre*], *The Irish Book Lover* (Dublin), IV (February 1913), 128.

Reid, Forrest. *Private Road*, pp. 77-78. London, Faber and Faber, [1940]. [A brief biographical passage]

—————. *W. B. Yeats: A Critical Study*, p. 151. London, Martin Secker, 1915.

[Report from Maurice Bourgeois of articles on the Irish Theatre in *Phalange* and *La Revue du Mois*], *The Irish Book Lover* (Dublin), III (December 1911), 74. [Bourgeois refers specifically to: Jean

Florence (Professor Blum), "Le Théâtre irlandais", *Phalange* (Paris), 20 January 1911, p. 52; Madeleine L. Cazamian, "Le Théâtre de J. M. Synge", *La Revue du Mois* (Paris), XII (10 October 1911), 456-468]

[Report of Reading by Miss Hayden of Maurice Bourgeois's Paper on Synge at the National Literary Society, Dublin], *The Irish Book Lover* (Dublin), III (March 1912), 132-133. [A note about Synge's life in Paris, his reading habits, and the influence of Pierre Loti on him]

[Review of Francis Bickley, *J. M. Synge and the Irish Dramatic Movement*], *The Irish Book Lover* (Dublin), IV (November 1912), 70.

[Review of J. W. Luce and Co. edition, *The Aran Islands*], *American Library Association Booklist* (Chicago), VIII:4 (December 1911), 164.

Robinson, Lennox. "The Irish National Theatre", in *Abbey Theatre Dramatic Festival of Plays and Lectures*, pp. 6, 9, 10. Dramatic Festival Souvenir. Dublin, August 6th-20th, Cahill, 1938.

Ruyssen, Henri. "Le Théâtre irlandais", *Revue Germanique* (Paris), VII (January-February 1911), 69-70. [Dismisses *Tinker's Wedding* in one sentence and then speaks briefly about *Deirdre*]

Ryan, William Patrick. *The Pope's Green Island*, pp. 306-307. London, James Nisbet; Boston, Small, Maynard, 1912. [Comments briefly on *Playboy* and concludes that "Synge fared best with beggars and tinkers" and that "his work . . . will live longer as literature than as acting drama"]

Sargeant, Howard. [Notice of J. M. Synge, *Collected Works, Vol. I, Poems*, edited by Robin Skelton], *English* (London), XIV (Spring 1963), 164.

Schaff, Harrison Hale. "Introduction", in *Three Irish Plays*, p. 10. Boston, International Pocket Library Corporation, 1936. [Contains a short paragraph of biography]

Scudder, Vida D. "The Irish Literary Drama: An Address Delivered at the Opening of the Twentieth Century Club Series of Plays", *Poet-Lore* (Boston), XVI (Spring 1905), 40-53. [A brief discussion of *Riders*, see p. 51]

"Short Notices: Miscellaneous", *The Month* (London), CLX (August 1932), 189-190. [A review of Daniel Corkery, *Synge and Anglo-Irish Literature*]

Stamm, Rudolf. "Die neu-irische Theaterbewegung und wir", *Schweizer-Annalen* (Aarau, Switzerland), I:3 (1944), 156-166. [See pp. 161-162]

Starkie, Walter. "I, Yeats and the Abbey Theatre", in Walter Starkie and A. Norman Jeffares, *Homage to Yeats, 1865-1965*, pp. 3, 4, 5, 12, 21, 23, 24, 26, 35. Papers read at a Clark Library Seminar, 16 October 1965. University of California, Los Angeles, William Andrews Clark Memorial Library, 1966.

Stoll, Elmer Edgar. *Poets and Playwrights*, pp. 119-120. Minneapolis, University of Minnesota Press, 1930. [A brief discussion of Synge's speech and his aversion in the contemporary drama to its "sterility of speech"]

Strong, Leonard Alfred George. *Common Sense about Drama*, p. 53. New York, Knopf, 1937. [A short paragraph about time in *Riders*]

Sutton, Graham. *Some Contemporary Dramatists*, pp. 168, 174. London, Leonard Parsons, 1924. [Hints at Synge's influence on Eugene O'Neill]

Swander, Homer D. "Shields at the Abbey: A Friend of Cathleen", *Eire-Ireland* (St. Paul, Minnesota), V: 2 (Summer 1970), 25-41. [Contains a brief discussion of Arthur Shields in the role of Christy Mahon, see pp. 37-38, 40]

Trewin, John Courtenay. *Dramatists of Today*, p. 23. London, Staples Press, 1953. [Speaks of Synge's "transfiguring prose rhythms"]

Turner, Edward Raymond. *Ireland and England*, pp. 338-339. New York, Century, 1919. [A brief general comment about Synge's plays]

Ussher, Percy Arland. *Three Great Irishmen: Shaw, Yeats, Joyce*, p. 87. London, Victor Gollancz, 1952. [A brief, but interesting, comment about *Playboy*]

Vendler, Helen Hennessy. *Yeats's Vision and the Later Plays*, p. 44. Cambridge, Massachusetts, Harvard University Press; Oxford, Oxford University Press, 1963. [A brief discussion of Synge according to Yeats's description of him in *A Vision* as a "receptive" man]

W. B. Yeats: A Centenary Exhibition in the National Gallery of Ireland, pp. 67-68. Dublin, printed for the National Gallery of Ireland by The Dolmen Press, 1965. [A catalogue of paintings with biographical sketches]

Weldon, A. E. [Brinsley MacNamara]. *Abbey Plays: 1899-1948*. Dublin, Sign of the Three Candles, [1949].

Wells, Henry W. "Poetic Imagination in Ireland and India", *The Literary Half-Yearly* (Bangalore, Mysore, India), IX: 2 (1968), 37-48. [The author says that Synge "mastered flights of poetic rhetoric essentially lyrical and curiously like those in Sanskrit plays"; see pp. 47-48]

Weygandt, Cornelius. "The Art of the Irish Players: And a Comment on Their Plays", *The Book News Monthly* (Philadelphia), XXX (February 1912), 379-381. [Comments briefly about *Playboy* and

Well, and says "reading Synge I had held him the greatest dramatist in English of the last hundred years. Seeing him upon the stage I feel my judgment was true", see pp. 380-381]

—————. *Tuesdays at Ten: A Garnering from the Talks of Thirty Years on Poets, Dramatists and Essayists*. Philadelphia, University of Pennsylvania Press, 1928. [Miscellaneous information about Synge's plays and productions of Synge's plays]

Wilde, Percival. *The Craftsmanship of the One-Act Play*, pp. 38, 64, 272, 288. Boston, Little, Brown, 1923. [Contains brief but interesting comments on *Riders*]

Wilson, Edmund. *Axel's Castle: A Study in the Imaginative Literature of 1870-1930*, p. 43. New York and London, Scribner's, 1931. [A brief comment on Synge's work which he calls "the most authentic example of poetic drama which the modern stage has seen"]

Yeats, John Butler. *Early Memories: Some Chapters of Autobiography*, pp. 80, 81. Churchtown, Dundrum, Cuala Press, 1923. [Mentions Synge's attitude towards the Irish peasants and calls Synge "the most fastidious man I ever knew and the proudest"]

Yeats, William Butler. "The Bounty of Sweden: A Meditation", *The Dial* (Chicago), LXXVII (September 1924), 181-199. [See pp. 181, 196. The same article appears also in *The London Mercury* (see below, next entry)]

—————. "The Bounty of Sweden: A Meditation", *The London Mercury*, X (September 1924), 466-479. [See pp. 466, 477. Reprinted in *The Bounty of Sweden: A Meditation, and a Lecture Delivered Before the Royal Swedish Academy and Certain Notes by William Butler Yeats*. Dublin, Cuala Press, 1925]

—————. *Dramatis Personae*, pp. 38, 39, 64, 66, 68, 81, 87. Dublin, Cuala Press, 1935.

—————. "First Principles" *Samhain* (Dublin), No. 7 (November 1908), 6-12. [A sentence on *Playboy*, see pp. 7-8]

—————. "First Principles", *Samhain: 1904* (Dublin), No. 4 (December 1904), 12-24. [A brief mention of *Shadow*, see pp. 13 and 21. Reprinted in "The Irish Dramatic Movement", in the *Collected Works*, Vol. IV, 1908; and in *Plays and Controversies, 1923*]

—————. "The Irish National Theatre", in *Convegno di lettere, 8-14 Ottobre 1934; Tema: Il teatro drammatico*, IV, 386-392. Rome, Reale Accademia d'Italia, 1935. [Has some interesting comments on *Playboy* and on Synge; see pp. 387-389]

—————. "More Memories", *The Dial* (Chicago), LXXII (May 1922), 449-462. [Yeats remarks that had he not fought the Irish tendency in literature to melodramatize the past, this tendency "might have silenced in 1907 John Synge, the greatest dramatic genius of Ireland", see p. 454. Yeats also remarks that John O'Leary "would have hated *The Playboy of the Western World*, and his death a little before its performance was fortunate for Synge and myself", see p. 460. The same article appears in *The London Mercury* (see below, next entry). Reprinted in *The Trembling of the Veil*, 1922; and in *Autobiographies*, 1926]

——————. "More Memories—I", *The London Mercury*, VI (May 1922), 34-44. [See pp. 37 and 42]

——————. "Notes", *Samhain: 1903* (Dublin), No. 3 (September 1903), 3-8. [See pp. 5 and 7. Reprinted in "The Irish Dramatic Movement", in the *Collected Works*, Vol. IV, 1908; and in *Plays and Controversies*, 1923]

——————. *Per Amica Silentia Lunae*, pp. 14-15. London, Macmillan, 1918. [A brief but interesting discussion of the relationship of Synge's art to his health. New York, Macmillan, 1918 edition, pp. 22-23]

——————. "The Play, The Player, and The Scene", *Samhain: 1904* (Dublin), No. 4 (December 1904), 24-33. [A sentence about "the vivid, picturesque, ever-varied language of Mr. Synge's persons", see p. 26. Reprinted in "The Irish Dramatic Movement", in the *Collected Works*, Vol. IV, 1908; and in *Plays and Controversies*, 1923]

——————. *The Trembling of the Veil*, pp. 90, 99, 188, 220, 247. London, T. W. Laurie, 1922.

——————. *W. B. Yeats: Selected Prose*, edited by A. Norman Jeffares. London, Macmillan, 1964. [Concerns *Playboy* and Synge's genius; see pp. 117-118]

——————, and Lady Gregory. "Preface", in *The Unicorn from the Stars and Other Plays*. New York, Macmillan, 1908. [See p. vi: "it was only the coming of the unclassifiable, uncontrollable, capricious, uncompromising genius of J. M. Synge that altered the direction of the movement and made it individual, critical, and combative"]

INTRODUCTIONS TO EDITIONS

Bourgeois, Maurice. "Avant-Propos", in John M. Synge, *Les Îles Aran*, translated by Léon Bazalgette. Les Prosateurs étrangers modernes. Paris, F. Rieder et Cie, 1921.

——————. "Avant-Propos du traducteur" [to J. M. Synge, *Le Baladin du monde occidental*], *La Grande Revue* (Paris), LXXXII (25 November 1913), 217-226.

——————. [Preface and Notes], in J. M. Synge, *Théâtre*, translated by Maurice Bourgeois. Paris, Gallimard, 1942.

Fisher, Charles H., and Sil-Vara [G. Silberer]. "Zur Einführung", in J. M. Synge, *Der Held des Westerlands*, translated by Charles H. Fisher and Sil-Vara. Munich, Georg Müller, 1912.

Grønbech, Vilhelm. "Indledning", in *J. M. Synge, I Kløftens Skygge [and] De Rider Mod Havet* [*In the Shadow of the Glen* and *Riders to the Sea*], translated by Gunnar Robert-Hansen. Copenhagen, 1925.

Hansen, Gunnar Robert. "Oversaetterens Forord", in J. M. Synge, *I Kløftens Skygge* [and] *De Rider Mod Havet* [*In the Shadow of the Glen* and *Riders to the Sea*], translated by Gunnar Robert-Hansen. Copenhagen, 1925.

Henn, Thomas Rice, ed. "General Introduction and Notes", in *The Plays and Poems of J. M. Synge*. London, Methuen, 1963.

——————. "Introduction", in J. M. Synge, *The Playboy of the Western World*. London, Methuen, 1961.

——————. "Introduction and Notes", in J. M. Synge, *The Playboy of the Western World*. Methuen's Modern Classics. London, Methuen, 1960.

——————. "Introduction and Notes", in J. M. Synge, *Riders to the Sea* and *In the Shadow of the Glen*. Methuen's Modern Classics. London, Methuen, 1961.

Ichikawa, Sanki. "Introduction and Notes" [in Japanese], in John M. Synge, *Plays*. Kenkyusha English Classics. Tokyo, 1923. Kenkyusha British and American Classics, No. 186. Tokyo, Kenkyusha, 1954.

"Introduction [and] Note", in J. M. Synge, *The Works of John M. Synge, Vol. I, Plays*. Revised collected edition, London, Allen and Unwin, 1932. [The introduction includes "Extracts from Note Books of J. M. Synge" (1907) and (1908), and "A Letter to a Young Man" (19 February 1907). The note concerns the chronology of the plays and the rewriting of some of them]

Jiménez, Juan Ramón, and Zenobia Camprubí de Jiménez. [Introduction], in John M. Synge, *Jinetes hacia el mar* [*Riders to the Sea*], translated by Zenobia Camprubí de Jiménez and Juan Ramón Jiménez. Madrid, Editores De Su Propia y Sola Obra, 1920.

Kovalev, Iu. "Dramaturgiia Ddzona Singa" [Dramaturgy of John Synge], in *Ddzon Millington Sing: Dramy,* translated by V. Metalnikov, and notes by N. Sitnikovaia, Biblioteka dramaturga. Leningrad and Moscow, Iskysstvo, 1964. [See pp. 5-33]

Linati, Carlo. "Introduzione", in John M. Synge, *Deirdre l'addolorata,* translated by Carlo Linati. Teatro Moderno. Milan, Rosa e Ballo, 1944.

——————. "Introduzione", in John M. Synge, *Il furfantello dell' ovest,* translated by Carlo Linati. Milan, Rosa e Ballo, 1944.

——————. "Prefazione", in *Il furfantello dell' ovest e altri drammi,* translated by Carlo Linati. Milan, Studio Editoriale Lombardo, 1917.

Mac Liammóir, Micheál. "Introduction", in *J. M. Synge's Plays, Poems, and Prose.* Everyman's Library No. 968. London, Dent, 1941.

O'Brien, Edward J. "Introduction", in J. M. Synge, *The Aran Islands.* Boston, J. W. Luce, 1928.

——————. "Introduction", in J. M. Synge, *Riders to the Sea.* Boston, J. W. Luce, 1911.

Price, Alan F., ed. "Introduction", in J. M. Synge, *Collected Works, Vol. II, Prose.* London, Oxford University Press, 1966.

"Publisher's Note", in J. M. Synge, *The Works of John M. Synge,* Vol. I. First Collected edition. Dublin, Maunsel, 1910. [Bibliographical information about the plays, poems and prose]

Rhys, Ernest. "Introduction", in *John M. Synge: Plays, Poems, and Prose.* Everyman's Library No. 968. London, J. M. Dent and Sons, 1941.

Rodgers, William Robert. "Introduction", in John M .Synge, *Collected Plays.* Penguin Books 845. Harmondsworth, Middlesex, Penguin, 1952.

Saddlemyer, Ann, ed. "Introduction", in J. M. Synge, *Collected Works, Vol. III, Plays.* London, Oxford University Press, 1968.

——————, ed. "Introduction", in J. M. Synge, *Collected Works, Vol. IV, Plays.* London, Oxford University Press, 1968.

Simons, Leo. "J. M. Synge", in J. M. Synge, *De Heiligenbron* [*The*

Well of the Saints], translated by Leo Simons. Tooneelbibliotheek onder Leiding van Leo Simons uitgegeven door de maatschappij voor Goede en Goedkoope Lectuur. [Drama library under the direction of Leo Simons published by the Society for Good and Cheap Literature] Amsterdam, 1912.

Skelton, Robin, ed. "Introduction", in J. M. Synge, *Collected Works, Vol. I, Poems.* London, Oxford University Press, 1962.

——————, ed. "Introduction", in J. M. Synge, *Four Plays and The Aran Islands.* World's Classics No. 585. London and New York, Oxford University Press, 1962.

——————, ed. "Introduction", in J. M. Synge, *Riders to the Sea.* Edited from the Manuscript in the Houghton Library in Harvard University. Dublin, Dolmen Press; London, Oxford University Press, 1969.

——————, ed. "Introduction" in J. M. Synge, *Translations.* Edited from the Original Manuscripts. Dublin, Dolmen Press; London, Oxford University Press, 1961.

Sultan, Stanley, ed. "Introduction", in J. M. Synge, *The Playboy of the Western World,* pp. 9-40. Barre, Mass., Imprint Society, 1970.

Tracy, Robert, ed. "General Introduction", in J. M. Synge, *The Aran Islands and Other Writings.* Vintage Books. New York, Random House, 1962.

Ungvári, Tamás. "John Millington Synge (1871-1909)", in J. M. Synge, *A Nyugati Világ Bajnoka [The Playboy of the Western World],* translated by Tamás Ungvári, pp. 67-75. Szeged, Európa, 1960.

Yeats, William Butler. "Introduction: Mr. Synge and His Plays", in *The Well of the Saints* by J. M. Synge. Being Volume Four of Plays for an Irish Theatre. London, A. H. Bullen, 1905.

——————. "John M. Synge", in J. M. Synge, *Poems and Translations,* pp. vi-xiv. Churchtown, Dundrum, Cuala Press, 1909.

——————. "Preface", in *Deirdre of the Sorrows: A Play by John M. Synge.* Churchtown, Dundrum, Cuala Press; New York, Printed for John Quinn, 1910.

Yetkin, Suut Yemal. "Önsöz", in J. M. Synge, *Denize Giden Atlilar [Riders to the Sea],* translated by Orhan Burian. Istanbul, Maarif Matbaasi, 1940.

RECORDINGS

The Playboy of the Western World. Angel recordings 35357 and 35358, with Cyril Cusack and Siobhan McKenna.

The Playboy of the Western World. Columbia recording with Cyril Cusack and Siobhan McKenna.

Riders to the Sea and *In the Shadow of the Glen.* Spoken Arts recording, 743. Radio Eireann Players' Production.

LETTERS

Dodds, Eric Robertson, ed. *Journal and Letters of Stephen MacKenna.* New York, William Morrow, 1937.

Hone, Joseph, ed. *J. B. Yeats: Letters to His Son W. B. Yeats and Others, 1869-1922.* London, Faber and Faber, 1944.

Meyerfeld, Max. "Letters of John Millington Synge: From Material Supplied by Max Meyerfeld", *Yale Review* (New Haven), n.s. XIII (July 1924), 690-709.

Saddlemyer, Ann, ed. *J. M. Synge to Lady Gregory and W. B. Yeats* Dublin, Cuala Press, 1971.

—————, ed. *Letters to Molly: John M. Synge to Maire O'Neill. 1906-1909* Cambridge, Massachusetts, Belknap Press of Harvard University Press, 1971.

—————, ed. "Synge to MacKenna: The Mature Years", *The Massachusetts Review* (Amherst), V (Winter 1964), 279-296.

—————, ed. *Theatre Business, Management of Men. The Letters of the First Abbey Theatre Directors.* New York, New York Public Library, 1971.

Synge, Rev. Samuel. *Letters to My Daughter: Memories of John Millington Synge.* Dublin and Cork, Talbot Press, 1931.

Triesch, Manfred. "Some Unpublished J. M. Synge Papers", *English Language Notes* (Boulder, Colorado), IV (September 1966), 49-51.

Wade, Allan, ed. *The Letters of W. B. Yeats.* New York, Macmillan, 1955.

Wilson, Lawrence. *John Millington Synge: Some Unpublished Letters and Documents of J. M. Synge Formerly in the Possession of Mr. Lawrence Wilson of Montreal and Now for the First Time Published for Him by The Redpath Press.* Montreal, Redpath Press, 1959.

POEMS ABOUT SYNGE

"The Blushes of Ireland", *The Dublin Evening Mail*, 9 February 1907, p. 4.

Carnevali, Emanuel. "Synge's Playboy of the Western World: Variation", *The Dial* (Chicago), LXVI (5 April 1919), 340.

"A Difference in Artistic Ideals", *Sunday Independent* (*Dublin*), 3 February 1907, p. 1.

Farren, Robert [O Faracháin, Roibeárd]. "The Western World", in *Rime, Gentlemen, Please*, pp. 37-38. London and New York, Sheed and Ward, 1945. [Reprinted in *Selected Poems* (see below, next entry)]

—————. *Selected Poems*, p. 157. London and New York, Sheed and Ward, 1951.

Guiterman, Arthur. "The Neo-Celtic Criticism", *The Sun* (New York), 30 November 1911, p. 6.

Letts, Winifred M. "Synge's Grave", *Westminster Gazette* (London), 20 December 1912, p. 3. [Reprinted in *Songs from Leinster* and in *The Bibelot* (see below, next two entries)]

—————. *Songs from Leinster*, p. 55. London, Smith, Elder, 1913.

—————. "Synge's Grave", *The Bibelot* (Portland, Maine), XIX (1913), 246.

McDonnell, Randal. "A Seven Days' Wonder; or, Art at the Abbey", *The Leader* (Dublin), 9 February 1907, p. 407.

"'The Man That Killed His Da'", *Evening Telegraph* (Dublin), 2 February 1907, p. 5.

Nesbitt, T. A. "'The Playboy of the Western World': A Criticism", *The Irish World and Industrial Liberator* (New York), 11 November 1911, p. 7; *The New York Freeman's Journal*, 11 November 1911, p. 8.

S., T. D. "Our New 'Irish' Play", *The Irish Independent* (Dublin), 2 February 1907, p. 7; *Sunday Independent* (Dublin), 3 February 1907, p. 5.

Skelton, Robin. "The Death of Synge", *The Massachusetts Review* (Amherst), V (Winter 1964), 278.

Yeats, William Butler. "Beautiful Lofty Things", in *Collected Poems*, p. 348. Second edition, with later poems added. London, Macmillan, 1950.

——————. "The Municipal Gallery Revisited", in *Last Poems and Plays*, pp. 48-50. New York, Macmillan, 1940.

——————. "On Those Who Dislike The Playboy", *The Irish Review* (Dublin), I (December 1911), 476. [Reprinted, under the title "The Attack on the 'Play Boy' ", in *The Green Helmet and Other Poems* (see below, next entry)]

——————. "The Attack on the 'Play Boy'", in *The Green Helmet and Other Poems*, p. 26. New York and London, Macmillan, 1912.

PART II

NEWSPAPERS

ABERDEEN (Scotland)

The Aberdeen Free Press

"Irish National Theatre: Extraordinary Scenes in Dublin", 31 January 1907, p. 6.

"Statement by Mr. W. B. Yeats", 31 January 1907, p. 6.

"Irish National Theatre: More Disorderly Scenes", 1 February 1907, p. 6.

"Literature: Irish Literary Movement", 6 February 1911, p. 3. [Review article of Maunsel edition, *The Works*]

BELFAST (Northern Ireland)

The Belfast News-Letter

"Uproar in a Dublin Theatre", 29 January 1907, p. 7, col. 8.

"Dublin's Unpopular Play", 31 January 1907, p. 11.

"Literature of the Day: In the Wild West", 27 June 1907, p. 5. [Review of the Maunsel edition of *The Aran Islands*]

"Literature of the Day: The Playboy of the Western World", 27 June 1907, p. 5. [Review of the Maunsel edition of *The Playboy*]

"Theatre Royal: The Irish Players", 4 December 1908, p. 9. [*Riders*]

"Irish Author and Playwright", 25 March 1909, p. 8. [Obituary]

"Grand Opera House: The Playboy of the Western World", 4 August 1909, p. 10. [Review]

"Amusements: Grand Opera House", 5 April 1910, p. 8. [*Riders*]

"Grand Opera House: The Visit of the Abbey Theatre Company", 6 April 1910, p. 9. [*Well*]

The Irish News and Belfast Morning News

"The Irish National Theatre", 9 October 1903, p. 5. [*Shadow*]

"An Alleged Irish Comedy", 29 January 1907, p. 5. [*Playboy*]

[The Row over *The Playboy*], 30 January 1907, p. 4, col. 7. [Editorial]

"Mr. Synge's Disgusting Travesty", 30 January 1907, p. 8.

" 'Pegeen Mike'—A Parricide—Personalities—and Pretences", 31 January 1907, p. 4. [Long editorial]

J., P. "Ireland on the Stage", 4 February 1907, p. 4. [A specially contributed, long editorial]

[*The Playboy* in London], 17 June 1907, p. 4. col. 7

"Amusements: The Abbey Company at the Theatre Royal", 1 December 1908, p. 3. [*Shadow*]

"Theatre Royal: The Abbey Theatre Company in Four Plays, Fine Performances", 4 December 1908, p. 5. [*Riders*]

"Death of Mr. J. M. Synge: Clever Irish Playwright Dies in Dublin Hospital", 25 March 1909, p. 8.

"Abbey Theatre Co.: 'The Playboy' and Other Pieces at the Grand Opera House", 4 August 1909, p. 5. [*Playboy*]

"The Irish Players", 5 August 1909, p. 8. [*Shadow*]

"Amusements: The Abbey Theatre Company at the Opera House", 5 April 1910, p. 8. [*Riders*]

"The Book Corner: 'J. M. Synge and the Irish Dramatic Movement' ", 5 October 1912, p. 7. [Review of Francis Bickley, *J. M. Synge and the Irish Dramatic Movement*]

The Irish Weekly and Ulster Examiner

Ouine, Sean. "Talk Upon Topics", 2 February 1907, p. 1. [*The Playboy* and the Dublin riots]

"To the Point", 2 February 1907, p. 4. [Editorial on *The Playboy*]

"An Alleged Irish Comedy: Scenes in the Abbey Theatre", 2 February 1907, p. 5. [*Playboy*]

"The 'Playboy' Disturbances", 9 February 1907, p. 12.

"Yeats's Fishy Yarn: Curious Genesis of the 'Playboy' ", 9 February 1907, p. 12.

Ouine, Sean. "Talk Upon Topics", 15 June 1907, p. 1.

The Northern Whig

"Dublin", 6 February 1905, p. 9. [*Well*]

"Dublin", 28 January 1907, p. 8. [*Playboy*]

"Another Scene at the Abbey Theatre", 30 January 1907, p. 9.

"Scenes in a Dublin Theatre", 31 January 1907, p. 11.

"Dublin", 4 February 1907, p. 7. [*Playboy*]

"Quill". " 'The Playboy of the Western World' ", 4 May 1907, p. 10. [Review article of Maunsel edition of *Playboy*]

"Irish Plays in London", 11 June 1907, p. 11. [*Playboy*]

"Theatre Royal: Visit of the Abbey Players, A Triple Bill", 1 December 1908, p. 2. [*Shadow*]

"Theatre Royal: Visit of the Abbey Company", 4 December 1908, p. 9. [*Riders*]

"Death of Mr. J. M. Synge: A Distinguished Irish Dramatist", 25 March 1909, p. 9.

"Grand Opera House: 'The Playboy of the Western World' ", 4 August 1909, p. 12.

"Grand Opera House: The Abbey Players", 5 August 1909, p. 11. [*Shadow*]

"Grand Opera House: The Abbey Players", 5 April 1910, p. 11. [*Riders*]

"Grand Opera House: 'The Well of the Saints' ", 6 April 1910, p. 11. [*Well*]

The Ulster Echo

"Theatre Royal: The Irish Players", 1 December 1908, p. 3. [*Shadow*]

"Theatre Royal: Abbey Theatre Company", 4 December 1908, p. 3. [*Riders*]

"Grand Opera House: The Abbey Company", 4 August 1909, p. 3. [*Playboy*]

BIRMINGHAM (England)

The Birmingham Daily Mail

"An Unpopular Play: Uproar at the Irish Theatre", 30 January 1907, p. 5.

The Birmingham Daily Post

"Disturbance in an Irish Theatre", 30 January 1907, p. 7, col. 2.

"Theatrical Novelties in London: The Irish Season", 12 June 1907, p. 5. [*Playboy*]

"The Works of J. M. Synge", 1 February 1911, p. 4. [Review article of Maunsel edition, *The Works*]

BOSTON (U.S.A.)

The Boston American

"Irish Play Wins Censor", 17 October 1911, p. 1. [*Playboy*]

Young, Nicholas. "Finished Acting by Irish Players: 'The Playboy of the Western World' at Plymouth Big Hit Despite Interruptions", 17 October 1911, p. 14.

The Boston Daily Advertiser

Williams, S. C. "The Abbey Players at the Plymouth", 25 September 1911, p. 5. [*Shadow*]

"Music and Drama: Plymouth Theatre", 26 September 1911, p. 5. [*Well*]

Williams, S. C. "The Abbey Players Score Again", 27 September 1911, p. 5. [*Well*]

C., J. V. "Music and Drama: 'Riders to the Sea' at Plymouth Theatre", 3 October 1911, p. 5. [Sub-headline reads: "First Production of Tragedy in America"]

The Boston Daily Globe

"New Plays at the Theatre: Irish Players at the Plymouth", (Morning), 26 September 1911, p. 8.

"Seek to Rouse Irish by Drama: Yeats Describes New National Theatre", (Morning), 29 September 1911, p. 5.

"Comes to Direct Irish Players", (Morning), 30 September 1911, p. 4.

"Irish Players at the Plymouth", (Morning), 3 October 1911, p. 17. [Reprinted in *The Boston Daily Globe* (Evening), 3 October 1911, p. 15]

"Doesn't Need Expurgation: Boston Opinion of 'The Playboy' ", (Evening), 17 October 1911, p. 6.

"Representative Boston Men Criticise 'The Playboy of the Western World': Play That Caused Riot in Dublin Discussed in the Globe by James B. Connolly, Michael J. Jordan, Thomas A. Mullen, P. O'Neil Larkin and A. J. Philpot", (Morning), 17 October 1911, p. 9. [Reprinted in *The Boston Daily Globe* (Evening), 17 October 1911, p. 8.]

Connolly, James B. "Sincere in His Art", (Morning), 17 October 1911, p. 9.

Jordan, Michael J. "Vulgar, Brutalizing", (Morning), 17 October 1911, p. 9.

Larkin, P. O'Neil. "Declared Untrue", (Morning), 17 October 1911, p. 9.

Mullen, Thomas A. "Shocking Travesty", (Morning), 17 October 1911, p. 9.

Philpott, A. J. "Taken Too Seriously", (Morning), 17 October 1911, p. 9. [The name A. J. Philpott is spelled Philpot in the headline]

"Satiric Drama by the Irish Players", (Morning and Evening), 17 October 1911, p. 15.

The Boston Evening Record

Williams, S. C. "Irish Players Open Plymouth Theatre", 25 September 1911, p. 6. [*Shadow*]

"Plymouth Theatre", 26 September 1911, p. 6. [Interview with Yeats about *Well*]

Williams, S. C. "Abbey Players in New Bill", 27 September 1911, p. 6. [*Well*]

C., J. V. "New Bill by Irish Players", 3 October 1911, p. 6. [*Riders*]

"Plymouth Theatre", 14 October 1911, p. 6. [A discussion of the forthcoming performance of *Playboy*]

"Irish Protest 'Playboy' ", 16 October 1911, p. 5.

"Singe's [sic] Playboy Pleases", 17 October 1911, p. 5.

The Boston Evening Transcript

Moore, George. "George Moore on the Irish Theatre", 23 September 1911, p. 8. [A letter to the Editor, signed Dublin, and dated 14 September. Contains good material on Synge]

"The Irish Players", 23 September 1911, p. 9. [*Well*]

P., H. T. "The Irish Players: An Evening of New and Rare Impressions", 25 September 1911, p. 12. [*Shadow*]

P., H. T. "Two More Irish Plays: One Puzzling and One Pungent Comedy", 27 September 1911, p. 19. [*Well*]

M., K. "Synge's Posthumous Play", 27 September 1911, p. 19. [*Deirdre*]

"Yeats Upon Irish Drama: His Speech before the Drama League", 29 September 1911, p. 12. [Late edition: p. 14]

"The Abbey Theatre", 3 October 1911, p. 13. [Late edition: p. 14]

P., H. T. "More Irish Plays: Riders to the Sea", 3 October 1911, p. 13. [Late edition: p. 14]

"New Plays and New Music: Signs in the Irish Heavens", 5 October 1911, p. 14.

Fuller, Eunice. "The Abbey Theatre", 7 October 1911, Part 3, p. 4.

P., H. T. "Plays and Players: The Debate Over the Irish Plays", 9 October 1911, p. 13.

"Plays and Players: Mr. Yeats Explains", 13 October 1911, p. 14.

M., K. "Dublin and 'The Playboy' ", 14 October 1911, Part 3, p. 4.

P., H. T. "The Embattled 'Playboy' ", 17 October 1911, p. 12. [Late edition: p. 13]

"Approves the Irish Play", (Late edition), 17 October 1911, p. 3.

"The Irish Players: The Victory for 'The Playboy' ", 18 October 1911, p. 23.

M., K. "The Tinker's Wedding", 18 October 1911, p. 23.

"An Irish Anthology", 19 October 1911, p. 12. [Late edition: p. 14]

"News of the Theatre: Providence and 'The Playboy' ", 31 October 1911, p. 13.

" 'The Playboy' in New York", 28 November 1911, p. 14. [Late edition: p. 16]

"Pursuing 'The Playboy' ", 29 November 1911, p. 22.

The Boston Herald

"Irish Players at Plymouth", 26 September 1911, p. 5. [*Well*]

"Drama, Farce at Plymouth", 27 September 1911, p. 10. [*Well*]

"Tells Story of Irish Stage: William Butler Yeats Speaks Before the Boston Drama League", 29 September 1911, p. 3.

Hale, Philip. "Two Successes at Plymouth: Irish Players Delight Audience with the Grim Tragedy 'Riders to the Sea' ", 3 October 1911, p. 5.

"Yeats Defends 'The Playboy' ", 12 October 1911, p. 8.

Hale, Philip. "Double Bill at the Plymouth: Scattered Hissing at 'Playboy of the Western World' Resented by the Audience", 17 October 1911, p. 12. [*Playboy*]

"Ask 'Playboy's' Withdrawal", 18 October 1911, p. 2.

The Boston Journal

"Irish Players Happy Choice for Plymouth Theatre's Dedication", 24 September 1911, p. 3. [*Shadow*]

" 'Well of Saints' Superb Comedy", 27 September 1911, p. 7.

"Champions Irish National Theater: Playwright Yeats Tells Drama League How Plan Succeeded", 29 September 1911, p. 7.

"Irish Players in New Bill", 3 October 1911, p. 9. [*Riders*]

"Sensational Drama Plymouth Offering", 15 October 1911, p. 8.

"Irish Actors Give 'Playboy' ", 17 October, 1911, p. 4.

The Boston Post

"New Plays at the Plymouth", 27 September 1911, p. 6. [*Well*]

"Plymouth Theatre", 3 October 1911, p. 9. [*Riders*]

"Yeats Replies to His Critics: Defends Irish Plays Being Produced Here", 5 October 1911, p. 8.

Crosby, Edward H. "New Plays Last Evening: Plymouth Theatre", 17 October 1911, p. 9. [*Playboy*]

"Condemn Play by the Irish Players", 18 October 1911, p. 7.

"No Booing at Irish Players", 18 October 1911, p. 7.

"Protests the Irish Players: Central Council Terms the 'Playboy' Infamous", 24 October 1911, p. 5.

The Boston Sunday Globe

"Opened with the New Irish Drama", (Morning), 24 September 1911, p. 9.

"Simple and Real", (Morning), 24 September 1911, p. 9. [*Shadow*]

"Attractions at the Theatres: 'The Playboy of the Western World' at the Plymouth", (Morning), 15 October 1911, p. 58.

The Boston Sunday Post

"Plymouth Theatre", 15 October 1911, p. 28. [*Playboy*]

The Boston Traveler

Biggers, Earl Derr. "The New Plays", 25 September 1911, p. 4. [*Shadow*]

Biggers, Earl Derr. "The New Plays", 28 September 1911, p. 4. [*Well*]

Biggers, Earl Derr. "The New Plays", 4 October 1911, p. 4. [*Riders*]

Biggers, Earl Derr. "The New Plays", 17 October 1911, p. 6. [*Playboy*]

The Christian Science Monitor

Egerton, George. "Irish National Drama Real Says Noted English Writer", 23 September 1911, p. 25.

"Irish Players Delight Boston With Sincerely Acted Dramas", 25 September 1911, p. 4. [*Shadow*]

"The Theatrical World: Irish Players Change Bill", 27 September 1911, p. 12. [*Well*]

"Irish Players in New Bill", 3 October 1911, p. 5. [*Riders*]

"Irish Players to Act 'The Playboy' ", 14 October 1911, p. 14.

" 'The Playboy of the Western World' ", 17 October 1911, p. 4.

The Pilot

Mahon, M. P. "The Irish Players: A Critique", 21 October 1911, p. 3. [*Playboy*]

The Sunday Herald

Hale, Philip. "Boston's New Theatre Opens", 24 September 1911, p. 4. [*Shadow*]

Hale, Philip. "Dramatic and Musical Review: Mr. W. B. Yeats and J. M. Synge", 1 October 1911, p. 24.

"Isabella Augusta, Lady Gregory, 'The Comedy Spirit of Ireland': A Grand-Mother Author and Says She Has a Right to Laugh", 1 October 1911, Magazine section, [p. 4]

Hale, Philip. "Dramatic and Musical Review: How Dublin Misunderstood 'The Playboy' ", 15 October 1911, p. 24.

BRADFORD (England)

The Yorkshire Observer

"Irish Players in Leeds", 15 April 1910, p. 7. [*Playboy*]

"Irish Players in Leeds", 18 April 1910, p. 9. [*Shadow*]

BRIGHTON (England)

The Sussex Daily News

"London Correspondence: An Irish Play", 11 June 1907, p. 8. [*Playboy*]

BRISTOL (England)

The Bristol Daily Mercury

"London Letter: An Irish Comedy", 11 June, 1907, p. 4. [*Playboy*]

BROOKLYN (New York, U.S.A.)

The Brooklyn Daily Eagle

"Irish Players Consist Largely of Humbug", 24 November 1911, p. 6. [*Well*]

" 'Playboy' to Go on in Spite of Rioters", 28 November 1911, p. 3.

"A Poor Way to Treat Poor Plays", 28 November 1911, p. 4. [Editorial]

" 'Playboy' Causes Riot: Irish Players in Drama That Caused Wild Riot in Theater Last Evening", 28 November 1911, p. 6.

"Irish Players Again: Synge's Tragedy, 'Riders to the Sea', Proves Most Effective of Company's Repertoire", 5 December 1911, p. 6.

"Irish Players Again: Seen in One Act Play by Synge", 16 December 1911, p. 9. [*Shadow*]

CAPE TOWN (South Africa)

The Cape Times

"Society & the Drama", 22 February 1907, p. 5. [Dated London, 1 February 1907. See paragraph four for a discussion of *Playboy* and the Abbey Theatre disturbance]

CHICAGO (Illinois, U.S.A.)

The Chicago American

"Ask Mayor to Bar Irish Players Here", (One O'Clock Saturday Sporting Special; [1st] Home Edition), 27 January 1912, p. 2.

"Defies Council to Stop Play", (8th Edition; 9th Sporting Edition; 10th Edition; Last 10th Edition; Extra), 30 January 1912, p. 2.

"Irish Play Ban up to Harrison", (2nd Edition; [1st] Home Edition;

Third One O'Clock Edition; [2nd] Home Edition), 30 January 1912, p. 2.

"Irish Play in Mayor's Hands", (Seventh and Home Edition), 31 January 1912, p. 1.

"Irish Play in Mayor's Hands", (8th Edition; 9th Edition; 10th Edition; Last 10th Edition), 31 January 1912, p. 2. [Expanded story from earlier edition]

Lait, Jack. "Irish Players Do 'The Playboy' ", ([2nd] Home Edition; [3rd] Home Edition; Seventh and [4th] Home Edition; 8th Edition; 9th Edition; 10th Edition; Last 10th Edition), 7 February 1912, p. 12.

The Chicago Citizen

Henry-Ruffin, Mrs. M. E. (L. H. D.) "The Irish (?) Plays", 13 January 1912, p. 3. [Undated letter to the Editor]

Forhan, Simon J. "The Irish Players", 17 February 1912, p. 3.

Ryan, Joseph E. "A Playboy Post Mortem", 2 March 1912, p. 3. [Undated letter to the Editor]

The Chicago Daily Journal

"Irish Delay Play Protest", 29 January 1912, p. 5.

"Mayor Will Prohibit Play: Lady Gregory Defends It", 30 January 1912, p. 3.

" 'The Playboy of the Western World' and *Why* It Stirs the Irish Wrath", 31 January 1912, p. 3.

"Threaten Injunction to Foil Ban on Play", 31 January 1912, p. 3.

"Rules on 'Playboy' Row", 1 February 1912, p. 3.

Hall, O. L. "Act 'Playboy' Without Fight", 7 February 1912, p. 5.

Hall, O. L. "Irish Co. in Three Plays", 14 February 1912, p. 7. [*Riders*]

Hall, O. L. "Irish Co. in Three Plays", 22 February 1912, p. 8. [*Shadow*]

Hall, O. L. "News and Gossip of the Theaters", 28 February 1912, p. 7. [*Well*]

The Chicago Daily News

Leslie, Amy. "Synge With His Types", 7 February 1912, p. 14. [*Playboy*]

Leslie, Amy. "Varied Bill at Grand: Tragic Hour With Synge", 13 February 1912, p. 14. [*Riders*]

Leslie, Amy. "Four Fine Irish Plays: Synge's Effort in Satire", 22 February 1912, p. 14. [*Shadow*]

Leslie, Amy. "Three New Irish Bits: Synge's 'The Well of the Saints': A Deeply Tender Philosophical Study", 29 February 1912, p. 5.

The Chicago Daily Socialist

" 'Playboy' May Not Play Here", 30 January 1912, p. 1.

The Chicago Daily Tribune

Peattie, Elia W. "Among the New Books: Synge as Playwright, and Master of English", 21 January 1911, p. 11. [Review of Maunsel edition, *The Works*]

Hackett, Francis. "An Irishman's Defense of Synge", 30 January 1912, p. 11.

"Nullifies Order to Stop 'Playboy' ", 1 February 1912, p. 19.

Hammond, Percy. "The Delightful Irish Actors at the Grand", 7 February 1912, p. 13. [Appears under the headline: "First Performance in Chicago of 'The Playboy of the Western World', No Riots"]

O'Shaughnessy, James. "O'Shaughnessy Calls It a 'Harmless Hoax' ", 7 February 1912, p. 13. [Appears under the headline: "First Performance in Chicago of 'The Playboy of the Western World', No Riots"]

Hammond, Percy. "The Delightful Irish Actors at the Grand", 8 February 1912, p. 9.

O'Shaughnessy, James. "An Irishman's Views", 8 February 1912, p. 9.

Hammond, Percy. "Music and the Theaters", 15 February 1912, p. 9. [*Riders*]

Hammond, Percy. " 'The Well of the Saints' by the Irish Players", 29 February 1912, p. 7.

The Chicago Evening Post

"An Irish Comedy in Dublin Last January", 20 April 1907, p. 6. [*Playboy*]

Hackett, Francis. "The Book of the Week: Synge", *Friday Literary Review*, 2 July 1909, p. 1. [Review of Cuala Press edition, *Poems and Translations*]

Hackett, Francis. "Says 'Playboy' Foes Have Had Their Day", 3 February 1912, p. 3. [Letter to the Editor, dated 2 February]

Hatton, Frederic. "Bouquets, Not Bricks, Greet 'The Playboy' ", 7 February 1912, p. 5.

Hatton, Frederic. "Triple Bill Enhances Irish Players' Week", 22 February 1912, p. 5. [*Shadow*]

Hatton, Frederic. "Irish Players Reveal Poetical Synge Play", 28 February 1912, p. 5. [*Well*]

The Chicago Examiner

Dillon, William. "Play Pictures Peasant from Viewpoint of Landlord and is not Faithful Portrayal", 27 January 1912, p. 4. [Appears under headline: "Lady Gregory Denies Harm in 'The Playboy': 10,000 Irish to Protest Its Coming to Chicago"]

Field, Roswell. "Conductor of Irish Players Asserts Critics Are Confused as to Intent of Author: Surprised at Opposition", 27 January 1912, p. 4. [Appears under headline "Lady Gregory Denies Harm in 'Playboy': 10,000 Irish to Protest Its Coming to Chicago"]

"Mayor to be Urged to Bar Production", 27 January 1912, p. 4.

"Irish 'Playboy' Barred by Aldermen", 30 January 1912, p. 1.

Mayor Studies 'Playboy' to Determine Its Morality: Examiner Arranges Notable Discussion of Play", 31 January 1912, p. 3.

"Mrs. John Cudahy Praised for Snubbing 'The Playboy' ", 5 February 1912, p. 10.

"Says 'Playboy' Libels Women: [Seumas] MacManus Assails the Drama", 6 February 1912, p. 4.

"1,500 Greet Irish Players Without Disturbance", 7 February 1912, p. 7. [Appears under headline: " 'Playboy of the Western World', Draws Throngs of Chicago Society Folk"]

Stevens, Ashton. " 'Playboy' is Foolish Satire, Burlesquing the Burlesque", 7 February 1912, p. 7. [Appears under headline: " 'Playboy of the Western World' Draws Throngs of Chicago Society Folk"]

" 'Playboy' Again Given Without Disturbance", 8 February 1912, p. 7.

Stevens, Ashton. " 'Well of Saints' is Grim, Gray Comedy", 28 February 1912, p. 7.

The Chicago Record-Herald

Bennett, James O'Donnell. "News of the Stage", 14 April 1909, p. 8. [Review of *The Playboy* performed at the Illinois Theater, 13 April 1909. This is the first American performance of *The Playboy*]

B[ennett]., J[ames]. O'D[onnell]. "Music and the Drama: A Note about 'The Playboy' ", 17 April 1909, p. 8.

Bennett, James O'Donnell. "Mrs. Fiske Presents Two Plays", 1 November 1910, p. 8. [*Shadow*]

"Truce on Irish Play Until Mayor Reads It", 31 January 1912, p. 13.

"The Mayor and the 'Play Boy' ", 31 January 1912, p. 14. [Editorial]

"Irish Play Ban Void, City Lawyer Holds", 1 February 1912, p. 1.

"The First Lady of Ireland" [Lady Augusta Gregory], 4 February 1912, Part 6, p. 1.

"Peace at Irish Play: Titters, Not Bricks", 7 February 1912, p. 1.

Bennett, James O'Donnell. "The Theatre: 'The Playboy of the Western World' ", 8 February 1912, p. 8. [*Playboy*]

Bennett, James O'Donnell. "Drama and Music: Ireland's Smiles and Tears", 15 February 1912, p. 6. [*Riders*]

Bennett, James O'Donnell. "Drama of the Day: Synge on Compensations", 29 February 1912, p. 6.

The Chicago Sunday Examiner

"Irish Players Will Produce 'Playboy' Despite Protest", 28 January 1912, Part I, p. 9.

"Mrs. Cudahy Disavows 'Playboy': 'I am not Patroness', She says: Insists Name be Taken Off List", 4 February 1912, Part I, pp. 1 and 9.

" 'Playboy' is Merely Stupid, says Rabbi", 4 February 1912, Part I, p. 9.

The Chicago Sunday Tribune

Hammond, Percy. "Cause of the Irish Riots; Peaceful Outlook Here", 4 February 1912, Part 2, p. 1.

The Daily Calumet

"Irish Up in Arms Against 'Playboy' ", 2 February 1912, p. 1.

The Inter Ocean

"Irish Play Moral, Says Lady Gregory", 31 January 1912, p. 7.

"Ban is not Issued: 'Playboy' Stupid in Opinion of Mayor", 1 February 1912, pp. 1 and 3.

Delamarter, Eric. "That Brick-Batted 'Playboy' ", 8 February 1912, p. 6.

Delamarter, Eric. "With the Irish Players", 29 February 1912, p. 6. [*Well*]

The Sunday Record-Herald

Bennett, James O'Donnell. "The Stage: 'The Playboy of the Western World', For the First Time in America", 11 April 1909, Part 5, p. 4.

Eaton, Walter Prichard. "Viewing Irish Players in the Light of Reason: Synge's Pre-Eminence", 17 December 1911, Part 7, p. 3. [A lengthy discussion of *Riders*]

"Fight Irish Plays: Mayor is Appealed to", 28 January 1912, Part 1, p. 8.

Gregory, Lady Augusta. "Our Trials and Triumphs", 4 February 1912, Part 7, p. 1.

Moore, George. "From the Beginning", 4 February 1912, Part 7, p. 1.

Rolleston, T. W. "Thanking God for Synge", 4 February 1912, Part 7, p. 1.

Yeats, W. B. "What We Try to Do", 4 February 1912, Part 7, p. 1.

Masefield, John. "Glimpses of the Author of 'The Playboy' ", 11 February 1912, Part 7, p. 3.

CORK (Ireland)

The Cork Constitution

"A Queer Country: An Irish Play Hissed Down", 29 January 1907, p. 5.

"Irish Theatre: More Disturbances", 30 January 1907, p. 5.

"The Abbey Theatre: Continued Disturbances", 1 February 1907, p. 3.

[The Irish National Theatre], 4 February 1907, p. 4. [Long editorial]

"Abbey Theatre: Another Prosecution", 4 February 1907, pp. 5 and 6.

"Opera House: Abbey Theatre Company in 'Deirdre' and 'The Playboy of the Western World' ", 30 August 1910, p. 6. [*Deirdre* and *Playboy*]

O'Connor, Eily. "Correspondence: 'The Playboy of the Western World' ", 31 August 1910, p. 5. [Undated letter to the Editor]

Ray, R. J. "Correspondence: 'The Playboy of the Western World' ", 1 September 1910, p. 8. [Letter to the Editor, dated 31 August. Replies to Eily O'Connor's letter of 31 August]

Wyat, James. "Correspondence: 'The Playboy of the Western World' ", 1 September 1910, p. 8. [Letter to the Editor, dated 31 August]

J., M. "Correspondence: 'The Playboy of the Western World' ", 2 September 1910, p. 8. [Undated letter to the Editor. Replies to commend Eily O'Connor's letter of 31 August]

O'Callaghan, T. J. "Correspondence: 'The Playboy of the Western World' ", 2 September 1910, p. 8. [Letter to the Editor, dated 2 September 1910. Replies to R. J. Ray's letter of 1 September]

O'Connor, Eily. "Correspondence: 'The Playboy of the Western World' ", 2 September 1910, p. 8. [Letter to the Editor, dated 1 September. Replies to R. J. Ray's letter of 1 September]

Wyett, James. "Correspondence: 'The Playboy of the Western World' ", 2 September 1910, p. 8. [Letter to the Editor, dated 1 September. Replies to R. J. Ray's letter of 1 September]

Ray, R. J. "Correspondence: 'The Playboy of the Western World' ", 3 September 1910, p. 10. [Undated letter to the Editor. Replies to all his critics]

"Go On". "Correspondence: 'The Playboy of the Western World' ", 5 September 1910, p. 3. [Letter to the Editor, dated 3 September. Replies to R. J. Ray's letter of 3 September]

O'Callaghan, T. J. "Correspondence: 'The Playboy of the Western World' ", 5 September 1910, p. 3. [Letter (i.e., a poem) to the Editor, dated 3 September. Replies in verse to R. J. Ray's letter of 3 September]

Wyett, James. "Correspondence: 'The Playboy of the Western World' ", 5 September 1910, p. 3. [Undated letter to the Editor. Replies to R. J. Ray's letter of 3 September]

J., M. "Correspondence: 'The Playboy of the Western World' ", 6 September 1910, p. 8. [Undated letter to the Editor. Replies to R. J. Ray's letter of 3 September]

O'Connor, Eily. "Correspondence: 'The Playboy of the Western World' ", 6 September 1910, p. 8. [Undated letter to the Editor. Replies to R. J. Ray's letter of 3 September]

Ray, R. J. "Correspondence: 'The Playboy' ", 7 September 1910, p. 8. [Undated letter to the Editor. Replies to M. J.'s letter of 6 September]

C., B. "Correspondence: 'The Playboy' ", 8 September 1910, p. 6. [Letter to the Editor, dated 7 September]

R., T. B. "Correspondence: 'The Playboy' ", 8 September 1910, p. 6. [Letter to the Editor, dated 7 September. Replies to R. J. Ray's letter of 7 September]

J., M. "Correspondence: 'The Playboy' ", 9 September 1910, p. 6. [Undated letter to the Editor. Replies to R. J. Ray's letter of 7 September]

Ray, R. J. "Correspondence: 'The Playboy of the Western World' ", 12 September 1910, p. 2 [Undated letter to the Editor. Replies to M. J.'s letter of 9 September]

"Reviews of Books", 16 October 1912, p. 2. [Brief review of Francis Bickley, *J. M. Synge and the Irish Dramatic Movement*]

The Cork Examiner

"Scene at a Dublin Theatre", 29 January 1907, p. 5.

"Abbey Theatre: More Scenes", 30 January 1907, p. 6.

"Notes and Comments", 31 January 1907, p. 5. [*The Playboy* and the Abbey Theatre disturbance]

"Abbey Theatre: Another Prosecution", 1 February 1907, p. 6.

"Abbey Theatre: Further Prosecutions", 2 February 1907, p. 5.

"Abbey Theatre: More Prosecutions", 4 February 1907, p. 8.

"Abbey Theatre: More Scenes", 5 February 1907, p. 6.

"Death of Mr. J. M. Synge", 25 March 1909, p. 6.

"Opera House: Abbey Theatre Plays", 30 August 1910, p. 7. [*Playboy*]

"Opera House", 1 September 1910, p. 7. [*Playboy*]

"Literary and Scientific Society: Synge's Dramatic Work", 11 November 1910, p. 8. [Report of Daniel Corkery's lecture on "The Drama of the late J. M. Synge" given in the Lecture Hall of the School of Art (Crawford Institute), 10 November]

The Cork Free Press

Ray, R. J. "Abbey Theatre Company", 27 August 1910, p. 8. [Undated letter to the Editor]

"Opera House", 30 August 1910, p. 8. [*Playboy*]

Mahon, Christy. " 'The Playboy of the Western World' ", 1 September 1910, p. 2. [Letter to the Editor, dated 31 August 1910]

L., P. J. " 'The Playboy of the Western World' ", 2 September 1910, p. 8. [Letter to the Editor, dated 1 September 1910]

O'Callaghan, T. J. " 'The Playboy of the Western World' ", 2 September 1910, p. 8. [Letter to the Editor, dated 1 September 1910]

"The Drama of Synge: His Life Story Told: Lecture by Mr. D. Corkery", 28 October 1910, p. 10. [Given in the Hall of the Crawford Institute, Cork]

"Literary and Scientific Society: The Drama of J. M. Synge", 11 November 1910, p. 7. [Report of Daniel Corkery's lecture on "The Drama of the late J. M. Synge", given in the Lecture Hall of the School of Art (Crawford Institute), 10 November]

The Cork Weekly News

"A Queer Country: An Irish Play Hissed Down", 2 February 1907, p. 3.

"Abbey Theatre: Another Prosecution", 9 February 1907, p. 5.

"Opera House: Abbey Theatre Company in 'Deirdre', and 'The Playboy of the Western World' ", 3 September 1910, p. 6.

O'Connor, Eily. "Correspondence: 'The Playboy of the Western World' ", 3 September 1910, p. 7. [Undated letter to the Editor]

DUBLIN (Ireland)

An Chlaidheamh Soluis

Mhag Ruaidhrí, Mícheál. "Dhá Chéad Bliadhain Deireannach, agus, a Ghrádh, nach Fada an Suan é?" 9 February 1907, p. 4.

"The Passing of Anglo-Irish Drama", 9 February 1907, p. 7.

MacUidhir, Art. "John M. Synge", 30 April 1910, p. 5.

The Daily Express

"Irish National Theatre Society", 9 October 1903, p. 5. [*Shadow*]

"Irish National Theatre Society: 'The Well of the Saints' ", 6 February 1905, p. 6.

"The Abbey Theatre: Mr. Synge's New Play", 28 January 1907, p. 6. [*Playboy*]

"Disturbances at the Abbey Theatre", 29 January 1907, p. 6.

"The Abbey Theatre: Further Disorderly Scenes: Mr. Yeats and the Critics", 30 January 1907, p. 5.

"Scenes at the Abbey Theatre: Renewal of Disturbances", 31 January 1907, p. 5.

"Abbey Theatre Play: A Fair Hearing Accorded: Interview with Mr. W. B. Yeats", 1 February 1907, p. 5.

"The Abbey Theatre Disturbance: Mr. Wall and the Rights of Playgoers", 2 February 1907, p. 7.

"The Abbey Theatre", 4 February 1907, p. 7.

"The Abbey Theatre Disturbances: Mr. Yeats on Mr. Synge's Play: Lively Debate", 5 February 1907, p. 8.

"Death of Mr. J. M. Synge", 25 March 1909, p. 4.

"The Abbey Theatre: Revival of 'The Playboy' ", 28 May 1909, p. 6.

"The Abbey Theatre: Production of Mr. Synge's Last Play", 14

January 1910, p. 5. [*Deirdre*]

"John M. Synge", 20 April 1911, p. 8. [Review article of Maunsel edition, *The Works*]

The Dublin Evening Mail
[Buff edition unless otherwise indicated]

M., R. "The National Theatre Society", 9 October 1903, p. 2. [*Shadow*]

M., R. "At the Abbey Theatre: Production of 'The Well of the Saints' ", 6 February 1905, p. 2.

"Abbey Theatre", 26 January 1907, p. 6.

D., H. S. "A Dramatic Freak: First Night at the Abbey Theatre", 28 January 1907, p. 2.

"The Abbey Theatre Disturbance", 29 January 1907, p. 2. [Editorial]

F., A. " 'I Don't Care a Rap': Mr. Synge's Defence", 29 January 1907, p. 2. [Includes a Post Script entitled: "Mr. T. W. Russell's Views"]

H., P. "Dramatic Criticism", 29 January 1907, p. 5. [Undated letter to the Editor]

"Last Night's Row at the Abbey", 30 January 1907, p. 2.

"This Evening's London Papers: 'The Playboy of the Western World' ", 30 January 1907, p. 3.

"The Abbey Theatre: Further Disorderly Scenes, Mr. Yeats and the Critics", 30 January 1907, p. 6.

"La Linge". " 'The Playboy' at the Abbey Theatre", 31 January 1907, p. 2. [Letter to the Editor, dated 31 January]

"Last Night's Row at the Abbey: Police Court Proceedings", 31 January 1907, p. 3.

"The Law and the Drama: Last Night's Row at the Abbey", 31 January 1907, pp. 3 and 4. [This title is found in the Late Buff edition only, not in the Buff edition]

Colum, Padraic. [Undated Letter to the Editor], 1 February 1907, p. 2.

"Crito". [Undated Letter to the Editor], 1 February 1907, p. 2.

"Mr. Wall Invited to the Abbey", 1 February 1907, p. 2.

Power, Ambrose. [Letter to the Editor, dated 31 January], 1 February 1907, p. 2.

"Abbey Theatre Play: Interview With Mr. W. B. Yeats", 1 February 1907, p. 5.

"The New Play at the Abbey Theatre", 2 February 1907, p. 4.

"Abbey Theatre Disturbances", 2 February 1907, p. 5.

"Mr. Synge's Secret", 5 February 1907, p. 2.

Horniman, A. E. F. "The Abbey Theatre: Letter from Miss Horniman", 12 February 1907, pp. 3-4. [Letter to the Editor, dated 11 February]

" 'The Playboy' in London: A Sheaf of Press Criticisms", 12 June 1907, p. 2.

"Mr. J. M. Synge", 30 October 1908, p. 2. [*Well*]

"Irish Playwright Dead: Mr. J. M. Synge Passes Away", 24 March 1909, p. 3.

"An Appreciation", 26 March 1909, p. 2. [Reprinted from "Mr. J. M. Synge", *The Manchester Guardian*, 25 March 1909, p. 7]

"The Late Mr. J. M. Synge", 26 March 1909, p. 2.

D., H. S. " 'Deirdre of the Sorrows': Mr. Synge's Last Play", 15 January 1910, p. 5.

"Abbey Players", 6 July 1911, p. 5.

The Evening Herald

"The Playboy at the Abbey", 29 January 1907, p. 2.

" 'Abbey' Scenes Sequel", 30 January 1907, pp. 1-2.

"The 'Playboy' at the Abbey", 30 January 1907, p. 5.

"Abbey Theatre Scenes", 31 January 1907, p. 2.

M.A.M. "Art in Trouble", 31 January 1907, p. 4.

" 'The Playboy' ", 31 January 1907, p. 5. [Includes cartoons]

"Mr. Wall on the Drama", 1 February 1907, pp. 1 and 5.

"Mr. Synge Beaming", 1 February 1907, p. 5.

" 'The Playboy' ", 1 February 1907, p. 5.

"The Poet Is Pleased", 1 February 1907, p. 5.

R., V. "Mr. Yeats's Invitation", 1 February 1907, p. 5.

"A Weeding-Out of Words", 1 February 1907, p. 5.

" 'The Playboy' at the Abbey: Merits and Demerits Debated", 5 February 1907, p. 5. [Includes cartoons]

M' C., F. "Irish National Theatre: 'The Well of the Saints' ", 6 February 1905, p. 3.

Horniman, A. E. F. " 'The Playboy of the Western World': Letter from Miss Horniman", 12 February 1907, p. 4. [Letter to the Editor, dated 11 February, defending *The Playboy*]

"Death of Mr. J. M. Synge, Famous Irish Playwright: Sketch of His Career", 24 March 1909, pp. 1-2.

Point, Jack. " 'The Playboy' Again at the Abbey", 28 May, 1909, p. 4. [Review]

Holloway, Joseph. "John Millington Synge as Critic of Boucicaultian Irish Drama", 10 July 1913, p. 2.

The Evening Telegraph [Last Pink edition and Special Pink edition correspond, unless otherwise indicated. When no edition is indicated, it is the Last Pink edition.]

"Irish National Theatre Society: Production of Two New Plays", 9 October 1903, p. 3. [*Shadow*]

"Irish National Theatre Society", 26 February 1904, p. 3. [*Riders*]

"The National Theatre: Mr. Synge's New Play", 6 February 1905, p. 5. [*Well*]

"The Abbey Theatre: Mr. Synge's New Play", 25 January 1907, p. 3. [*Playboy*]

"The Abbey Theatre: 'The Playboy of the Western World'; A Revolting Caricature", 28 January 1907, p. 2.

A Western Girl. [Letter to the Editor, dated 27 January], (Special Pink edition, Dublin), 28 January 1907, p. 2.

"Abbey Theatre 'Playboy' ", 29 January 1907, p. 2.

"The Author Interviewed", 29 January 1907, p. 2.

Justitia. [Letter to the Editor, dated 28 January], 29 January 1907, p. 2.

K., T. W. [Letter to the Editor, dated 29 January], 29 January 1907, p. 2.

"Mr. Denis O'Sullivan's Opinion", 29 January 1907, p. 2.

" 'The People and the Parricide': 'Calumny Gone Raving Mad' ", 29

January 1907, p. 2. [Extract from the editorial "The People and the Parricide", *Freeman's Journal*, 28 January 1907, p. 6]

"What His 'Enthusiastic Admirer' Says of Mr. Synge's 'Playboy'", 29 January 1907, p. 2. [Reprinted from S. F. S., "An Impression of 'The Playboy'", *The Irish Times*, 29 January 1907, p. 8. (Undated letter to the Editor)]

"What Lady Gregory Said", 29 January 1907, p. 2.

"Abbey Theatre Scene: Interview with Mr. W. B. Yeats", 29 January 1907, p. 3. [Special Pink edition, p. 4]

"Abbey Theatre Scenes: More Uproar Last Night", 30 January 1907, p. 2.

A Commonplace Person. "'The Sneer of the Decadent'", 30 January 1907, p. 2. [Letter to the Editor, dated 29 January]

J., D. J. "Mr. Harvey and 'The Spell'", 30 January 1907, p. 2. [Letter to the Editor, dated 30 January]

A Much Interested Foreigner. "A Lady Approves of the Play Because It Represents 'An Uncivilised, Savage, Ferocious People'", 30 January 1907, p. 2. [Undated letter to the Editor]

"Police-Protected Drama: Mr. W. B. Yeats Examined", 30 January 1907, p. 3.

"The Scene in the Theatre", 30 January 1907, p. 3.

"Another 'Western Playboy'", 30 January 1907, pp. 3 and 4. [Special Pink edition, p. 3]

An Old Parnellite. "Sinn Fein and Abbey Theatre", 30 January 1907, pp. 3 and 4. [Undated letter to the Editor]

B., T. F. "'From the Point of View of Art'", 31 January 1907, p. 2. [Letter to the Editor, dated 30 January]

Colum, Padraic. "Letter from Mr. Padraic Colum, Author of 'The Land'", 31 January 1907, p. 2. [Letter to the Editor, dated 30 January]

Ua Muineacháin, P. S. [Letter to the Editor, dated 30 January], 31 January 1907, p. 2.

"Under Police Protection: Another Night in 'The Abbey'", 31 January 1907, p. 2.

"Police and 'The Playboy'", 31 January 1907, p. 3.

"'Sinn Fein' on the Subject", 31 January 1907, pp. 3-4. [Reprinted from "The Abbey Theatre", *Sinn Féin,* 2 February 1907, p. 2]

" 'Freedom of the Theatre': Address by Mr. W. B. Yeats at the Abbey Theatre", 31 January 1907, p. 4. [Special Pink edition, p. 3]

An Irishwoman. "A Lady Defender of the Play", 31 January 1907, p. 4. [Letter to the Editor, dated 30 January. Special Pink edition, p. 3]

Markham, Thomas. " 'Singed His Wings' ", 31 January 1907, p. 4. [Letter to the Editor, dated 31 January. Special Pink edition, p. 3]

O Maoláin, Micheál. "Mr. Synge's Knowledge of the West", 31 January 1907, p. 4. [Letter to the Editor, dated 31 January. Special Pink edition, p. 3]

[Synge, J. M.]. "Letter from Mr. Synge", 31 January 1907, p. 4. [The same letter appears under the title "The 'Playboy' ", in *The Irish Times,* 31 January 1907, p. 5. Special Pink edition, p. 3]

"Abbey St. 'Parricide' ", 1 February 1907, p. 2.

[Boyle, William]. "Mr. Wm. Boyle's Protest: Withdraws All His Plays", 1 February 1907, p. 2. [Letter to the Editor, dated London, 31 January]

Hogan, Patrick A. "Trinity Students and 'The Abbey' ", 1 February 1907, p. 2. [Letter to the Editor, dated 31 January]

"Lame and Impotent", (Special Pink edition) 1 February 1907, p. 2.

Power, Ambrose. "The Language of the Play", 1 February 1907, p. 2. [Letter to the Editor, dated 31 January. Same letter was sent to *Sinn Féin*]

Ua Broin, G. C. " 'The Abbey's' Future Supporters", 1 February 1907, p. 2. [Letter to the Editor, dated 31 January]

"The Abbey 'Parricide' ", (Special Pink edition) 1 February 1907, p. 3. [The same article appears under the title "Police Court Matinee" in the Last Pink edition, pp. 3-4]

"Police Court Matinee: The Abbey 'Parricide' ", 1 February 1907, pp. 3-4. [Includes a sketch of W. B. Yeats on p. 3]

Britton, T. F. " 'Representative of Nothing in Nature' ", 1 February 1907, p. 4. [Letter to the Editor, dated 1 February]

Griffith, Arthur. "The Language of the Play", 2 February 1907, p. 3. [Letter to the Editor, dated 1 February]

Gwynn, Stephen. "Mr. Boyle and Mr. Synge: Letter from S. Gwynn, M.P.", 2 February 1907, p. 3. [Undated letter to the Editor]

"Under Police Protection", 2 February 1907, p. 3.

"Another 'Playboy' Matinee", 2 February 1907, p. 5.

"Connaught Ranger". "Free Speech 'in the Abbey' ", (Special Pink edition) 2 February 1907, p. 5. [Letter to the Editor, dated 1 February]

Knight, W. "Monday Night's Debate", (Special Pink edition) 2 February 1907, p. 5. [Letter to the Editor, dated 2 February]

"Last Night's Disturbances", 2 February 1907, p. 5.

"Mr. Yeats Talks Again to an Evening Telegraph Man, about the 'Western Playboy' ", (Special Pink edition) 2 February 1907, p. 5.

O'Grady, L. C. "The Police and 'The Playboy' ", (Special Pink edition) 2 February 1907, p. 5. [Letter to the Editor, dated 2 February]

"An Outside View", (Special Pink edition) 2 February 1907, p. 5.

Wheeler, A. "Police Prosecutions", (Special Pink edition) 2 February 1907, p. 5. [Undated letter to the Editor]

O'Donoghue, D. J. "A Reply to Mr. Gwynn", (Special Pink edition) 2 February 1907, p. 6. [Undated letter to the Editor in reply to Stephen Gwynn's letter, "Mr. Boyle and Mr. Synge", 2 February 1907, p. 3]

" 'The Playboy of the Western World': 'An Exaggeration Apropos', Said Mr. W. B. Yeats", (Special Pink edition) 2 February 1907, p. 6. [No article; only a cartoon of W. B. Yeats]

Vox Populi. " 'The Freedom of the Public' ", (Special Pink edition) 2 February 1907, p. 6. [Letter to the Editor, dated 1 February]

Boyle, William. "Letter from Mr. Wm. Boyle", 4 February 1907, p. 2. [Letter to the Editor, dated London, 3 February]

Justitia. "The Prestige of the Abbey: The Fiddler and His Fun", 4 February 1907, p. 2. [Letter to the Editor, dated 4 February]

Milligan, Alice L. "Letter from Miss Alice Milligan", 4 February 1907, p. 2. [Undated latter to the Editor]

O'Leary-Curtis, W. "Letter from Mr. O'Leary-Curtis", 4 February 1907, p. 2. [Undated letter to the Editor]

Oryza. " 'A Tramcar Conversation' in 'The Abbey' Stalls", 4 February 1907, p. 2. [Undated letter to the Editor. The writer quotes Synge]

"Passing of 'The Parricide' ", 4 February 1907, p.2.

O'Mangain, H. C. "The National Drama", 4 February 1907, p. 3. [The sub-heading reads: "Mr. Henry Mangan Discusses Mr. Yeats, Mr. Synge, Mr. Boyle, and Lady Gregory". Special Pink edition, p. 4]

" 'The Playboy' a Week After", 4 February 1907, pp. 3 and 6. [Special Pink edition, p. 4]

"The 'Long-Haired Men' and the 'Broad-Leafed Hats' and 'The Man That Killed His Da' ", 5 February 1907, p. 2.

A Lover of Liberty. "The 'Freedom of the Theatre' ", 5 February 1907, p. 2. [Undated letter to the Editor]

" 'The Parricide and the People': Discussion in 'The Abbey'; Mr. Yeats's Defence", 5 February 1907, p. 2.

Dillon, Edward. "A Contradiction", 6 February 1907, p. 3, col. 3. [Letter to the Editor, dated 5 February]

"Resolutions of Protest", (Special Pink edition) 6 February 1907, p. 3, col. 3.

Yeats, W. B. "Mr. Boyle's Plays: Letter from Mr. W. B. Yeats", 6 February 1907, p. 3, col. 3. [Letter to the Editor, dated 6 February]

"The Man That Killed His Father 'Out of a Tragic Incident' ", 8 February 1907, p. 2. [Extract from the article, "The Freedom of the Theatre", *Sinn Féin*, 9 February 1907, p. 2]

" 'The National Drama' ", 8 February 1907, p. 2. [Extract from the article, "A National Theatre", *Sinn Féin*, 9 February 1907, p. 2]

Horniman, A. E. F. "Abbey Theatre Affairs: Letter from Miss Horniman; Her Views on 'The Playboy' ", 12 February 1907, p. 2. [Letter to the Editor, dated 11 February]

"Mr. Yeats Unbosoms Himself on Literature and the Stage", 14 February 1907, p. 2.

"Mr. Synge's Slander on the Irish Peasantry: 'The Parricide' Greeted with Saxon Cheers", 11 June 1907, p. 2.

"Death of Mr. J. M. Synge", 24 March 1909, p. 3.

Lawrence, W. J. " 'The Playboy of the Western World'; Proposed Revival at Abbey Theatre of Mr. Synge's Drama", 19 May 1909, p. 3.

O'L., J. J. " 'The Playboy of the Western World': The Proposed Revival at the Abbey Theatre", 20 May 1909, p. 3. [Letter to the Editor, dated 20 May]

O'Neill, James J. " 'The Playboy of the Western World': The Proposed Revival at the Abbey Theatre", 20 May 1909, p. 3. [Letter to the Editor, dated 20 May]

"J. M. Synge and 'The Playboy' ", 26 May 1909, p. 5.

"The Abbey Theatre", 28 May 1909, p. 5. [*Playboy*]

" 'Mr. Synge's Art and Message' ", 29 May 1909, p. 7.

" 'The Playboy of the West': Production in London", 9 June 1909, p. 3.

"The Abbey Theatre: Production of Mr. J. M. Synge's Posthumous Work", 14 January 1910, p. 2. [*Deirdre*]

"The Abbey Theatre", 7 October 1910, p. 2. [*Shadow*]

Cahill, Patrick K. " 'The Playboy of the Western World' ", 3 May 1911, p. 6. [Letter to the Editor, dated 2 May]

"Abbey Theatre Players at Shakespeare Festival: 'Playboy of the West' Creates Unfavourable Impression", 4 May 1911, p. 2.

Another Irishman. " 'The Playboy of the Western World' ", 5 May 1911, p. 2. [Letter to the Editor, dated 4 May; satirically agrees with Cahill's letter of 3 May]

Dickson, W. A. " 'The Playboy of the Western World' ", 5 May 1911, p. 2. [Undated letter to the Editor]

O'D. Power, Victor. " 'Playboy of the Western World' ", 8 May 1911, p. 2. [Letter to the Editor, dated 4 May; replies to the quotations cited in Another Irishman's letter of 5 May]

" 'The Playboy' at Stratford-on-Avon", 8 May 1911, p. 6.

R[yan]., F[red]. "The Abbey Theatre: 'The Playboy of the West' and the Abbey Peasant: A Curious Development and its Inner History", 13 May 1911, p. 5.

[Colum, Padraic]. "The Irish Peasant in Abbey Theatre Plays: Reply by Padraic Colum to Mr. Fred Ryan's Article in Last Saturday's Evening Telegraph", 20 May 1911, p. 5.

R[yan]., F[red]. "The Irish Peasant and the Abbey Dramatists: Is He a Moral Freak? Reply to Padraic Colum by Mr. Fred Ryan", 3 June 1911, p. 4.

A Visitor from Tzardom. " 'The Playboy' Drama", 12 June 1911, p. 2. [Letter to the Editor, dated 10 June]

The Freeman's Journal

"Irish National Theatre Society", 9 October 1903, pp. 5-6. [*Shadow*]

"Irish National Theatre Society", 26 February 1904, p. 6. [*Riders*]

"Irish National Theatre: Mr. Synge's New Play", 6 February 1905, p. 5. [*Well*]

"The Abbey Theatre: Mr. Synge's New Play", 26 January 1907, p. 10.

"The Abbey Theatre: 'The Playboy of the Western World' ", 28 January 1907, p. 10. [*Playboy*]

A Western Girl. [Letter to the Editor, dated 27 January], 28 January 1907, p. 10.

"The People and the Parracide", 29 January 1907, p. 6. [Editorial; includes the frequently quoted line: "calumny gone raving mad"]

"The Abbey Theatre: Uproarious Scenes", 29 January 1907, p. 7.

[Editorial on *The Playboy*], 30 January 1907, p. 7.

"Abbey Theatre Scenes: More Uproar Last Night", 30 January 1907, pp. 7-8.

A Commonplace Person. [Letter to the Editor, dated 29 January], 30 January 1907, p. 8.

"Interview With Mr. W. B. Yeats: Mr. Synge's Version of the Objectionable Passage", 30 January 1907, p. 8.

"Mr. T. W. Russell's Views", 30 January 1907, p. 8. [Extract from A. F., "Mr. T. W. Russell's Views", *The Dublin Evening Mail*, 29 January 1907, p. 2]

A Much Interested Foreigner. "A Lady Approves of the Play, Because It Represents 'An Uncivilised, Savage, Ferocious People' ", 30 January 1907, p. 8. [Undated letter to the Editor]

[Editorial on *The Playboy*], 31 January 1907, p. 7.

"The Abbey Theatre: More Uproar", 31 January 1907, pp. 7-8.

B., T. F. " 'From the Point of View of Art' ", 31 January 1907, p. 8. [Letter to the Editor, dated 30 January]

Colum, Padraic "Letter from Mr. Padraic Colum, Author of 'The Land' ", 31 January 1907. p. 8. [Letter to the Editor, dated 30 January]

"Police Prosecutions: Mr. W. B. Yeats Examined", 31 January 1907, p. 8.

"The Scene in the Theatre", 31 January 1907, p. 8.

"Supporter of the Play", 31 January 1907, p. 8.

Ua Muineacháin, P. S. [Letter to the Editor, dated 30 January], 31 January 1907, p. 8.

[Editorial on the Abbey Theatre Disturbance], 1 February 1907, p. 4.

"The Abbey Theatre: A Rather Quiet Night", 1 February 1907, p. 5.

"Another Prosecution", 1 February 1907, pp. 5-6.

Boyle, William. "Mr. William Boyle's Protest", 1 February 1907, p. 6. [Letter to the Editor, dated 31 January]

Power, Ambrose. "The Language of the Play", 1 February 1907, p. 6. [Letter to the Editor, dated 31 January]

"The Abbey Theatre: One Arrest", 2 February 1907, p. 2.

Griffith, Arthur. "The Language of the Play", 2 February 1907, p. 2. [Letter to the Editor, dated 1 February]

Gwynn, Stephen. "Mr. Boyle and Mr. Synge: Letter from Mr. Stephen Gwynn, M.P.", 2 February 1907, p. 2. [Undated letter to the Editor]

"Two More Prosecutions", 2 February 1907, p. 2.

"The Abbey Theatre: Audience Overawed by Police", 4 February 1907, p. 4.

"Another Prosecution: Policeman's Description of the Play", 4 February 1907, p. 4.

Boyle, William. "Letter From Mr. William Boyle", 4 February 1907, p. 4. [Letter to the Editor, dated 3 February]

'Interview With Mr. Yeats", 4 February 1907, p. 4.

Milligan, Alice L. "Letter from Miss Milligan", 4 February 1907, p. 4. [Undated letter to the Editor]

O'Donoghue, D. J. "Letter from Mr. D. J. O'Donoghue", 4 February 1907, p. 4. [Undated letter to the Editor]

O'Leary-Curtis, W. "Letter from Mr. O'Leary-Curtis", 4 February 1907, p. 4. [Undated letter to the Editor]

"Parricide and Public: Discussion at the Abbey Theatre", 5 February 1907, pp. 6-7.

A Lover of Liberty. "The 'Freedom of the Theatre' ", 5 February 1907, p. 7. [Undated letter to the Editor]

Dillon, Edward. " 'Playboy' Prosecutions", 6 February 1907, p. 9. [Letter to the Editor, dated 5 February]

"The Western Peasant", 26 February 1907, p. 6. [Editorial prompted by the report of Dr. Sigerson's lecture on the peasants of the west]

"London Correspondence", 11 June 1907, p. 7. [*Playboy* in London]

"London Correspondence", 15 June 1907, p. 7. [*Playboy* in London]

"The Abbey Theatre", 15 May 1908, p. 10. [*Well*]

"Death of Mr. J. M. Synge", 25 March 1909, p. 7.

"The Late Mr. Synge: An English Appreciation", 27 March 1909, p. 5. [Reprinted from "Mr. J. M. Synge", *The Manchester Guardian*, 25 March 1909, p. 7]

"The Abbey Theatre", 14 May 1909, p. 10. [*Well*]

"The Abbey Theatre", 28 May 1909, p. 8. [*Playboy*]

"The Abbey Theatre: Production of Mr. J. M. Synge's Posthumous Work", 14 January 1910, p. 5. [*Deirdre*]

Observer. " 'The Playboy' ", 23 January 1912, p. 8. [Undated letter to the Editor]

"The Writings of J. M. Synge", 23 January 1912, p. 8. [Report of Maurice Bourgeois' paper, 22 January]

The Illustrated Irish Weekly Independent and Nation

"Two New Plays: Irish National Theatre", 17 October 1903, p. 21. [*Shadow*]

The Irish Catholic

O'Neill, George: "Some Aspects of Our Anglo-Irish Poets: The Irish Literary Theatre: Foreign Inspiration of Alleged Irish Plays", 23 December 1911, p. 5.

O'Neill, George. "Abbey Theatre Libels: Rev. George O'Neill, S.J., on 'Irish' Drama, I", 31 August 1912, p. 6. [Extract from "Irish Drama and Irish Views", *American Catholic Quarterly Review* (Philadelphia), XXXVII (April 1912), 322-332]

The Irish Independent

"Two New Plays: Irish National Theatre", 9 October 1903, p. 6. [*Shadow*]

"Irish National Theatre", 26 February 1904, p. 5. [*Riders*]

"The Abbey Theatre: 'The Well of the Saints' ", 6 February 1905, p. 7.

Jacques. "A Queer Hero", 28 January 1907, p. 4. [*Playboy*]

"Police In", 29 January 1907, p. 5.

O Neachtain, Eoghan. "Irish Ireland: A Leaguer's Point of View", 30 January 1907, p. 4. [The article is in Gaelic]

"The Previous Scenes: Messrs. Yeats' and Synge's View", 30 January 1907, p. 5.

"Wild Scene", 30 January 1907, p. 5.

"The 'National' Theatre", 31 January 1907, p. 4. [Editorial]

O Neachtain, Eoghan. "Irish Ireland: A Leaguer's Point of View", 31 January 1907, p. 4. [The article is in Gaelic]

B., T. F. " 'The Unreal and Untrue' ", 31 January 1907, p. 5. [Letter to the Editor, dated 30 January]

Colum, Padraic. [An undated letter to the Editor about the arrest of Colum's father who protested too loudly during a performance of *The Playboy*], 31 January 1907, p. 5.

F., G. "Appeal for Fair Hearing", 31 January 1907, p. 5. [Undated letter to the Editor]

O'C., S. " 'Slur on the Irish Race' ", 31 January 1907, p. 5. [Letter to the Editor, dated 30 January]

"The 'Playboy' Scenes", 31 January 1907, p. 5.

A Playgoer. "A Playgoer's Opinion", 31 January 1907, p. 5. [Undated letter to the Editor]

"Uproarious", 31 January 1907, p. 5.

O Neachtain, Eoghan. "Irish Ireland: A Leaguer's Point of View", 1 February 1907, p. 4. [The article is in Gaelic]

"A Comedy in Court", 1 February 1907, p. 5.

"Mr. Synge Beaming", 1 February 1907, p. 5.

"The Poet Is Pleased: Interview with Mr. Yeats", 1 February 1907, p. 5.

Power, Ambrose. "Not a 'Play with a Purpose' ", 1 February 1907, p. 5. [Undated letter to the Editor]

"A Protest from the West", 1 February 1907, p. 5.

"Quieter", 1 February 1907, p. 5.

"A Weeding-Out of Words", 1 February 1907, p. 5.

"Who's Who at the Abbey Theatre", 1 February 1907, p. 7. [Cartoons of the major figures in the Abbey Theatre disturbance]

Costello, Mary. "Decay of Humour: Do We Scream at the Prick of a Pin", 2 February 1907, p. 4.

"A Dramatist's Protest", 2 February 1907, p. 5.

"More Peaceful Now", 2 February 1907, p. 5.

"Mr. Synge's Defence—A Reply", 2 February 1907, p. 5.

"Mr. Wall on the Plays", 2 February 1907, p. 5.

"Playboys and Policemen", 2 February 1907, p. 7. [Cartoons of the Abbey Theatre audience and the police]

"Exit 'The Playboy' ", 4 February 1907, p. 5.

Keane, Michael. "Police-Aided Drama", 4 February 1907, p. 5. [Letter to the Editor, dated 2 February]

" 'Ten Bob a Hiss' ", 4 February 1907, p. 5.

"Matters of Moment: Freedom of the Drama", 5 February 1907, p. 4. [Editorial]

" 'Playboy': Abbey Theatre Debate", 5 February 1907, pp. 5-6.

One Who Enjoys a Joke. "Police-Aided Drama", 5 February 1907, p. 6. [Undated letter to the Editor]

"Anti-'Playboy' Protests from Indignant Connachtmen", 6 February 1907, p. 5.

Dillon, Edward. "Anti-'Playboy' Protests", 6 February 1907, p. 5. [Letter to the Editor, dated 5 February]

"Sovey". "Anti-'Playboy' Protests", 6 February 1907, p. 5. [Undated letter to the Editor]

Horniman, A. E. F. "The Abbey Theatre: Letter from Patentee: Her Defence of 'The Playboy' ", 13 February 1907, p. 4. [Letter to the Editor, dated 11 February]

"More Condemnation", 13 February 1907, p. 4. [This brief note follows Miss Horniman's letter]

Rolleston, T. W. "The 'Playboy' as a Book: Mr. Rolleston's Appreciation", 6 March 1907, p. 7. [A long, important letter to the Editor, dated 5 March]

" 'The Playboy' in London", 11 June 1907, p. 6.

"Young Irish Playwright: Death of Mr. John M. Synge", 25 March 1909, p. 4. [Pencil sketch of Synge on p. 7]

O'Donoghue, D. J. "John M. Synge: A Personal Appreciation", 26 March 1909, p. 4.

"The Late Mr. Synge: An English Writer's Tribute", 26 March 1909, p. 6.

Jacques. "The 'Playboy' Again", 28 May 1909, p. 6, col. 8.

"A Saddening Play: 'Deirdre of the Sorrows' ", 14 January 1910, p. 7.

O'Donoghue, D. J. "The Synge Boom", 21 August 1911, p. 4.

O'Byrne, J. K. " 'The Synge Boom' ", 23 August 1911, p. 6, col. 5. [Letter to the Editor, dated 22 August]

Irishman. " 'The Synge Boom' ", 24 August 1911, p. 6, col. 6. [Undated letter to the Editor]

O'Byrne, J. K. " 'The Synge Boom' ", 26 August 1911, p. 6, col. 6. [Letter to the Editor, dated 24 August]

Tomas. " 'The Synge Boom' ", 28 August 1911, p. 6, cols. 6-7. [Undated letter to the Editor]

O'Byrne, J. K. " 'The Synge Boom' ", 29 August 1911, p. 6, col. 3. [Letter to the Editor, dated 28 August]

"Irish Players Assailed: Riot in a New York Theatre", 29 November 1911, p. 5, col. 2.

"The 'Playboy' Uproar: Mayor Will Take No Action", 30 November 1911, p. 6, col. 4.

"Abbey Players' Co. Arrested: Synge's 'Playboy' the Cause: Sensation in 'Quaker' City", 19 January 1912, p. 5. [Report of Philadelphia arrest of the Irish Players, 18 January]

" 'The Playboy': A Stay in the Court Proceedings: Mr. Yeats Interviewed", 20 January 1912, p. 5.

" 'Playboy' Banned: No Performance in Chicago: Fears of Disturbance", 31 January 1912, p. 5. [The report is untrue]

Quinn, John "Irish Players' Tour: The Opinion in New York", 31 January 1912, p. 5. [A long letter to the Editor, dated 8 January, explaining the facts surrounding the Irish Players' tour]

The Irish Nation [and The Peasant]

"Synge, the Sea, Sex and an Altar to Beauty", 1 May 1909, p. 2. [Obituary article; Synge's work is discussed generally]

Cairdre: "The Abbey Players in Belfast: 'The Playboy' ", 14 August 1909, p. 7.

[Yeats, Jack B.]. "Jack Yeats's Memories of Synge", 14 August 1909,

p. 7. [Reprinted from Jack Yeats, "J. M. Synge", *The Evening Sun* (New York), 20 July 1909, p. 4]

Mac C., S. "Localising Synge's 'Playboy' ", 21 August 1909, p. 7.

"Synge's 'Deirdre' at the Abbey", 15 January 1910, p. 5.

Firín. "Synge's 'Deirdre' at the Abbey", 22 January 1910, p. 1.

O h-Eigeartaigh, P. S. "Dramatic Impressions: I.—Synge", 16 July 1910, p. 1.

L., W. A. "The Playboy", 17 September 1910, p. 2.

The Irish People

"Mr. Synge's 'Playboy' ", 9 February 1907, p. 6.

The Irish Press [Scéala Eireann]

Rahilly, Sean O'Mahony. "Synge and the Early Days of the Abbey", 21 April 1949, p. 4. [Interview with Miss Maire O'Neill]

The Irish Statesman

Yeats, William Butler. "A People's Theatre: A Letter to Lady Gregory", 29 November 1919, pp. 547-549; and 6 December 1919, pp. 572-573. [Reprinted in *The Dial* (Chicago), LXVIII (April 1920), 458-468; included in the section "The Irish Dramatic Movement", in *Plays and Controversies*, 1923]

Yeats, W. B. "A Memory of Synge", 5 July 1924, pp. 530, 532.

H[oughton]., C. H. "John Synge as I Knew Him", 5 July 1924, pp. 532 and 534.

O Faoláin, Seán. "Literature and Life: Yeats on Synge", 29 September 1928, pp. 71-72. [Review article of W. B. Yeats, *The Death of Synge and Other Passages from an Old Diary*]

Lynch, Arthur. "Synge", 20 October 1928, p. 131. [Undated letter to the Editor. Corrects some misstatements Seán O Faoláin made in his article, "Yeats on Synge", 29 September 1928, pp. 71-72]

MacKenna, Stephen. "Correspondence: Synge", 3 November 1928, pp. 169-170. [Undated letter to the Editor. Corrects a misstatement Arthur Lynch made in his article, "Synge", 20 October 1928, p. 131]

The Irish Times

"Irish National Theatre", 9 October 1903, p. 8. [*Shadow*]

"Irish National Theatre Society", 26 February 1904, p. 5. [*Riders*]

C., E. T. "Mr. Synge's New Play", 27 February 1904, p. 6. [An undated letter to the Editor about *Riders*]

Moore, George. "The Irish Literary Theatre", 13 February 1905, p. 6. [Letter to the Editor about *Shadow*, dated 8 February]

"Platform and Stage", 26 January 1907, p. 9. [Description of Synge's background and announcement of forthcoming play, *The Playboy of the Western World*]

"Public Amusements: Abbey Theatre", 28 January 1907, p. 7. [Review of *Playboy*. Reprinted in A. C. Ward, editor, *Specimens of English Dramatic Criticism XVII-XX Centuries*, pp. 248-250]

" 'The Playboy of the West': Disturbance at the Abbey Theatre", 29 January 1907, p. 5.

S., F. S. "An Impression of 'The Playboy' ", 29 January 1907, p. 8. [Undated letter to the Editor]

[Editorial on *The Playboy*], 30 January 1907, p. 6. [Reprinted in A. C. Ward, editor, *Specimens of English Dramatic Criticism XVII-XX Centuries*, pp. 250-253]

" 'Playboy of the West' ", 30 January 1907, p. 8.

Pat [P. D. Kenny]. "That Dreadful Play", 30 January 1907, p. 9. [Defends *The Playboy*. Reprinted in A. C. Ward, editor, *Specimens of English Dramatic Criticism XVII-XX Centuries*, pp. 254-259]

Duncan, Ellen. "The 'Playboy' ", 31 January 1907, p. 5. [Letter to the Editor, dated 29 January]

" 'The Playboy of the Western World': More Disturbances at the Abbey Theatre", 31 January 1907, p. 5.

Synge, J. M. "The 'Playboy' ", 31 January 1907, p. 5. [Undated letter to the Editor. The same letter appears under the title "Letter from Mr. Synge", in the *Evening Telegraph*, 31 January 1907, p. 4]

Colum, Padraic. "The 'Playboy' ", 1 February 1907, p. 6. [Undated letter to the Editor]

" 'The Playboy of the Western World': Comparative Quiet at the Abbey Theatre", 1 February 1907, p. 6.

"Abbey Theatre", 2 February 1907, p. 5. [*Playboy*]

"The Abbey Theatre", 4 February 1907, p. 9.

"The Freedom of the Play: Discussion at the Abbey Theatre", 5 February 1907, p. 8.

[Editorial on Irish Historical Drama], 7 February 1907, p. 4. [Brief mention of Synge]

Dillon, Edward. "Letter to the Editor: The Disturbance at the Abbey Theatre", 7 February 1907, p. 6. [Letter to the Editor, dated 5 February]

O'Dempsey, Michael. "Letter to the Editor: The Disturbance at the Abbey Theatre", 11 February 1907, p. 8. [Letter to the Editor, dated 7 February]

Horniman, A. E. F. "Letters to the Editor: The Disturbance at the Abbey Theatre", 13 February 1907, p. 9. [Letter to the Editor, dated 11 February]

"Books of the Week: The Aran Islands", 7 June 1907, p. 9. [Review of Maunsel edition, *The Aran Islands*]

"London Correspondence", 12 June 1907, pp. 6-7 [*Playboy* in London; see top of p. 7, col. 1]

"Public Amusements: Abbey Theatre", 4 August 1908, p. 6. [*Riders*]

[Obituary Editorial on Synge], 25 March 1909, p. 6.

"Obituary: Mr. J. M. Synge", 25 March 1909, p. 8.

"Funeral of Mr. J. M. Synge", 27 March 1909, p. 8.

"Abbey Theatre", 14 May 1909, p. 6. [*Well*]

"Abbey Theatre", 28 May 1909, p. 6. [*Playboy*]

" 'Deirdre of the Sorrows': The Late J. M. Synge's Play", 14 January 1910, p. 10.

"J. M. Synge: His Works and Genius", 23 January 1911, p. 7. [Review of Maunsel edition, *The Works*]

"The Stage Irishman: His Origins and Development", 8 February 1912, p. 7. [Report of a lecture by Rev. J. O'Hannay at the Royal Dublin Society Theatre, 7 February]

Starkie, Walter. "The Playboy Riots", 7 October 1963, p. 8.

Clarke, Austin. "John Synge Comes Next", 1 November 1969, p. 10. [Review article of J. M. Synge, *Riders to the Sea*, edited by Robin Skelton]

The Irish Truth

The Editor. " 'The Play-boy of the Western World' ", 2 February 1907, pp. 6795-6796.

The Editor. "The Abbey Theatre Debate", 9 February 1907, pp. 6811-6812.

Horniman, A. E. F. [A letter to the Editor explaining her relationship to the Abbey Theatre and expressing her approval of Playboy], 16 February 1907, p. 6836.

The Irish Weekly Independent

"Tumult in a Theatre", 2 February 1907, pp. 1 and 5. [Playboy]

" 'Playboy of the Western World' ", 9 February 1907, p. 6.

The Leader

Chanel. "Plays with Meanings", 17 October 1903, pp. 124-125. [Shadow]

Chanel. "The National Theatre", 5 March 1904, pp. 27-28. [Riders]

Bull, J. "As Others See Us", 15 December 1906, pp. 265-266. [A satiric letter supposedly from an Englishman residing in Dublin which tells of a visit to the Abbey Theatre]

"Monday Night at the Abbey Theatre", 2 February 1907, pp. 384-385. [Playboy]

Avis. "The Playboys in the Abbey", 2 February 1907, pp. 387-388.

"Mr. Yeats and Mr. Boyle's Plays", 9 February 1907, pp. 397-398.

"The Comedy Off the Stage", 9 February 1907, pp. 401-402.

Avis. "The Ruined 'Abbey' ", 9 February 1907, p. 412.

"Miss Horniman and the Abbey Theatre", 16 February 1907, pp. 415-416.

"Miss Horniman and the Abbey Theatre", 23 February 1907, pp. 1-2. [Includes a letter to the Editor, dated 16 February, which replies to The Leader article of the same date]

"Current Affairs: [The death of Mr. J. M. Synge]", 3 April 1909, p. 164.

"The 'Playboy' Again", 3 September 1910, p. 53.

"The 'Playboy' in England", 3 June 1911, p. 365.

"Yeats and Co. in America", 21 October 1911, pp. 229-230. [Extract from M. Kenny, "The 'Irish' Players and Playwrights", *America* (New York), V (30 September 1911), 581-582]

"Pensioner Yeats in the Western World", 28 October 1911, p. 252. [Quotes from J. F. Gallagher, "The Carrion Crows of Stageland", *The Irish World and American Industrial Liberator* (New York), 14 October 1911, p. 7; and from *The Irish-American* (New York), 14 October 1911]

" 'America' on Mr. Yeats", 4 November 1911, pp. 279-280. [Refers to W. B. Yeats, "Irish 'Paganism' ", *The Sun* (New York), 8 October 1911, Section One, p. 8 (Letter to the Editor, dated Boston, 6 October); and reply to John B. Yeats's letter to *The Sun*, 10 October (?)]

"A Jesuit on Yeats and Synge", 18 November 1911, p. 326. [Extract from M. Kenny, "The Plays of the 'Irish' Players", *America* (New York), VI (4 November 1911), 78-79]

"The Showing Up of Pensioner Yeats", 25 November 1911, pp. 348-349.

[The Irish Players in New York], 9 December 1911, pp. 399-400. [Extracts from "Plays That May Not Be Patronized", *America* (New York), VI (25 November 1911), 159-160; and from "The Un-Irish Players in New York", *The Irish World and American Industrial Liberator* (New York), 25 November 1911, p. 7]

"The 'Playboy' in New York" 16 December 1911, pp. 441-442. [Extracts from the *Public Ledger* (Philadelphia), 28 November 1911; and from "The 'Irish' Players", *The Irish World and American Industrial Liberator* (New York), 2 December 1911, p. 3]

"The 'Playboy' in New York", 23 December 1911, p. 466. [Extracts from "Music and Drama: 'The Playboy of the Western World' ", *The New York Evening Post*, 28 November 1911, p. 9; M. W. Benjamin, "The Irish Play", *The New York Evening Post*, 28 November 1911, p. 8 (Undated letter to the Editor); An Irish-American, "The 'Playboy' Again", *The New York Evening Post*, 1 December 1911, p. 8 (Letter to the Editor, dated 29 November); "Music and Drama: The Irish Players", *The New York Evening Post*, 24 November 1911, p. 9; "Irish Players as Wild Westerners", *The New York Times*, 24 November 1911, p. 13]

"The 'Players' in New York", 30 December 1911, p. 489. [Extracts from "Irish Players Condemned on All Sides", *The Irish World and American Industrial Liberator* (New York), 16 December 1911, p. 5; "Irish Players Consist Largely of Humbug", *The Brooklyn Daily Eagle*, 24 November 1911, p. 6; "League Disowns the Irish Players",

The New York Times, 4 December 1911, p. 13; "The Press and The Playboy", *The Irish-American* (New York), 9 December 1911, p. 4]

"The Abbey Players Arrested", 27 January 1912, pp. 587-588.

"The Return of the Pegeen-Mikes", 23 March 1912, p. 129.

"The Pegeen-Mike Reception", 30 March 1912, p. 150.

The Morning Mail and Irish Daily Mail

"Disturbance at the Abbey Theatre", 29 January 1907, p. 3.

"The Abbey Theatre: Further Disorderly Scenes", 30 January 1907, p. 4.

"Scenes at the Abbey Theatre: Renewal of Disturbances", 31 January 1907, p. 3.

"The Scenes at the Abbey Theatre", 1 February 1907, p. 4.

"The Abbey Theatre Disturbances: Mr. Yeats on Mr. Synge's Play", 5 February 1907, p. 3.

The Peasant and Irish Ireland

"Heard in the Capital", 9 February 1907, [p. 4]. [A brief, sarcastic note concerning Yeats, Synge and the question of art for art's sake]

Sheehy-Skeffington, F. "Dialogues of the Day", 9 February 1907, [p. 4]. [Concerns the Abbey Theatre Disturbance]

"Cois na Teineadh: Drama and Dry Humour", 13 April 1907, [p. 2]. [Criticizes the pro-Synge stand taken in the following article by George Roberts, "A National Dramatist", *The Shanachie* (Dublin), No. 3 (March 1907), 57-60]

"Mr. Synge's Fairy-Tale: One in which the Characters Are All Bad", 20 April 1907, [p. 7]. [A reprint of " 'The Playboy' ", *Inis Fáil* (London), No. 31 (April 1907), 3-4]

O h-Eigeartaigh, P. S. "Playboy Week in London", 22 June 1907, [p. 5]

O h-Eigeartaigh, P. S. "The 'Playboy' ", 29 June 1907, [p. 5] [The author makes a correction in a sentence from his article of 22 June]

The Saturday Herald

" 'The Playboy' at the Abbey", 2 February 1907, pp. 1-2.

"Matinee at the Abbey Theatre", 2 February 1907, p. 2.

B., M. P. "Rafferty at the New Play", 2 February 1907, p. 3. [Dialogue satirizing the disturbance at the Abbey Theatre]

"Pith of the London Evening Papers: 'The Playboy' ", 15 June 1907, p. 1.

Sinn Féin (Daily edition)

"Deirdre", 14 January 1910, p. 1.

" 'Deirdre of the Sorrows': Production at the Abbey Theatre", 14 January 1910, p. 3.

Sinn Féin (Weekly edition)

"The Abbey Theatre", 2 February 1907, p. 2. [*Playboy*]

"The Freedom of the Theatre", 9 February 1907, p. 2.

"A National Theatre", 9 February 1907, p. 2.

" 'The Playboy of the West' ", 9 February 1907, p. 2.

"Britannia Rule-the-Wave: A Comedy (In One Act and in Prose)", 9 February 1907, p. 3. [A dramatic scene, done satirically, parodying Yeats's insistence that *The Playboy* should receive a fair public hearing]

K., P. M. E. "A Plea for 'The Playboy' ", 9 February 1907, p. 3.

Shanganagh. "The Fable of the Fiddler", 9 February 1907, p. 3. [Short piece of satiric dialogue parodying the idea that the author is the best judge of his own work, and of what the audience wants. Clearly, it is aimed at Synge and Yeats]

"The Abbey Theatre", 16 February 1907, p. 7. [Extracts from a letter which Miss Horniman wrote to the Editor, *Sinn Féin*, in defence of *The Playboy*]

A. "The King of England as a Patron of Art", 23 February 1907, p. 3. [The title of the article refers to the English police force in Dublin restoring order at the Abbey Theatre]

"The 'Playboy' Abroad", 15 June 1907, p. 2.

"Plays and Playboys", 22 June 1907, p. 2.

O Cuisín, Seumas [James H. Cousins]. "J. M. Synge: His Art and Message", 17 July 1909, p. 1. [The substance of a lecture delivered in Dublin, May 1909]

"Deirdre", 22 January 1910, p. 1.

"Che Buono" [William Bulfin]. "Synge as a Playwright", 2 April 1910, p. 3.

MacDonald, H. "The Playboy in France", 10 February 1912, p. 3. [Refers to the following article: Philippe Millet, "Un Théâtre irlandais", *Le Temps* (Paris), 23 January 1912, pp. 4-5]

Fitzgerald, Maurice. "The Future of the Peasant Play", 15 March 1913, pp. 6-7.

The Sunday Independent

"Better Than the Play Itself", 3 February 1907, p. 1.

"Latest News: End of 'The Playboy' ", 3 February 1907, p. 1. [Same news release appears in second section, p. 7]

"A Dramatist's Protest", 3 February 1907, second section, p. 7.

"Getting Quieter", 3 February 1907, second section, p. 7.

"Latest News: End of 'The Playboy' ", 3 February 1907, second section, p. 7. [Same news release appears on p. 1]

"And Mr. Stephen Gwynn's Reply", 3 February 1907, second section, p. 7.

"Mr. Wall on the Plays", 3 February 1907, second section, p. 7.

"An Objection that Fell Through", 3 February 1907, second section, p. 7.

" 'Playboy of the Western World' ", 3 February 1907, second section, p. 7.

"Prosecutions in Police Court", 3 February 1907, second section, p. 7.

"Subsequent Street Scenes", 3 February 1907, second section, p. 7.

"Flashes from the Footlights", 16 June 1907, p. 4. [*Playboy* in England]

" 'Playboy of the West': Performance in London", 16 June 1907, p. 9.

"Irish Playwright Dead", 28 March 1909, p. 8.

Henderson, W. A. "The Irish Theatre Movement: The Molesworth Plays", 17 September 1922, p. 6.

The Sunday Press

Mac Síothcháin, D. "Picture of Ireland", 7 December 1969, p. 18. [Letter to the Editor, dated December 4. An example of present day hostility toward *Playboy*]

The United Irishman

Yeats, J. B. "Ireland Out of the Dock", 10 October 1903, p. 2. [*Shadow*]

[Review of *In the Shadow of the Glen*], 17 October 1903, p. 1.

Editor, *United Irishman*. [Reply to W. B. Yeats's "The Irish National Theatre and Three Sorts of Ignorance"], 24 October 1903, p. 2.

Yeats, W. B. "The Irish National Theatre and Three Sorts of Ignorance", 24 October 1903, p. 2.

Conn. "In a Real Wicklow Glen", 24 October 1903, p. 3. [A short dramatic scene done in reply to Synge's *Shadow*]

Editor, *United Irishman*. [Reply to J. B. Yeats's Letter, "The Irish National Theatre Society"], 31 October 1903, p. 7.

Yeats, J. B. "The Irish National Theatre Society", 31 October 1903, p. 7. [Undated letter to the Editor about *Shadow*]

[Brief review of *Riders to the Sea*], 5 March 1904, p. 1.

O'D., D. "The Irish National Theatre Company", 9 April 1904, p. 6.

Connolly, James. "Some Plays and a Critic", 7 May 1904, p. 6. [Reply to D. O'D.'s article of 9 April]

O'D., D. "Some Plays and a Critic", 21 May 1904, p. 3. [Reply to James Connolly's article of 7 May]

Connolly, James. "Dramatic Criticism", 4 June 1904, p. 6. [Reply to D. O'D.'s article of 21 May]

[Editorial about *In the Shadow of the Glen*], 7 January 1905, p. 5.

[Editor, *United Irishman*]. [Reply to W. B. Yeats's Letter of the Same Date], 28 January 1905, p. 1.

Yeats, W. B. [An undated Letter to the Editor in Reply to Criticism of *In the Shadow of the Glen* in *The United Irishman*, 7 January], 28 January 1905, p. 1.

[Editor, *United Irishman*]. [Reply to W. B. Yeats's Letter of the Same Date], 4 February 1905, p. 1.

Yeats, W. B. [An Undated Letter to the Editor in Reply to Criticism of *In the Shadow of the Glen* in *The United Irishman*, 7 and 28 January], 4 February 1905, p. 1.

[Editor, *United Irishman*]. [Reply to W. B. Yeats's Letter and to J. M. Synge's Letter of the Same Date], 11 February 1905, p. 1.

[Review of *The Well of the Saints*], 11 February 1905, p. 1.

Synge, J. M. [An Undated Letter to the Editor about the Source of *In the Shadow of the Glen* in Reply to Criticism in *The United Irishman*, 7 January], 11 February 1905, p. 1.

Yeats, W. B. [An Undated Letter to the Editor in Reply to Criticism of *In the Shadow of the Glen* in *The United Irishman*, 4 February], 11 February 1905, p. 1.

"The Irish Peasantry and the Stage: A Question of Psychopathy", 17 February 1906, pp. 2-3. [Report of George Sigerson's lecture to the National Literary Society]

The Weekly Freeman

"The Author Interviewed", 2 February 1907, p. 6.

"An Un-Irish Play", 2 February 1907, p. 6.

"What Lady Gregory Said", 2 February 1907, p. 6.

Allgood, Sara. "A Great Irish Actress of To-Day: An Autobiographical Sketch", 20 March 1909, p. 11. [Saint Patrick's Day No.]

The Weekly Irish Times

" 'Playboy of the West' ", 2 February 1907, p. 13.

GALWAY (Ireland)

The Connaught Champion

"Lionising a Murderer: 'Playboy' Production Condemned", 16 February 1907, p. 2.

"A Pathetic Picture of Life in the West: Eloquent Vindication of Connacht Peasants", 2 March 1907, p. 1. [Report of a lecture entitled "Among the Peasants of the West" given by George Sigerson, under the auspices of the National Literary Society]

"Vindicated! The Peasants of the West", 2 March 1907, p. 4. [Long editorial]

GLASGOW (Scotland)

The Glasgow Herald

"J. M. Synge: Dramatist", 16 February 1911, p. 12. [Review article of Maunsel edition, *The Works*]

Glasgow News

The Bookseller. "In the Book-Shop", 7 July 1910, p. 4. [Review of Cuala Press edition of J. M. Synge, *Deirdre of the Sorrows*]

"Views and Reviews: An Irish Dramatist", 2 February 1911, p. 2. [Review of Maunsel edition, *The Works*]

The Glasgow Observer

"In Ireland, Our Irish Letter: Uproarious Scenes in a Theatre", 2 February 1907, p. 6.

"Mr. Boyle Protests", 9 February 1907, p. 9.

"On the Screen: 'The Playboy' ", 16 February 1907, p. 9. [Editorial]

Boyle, William. "Irish Drama: New Style", 6 April 1907, p. 5. [A long, important statement by William Boyle explaining his reasons for withdrawing his plays from the Abbey Theatre]

JOHANNESBURG (South Africa)

The Transvaal Leader

"Modern Biographies: Synge and the Irish Drama", 17 December 1912, p. 10. [Review of Francis Bickley, *J. M. Synge and the Irish Dramatic Movement*]

LEEDS (England)

The Leeds Mercury

"The Irish Players", 11 May 1911, p. 3. [*Playboy*]

The Yorkshire Evening Post

"The Irish Players: Some Notes about the Company Who Visit Leeds this Week", 13 April 1910, p. 4.

"The Irish Players in Leeds", 15 April 1910, p. 5. [*Playboy*]

LIVERPOOL (England)

The Evening Express

"Irish Players' Triumph", 11 July 1911, p. 7. [*Shadow*]

The Liverpool Echo

"Life and Letters: The Drama of Synge", 2 July 1910, p. 7.

LONDON (England)

The Academy

Sidgwick, Frank. "Correspondence: A Human Document", 25 May 1907, p. 517. [Letter to the Editor, dated 21 May]

Shore, W. Teignmouth. " 'The Playboy of the Western World' ", 15 June 1907, p. 586.

"The Court Theatre", 10 June 1911, pp. 723-724. [*Playboy*]

"The Theatre: The Court Theatre", 24 June 1911, pp. 785-786. [*Shadow*]

"W. B. Yeats and J. M. Synge", 14 October 1911, pp. 485-486. [Review of W. B. Yeats, *Synge and the Ireland of His Time*]

The Athenaeum

"St. George's Hall: Performances of the National Theatre Society", 2 December 1905, pp. 771-772. [*Well*]

"Two Books on Ireland", 22 June 1907, pp. 754-755. [Review of Maunsel edition, *The Aran Islands*]

"Two Irish Plays", 5 October 1907, pp. 415-416. [*Playboy*]

"Irish Drama", 12 June 1909, p. 712. [*Playboy*]

"Irish Drama", 19 June 1909, p. 740. [*Riders* and *Well*]

"Verse", 14 August 1909, pp. 178-179. [Review of Cuala Press edition, *Poems and Translations*]

"Irish Drama", 4 June 1910, p. 684. [*Deirdre*]

"The Works of John M. Synge", 18 February 1911, pp. 182-183. [Review of Maunsel edition, *The Works*]

"Our Library Table: [*The Playboy of the Western World*]", 22 July 1911, p. 112. [Review of Maunsel edition, *The Playboy*]

"Memoirs: [*Synge and the Ireland of His Time*]", 26 August 1911, pp. 240-241. [Review of W. B. Yeats, *Synge and the Ireland of His Time*]

"The Irish Players", 8 June 1912, pp. 663-664. [*Playboy*]

"Four Irish Plays", 22 June 1912, p. 715. [*Well*]

"Synge and the Theatre", 29 June 1912, pp. 726-727. [Review of P. P. Howe, *J. M. Synge: A Critical Study*]

"The Irish Drama", 29 June 1912, p. 741. [*Shadow*]

"Irish Tragedy and Comedy", 6 July 1912, p. 24. [*Riders*]

' Notices of New Books: Bickley (Francis), *J. M. Synge and the Irish Dramatic Movement*", 5 October 1912, p. 387. [Brief review]

' Notices of New Books: Weygandt (Cornelius), *Irish Plays and Playwrights*", 1 March 1913, p. 260. [Brief review]

Black and White

L., R. W. "Some Books Worth Reading: A Writer Who Can Write", 11 May 1907, p. 658. [Review of Maunsel edition, *The Aran Islands*]

The Bystander

Jingle. "Irish Plays at the Court Theatre", 22 June 1910, pp. 598-600. [*Riders* and *Playboy*]

The Catholic Weekly

S., M. T. "The Playboy of the Western World: An Irish Literary Play", 21 June 1907, p. 3.

The Clarion

"Short Reviews: The Softly Falling Rain", 19 July 1907, p. 2. [Review of Maunsel edition, *The Aran Islands*]

Country Life

"Literature: A Book of the Week", 21 January 1911, pp. 102-103. [Review of Maunsel edition, *The Works*]

The Court Journal and Fashionable Gazette

"Great Queen-Street Theatre", 15 June 1907, p. 877. [*Playboy*]

Clifton, Arthur. "Court Theatre: The Irish National Theatre Society", 16 June 1909, pp. 872-873. [*Shadow* and *Riders*]

Clifton, Arthur. "Court Theatre: 'Deirdre of the Sorrows' ", 8 June 1910, p. 749.

The Daily Chronicle

"Irish Play's Success in London", 13 June 1907, p. 6. [*Playboy*]

"Books of the Day: An Irish Comedy", 13 September 1907, p. 3. [Review of Maunsel edition, *The Playboy*]

"Dublin's 'National Theatre' Company in London", 12 June 1909, p. 7. [*Playboy*]

"An Irish Poet", 26 July 1909, p. 3. Review article of Cuala Press edition, *Poems and Translations*]

"The Afternoon Theatre: Mr. Holbrooke's New Opera and Mr. Synge's Play", 12 November 1909, p. 5. [*Tinker's*]

"Irish Players: The Late J. M. Synge's Last Play at the Court", 31 May 1910, p. 1. [*Deirdre*]

Ryan, W. P. "Books of the Day: A Singer 'O' the Green' ", 4 February 1911, p. 6. [Review article of Maunsel edition, *The Works*]

The Daily Graphic

[Cartoons and Brief Comment on the Abbey Theatre Disturbance], 1 February 1907, p. 8.

"An Irish Comedy", 11 June 1907, p. 7. [*Playboy*]

The Daily Mail

"Irish Plays in London", 11 June 1907, p. 7. [*Playboy*]

"Irish Plays at the Court", 8 June 1909, p. 8. [*Playboy*]

H., A. "Irish Players", 31 May 1910, p. 8. [*Deirdre*]

"Books of the Week: 'A Drifting Silent Man', 'The Genius of J. M. Synge' ", 12 July 1912, p. 2. [Review of P. P. Howe, *J. M. Synge: A Critical Study*]

The Daily News [and Leader]

B[aughan], E. A. "Irish Plays: 'The Playboy of the Western World' ", 11 June 1907, p. 6.

L [ynd], R. "A Gifted Irishman: Personal Tribute to the Late J. M. Synge", 26 March 1909, p. 4.

"Irish Plays in London", 8 June 1909, p. 3. [*Playboy*]

Baughan, E. A. "Holbrooke's Lyric Drama", 12 November 1909, p. 5. [*Tinker's*]

"Irish Drama in London: Mr. Synge's 'Deirdre' Produced at the Court", 31 May 1910, p. 6.

Scott-James, R. A. "A Book of the Day: The Dramatist of Ireland", 1 February 1911, p. 3. [Review of Maunsel edition, *The Works*]

Lynd, Robert. "The Drama: Irish Plays and Players", 24 June 1911, p. 12.

" 'Playboy' in Trouble: Arrest of Irish Players at Philadelphia", (Late London edition), 19 January 1912, p. 1.

Ryan, Frederick. "An Irish View: Why the 'Playboy' Has Excited Hostility", (Late London edition), 19 January 1912, p. 1.

"Lady Gregory", 31 May 1912, p. 8. [Review of Lady Gregory, *Irish Folk-History Plays*]

"Dublin Players in London: 'The Playboy' at the Court Theatre", 5 June 1912, p. 5.

Lynd, Robert. "A Book of the Day: Syngolatry", 14 June 1912, p. 8. [Review of P. P. Howe, *J. M. Synge: A Critical Study*]

Baughan, E. A. "The Irish Players", 14 July 1913, p. 6.

The Daily Telegraph

"Great Queen-Street Theatre", 11 June 1907, p. 3. [*Playboy*]

"Court Theatre", 8 June 1909, p. 4. [*Playboy*]

"Afternoon Theatre", 12 November 1909, p. 8. [*Tinker's*]

"Court Theatre: Season of Irish Plays", 31 May 1910, p. 12. [*Deirdre*]

"The Irish Players", 6 June 1911, p. 11. [*Playboy*]

The Era

"Irish Plays", 15 June 1907, p. 12. [*Playboy* and *Riders*]

"Irish National Theatre: 'Deirdre of the Sorrows' ", 4 June 1910, p. 13.

The Evening News

"The Irish Players: The Class of Drama in Which the Green Isle Excels", 1 June 1910, p. 2. [*Deirdre*]

The Evening Standard and St. James's Gazette

"An Irish Play", 30 April 1907, p. 5. [Review of Maunsel edition, *The Playboy*]

"Topics of the Day: Playboys and Playthings", 15 June 1907, p. 3. [*Playboy*]

Palmer, Arnold. "The Voice of Ireland", 22 June 1910, p. 4.

P., A. "John Millington Synge", 24 January 1911, p. 5. [Review article of Maunsel edition, *The Works*]

"Notes: The Rowdiness of Drama", 6 May 1911, p. 3. [*Playboy*]

[Review of Francis Bickley, *J. M. Synge and the Irish Dramatic Movement*], 3 October 1912, p. 11.

James, W. P. "The Literary World", 12 October 1912, p. 9. [Brief review of Francis Bickley, *J. M. Synge and the Irish Dramatic Movement*]

"The Irish Theatre", 26 February 1913, p. 11. [Review of Cornelius Weygandt, *Irish Plays and Playwrights*]

The Eye-Witness

Ryan, Frederick. "The Cult of the 'Playboy' ", 1 February 1912, pp. 206-207.

The Financial News

"Amusement Notes", 6 June 1910, p. 8. [*Deirdre*]

The Gentlewoman

Momus. "Irish Plays in London", 22 June 1907, p. 862. [*Playboy*]

The Globe

"Dublin Theatre Scenes: Acting in Dumb Show", 30 January 1907, p. 3.

"Great Queen-Street Theatre: 'The Playboy of the Western World' ", 11 June 1907, p. 5.

"Court Theatre: The Irish Plays", 8 June 1909, p. 5. [*Playboy*]

"Court Theatre: 'Deirdre of the Sorrows' ", 31 May 1910, p. 10.

Hearth and Home

Lunn, Hugh. "An Interview with Mr. W. B. Yeats", 28 November 1912, p. 229. [Christmas Number]

"John Synge", 12 December 1912, p. 310. [Review of Francis Bickley, *J. M. Synge and the Irish Dramatic Movement*]

The Illustrated London News

"The Playhouses: The Dublin Abbey Theatre Company at Great Queen Street", 22 June 1907, p. 956. [*Playboy*]

"The Playhouses: Irish Theatre Society at the Court", 12 June 1909, p. 870. [*Playboy*]

"The Playhouses: 'Deirdre of the Sorrows' at the Court", 4 June 1910, p. 854.

Toye, Francis. "The Charm of Music", 12 March 1938, p. 428. [Review of Vaughan Williams, "Riders to the Sea"]

Trewin, J. C. "The World of the Theatre: Lovers' Meeting", 3 April 1948, p. 386. [Brief review of *Playboy*, with a photograph of the performance. See paragraph three]

Trewin, J. C. "Words and Music", 4 October 1958, p. 578. [*Playboy*]

The Illustrated Sporting and Dramatic News

"Vedette". "Round the Theatres", 22 June 1907, p. 694. [*Playboy* and *Riders*]

"Our Captious Critic: 'Deirdre of the Sorrows', at the Court Theatre", 18 June 1910, p. 662.

John Bull

P. "Among the Mummers", 22 June 1907, pp. 602-603. [*Playboy*]

Justice

H., P. P. "At the Theatre: Irish Plays and Players", 11 June 1910, p. 8. [*Playboy* and *Deirdre*]

H., P. P. "At the Theatre: Irish Plays and Players—III", 25 June 1910, p. 3. [*Playboy, Riders, Shadow*]

Ladies' Field

Gordon, Lady. "An Irish Genius: The Collected Works of J. M. Synge", 25 March 1911, pp. 176-177. [Review article of Maunsel edition, *The Works*]

The Listener

Hewitt, John [Review of David H. Greene and Edward M. Stephens, *J. M. Synge: 1871-1909*], 8 October 1959, p. 590.

Rodgers, W. R. "Talking Poetry", 5 December 1963, pp. 951-952.

[Review article of *The Plays and Poems of J. M. Synge,* edited by T. R. Henn]

Kitchin, Laurence. [Review of F. L. Lucas, *The Drama of Chekhov, Synge, Yeats and Pirandello*], 12 December 1963, pp. 993-994.

Hawkes, Terence. "Playboys of the Western World", 16 December 1965, pp. 991-993.

Trevor, William. "Notebooks of the Western World", 11 August 1966, p. 210. [Review of J. M. Synge, *Collected Works, Vol. II, Prose,* edited by Alan Price]

The Literary Post

H., P. P. "Irish Plays: The Season at the Court Theatre", 15 June 1910, pp. 202-203. [*Playboy* and *Deirdre*]

Lloyd's Weekly News

"Irish Players", 5 June 1910, p. 9. [*Deirdre*]

London Opinion

Rendle, T. McDonald. "The Peep Show: Ireland and the Drama", 9 February 1907, p. 204. [*Playboy* and the disturbance at the Abbey Theatre]

The Morning Leader

Archer, William. "Three Poets Departed", 15 May 1909, p. 4.

" 'Deirdre of the Sorrows': Irish Play Season at the Court", 31 May 1910, p. 1.

The Morning Post

" 'The Playboy of the Western World' ", 13 May 1907, p. 2. [Review of Maunsel edition, *The Playboy*]

"Great Queen Street Theatre: 'The Playboy of the Western World' ", 11 June 1907, p. 11.

"Court Theatre", 10 June 1909, p. 7. [*Shadow* and *Riders*]

"His Majesty's, The Afternoon Theatre: 'The Tinker's Wedding' ", 12 November 1909, p. 8.

"Court Theatre: Irish National Theatre Society", 31 May 1910, p. 10. [*Deirdre*]

Gosse, Edmund. "The Playwright of the Western World", 26 January 1911, p. 2. [Review of Maunsel edition, *The Works*]

The Nation [and Athenaeum]

"The Drama: The Troubles of the Irish National Theatre", 8 June 1907, pp. 560-561.

Bickley, Francis. "The Art of J. M. Synge", 3 April 1909, pp. 17-18. [Undated letter to the Editor]

Yeats, W. B. "The Art of J. M. Synge", 10 April 1909, p. 54. [Letter to the Editor, dated 6 April 1909]

Archer, William. "The Drama: The First-Fruits of Endowment", 19 June 1909, pp. 419-421.

"Life and Letters: John Synge's Art", 17 July 1909, pp. 563-564.

Colum, Padriac [sic]. "The Poetry of James Stephens: A Review of Stephens' 'Insurrections' ", 11 September 1909, pp. 857-858.

Archer, William. "The Art of the Artless", 4 June 1910, pp. 346-347. [*Deirdre*]

"Astringent Joy", 25 March 1911, pp. 1043-1044. [Review article of Maunsel edition, *The Works*]

M., H. W. "Half-Truth and Truth", 17 June 1911, pp. 430-431. [*Playboy*]

"The Virile Poet", 26 August 1911, pp. 767-768.

Omicron. "From Alpha to Omega", 24 October 1925, p. 150. [*Playboy*]

Birrell, Francis. "The Drama: The Artist and the Reporter", 4 June 1927, p. 304. [*Riders*]

The New Age

Jackson, Holbrook. "The Book of the Week: The Irish Playgoer and The Playboy", 2 May 1907, p. 7. [Review article of Maunsel edition, *The Playboy*]

Guest, L. Haden. "Drama: The Irish Theatre", 20 June 1907, pp. 124-125. [*Playboy*]

C., N. "Drama: The Irish Theatre (Court)", 17 June 1909, p. 162. [*Playboy*]

Dukes, Ashley. "Drama: The Irish Plays", 16 June 1910, pp. 160-161. [*Playboy* and *Deirdre*]

Hughes, Herbert. "Synge and Others", 13 April 1911, pp. 562-563. [Review article of Maunsel edition, *The Works*]

"Readers and Writers", 7 August 1913, p. 425. [Concerns translating *Well* into German]

New Ireland

K., T. M. "The Irish National Theatre Society", 17 October 1903, p. 5. [*Shadow*]

The New Statesman [and Nation]

S[haw]., G. B. "A Note on Irish Nationalism", 12 July 1913, pp. 1-2. [Supplement on "The Awakening of Ireland", Irish Supplement. Reprinted in Bernard Shaw, *The Matter with Ireland*, edited by Dan H. Laurence and David H. Greene, pp. 81-84. New York, Hill and Wang, 1962]

Shand, John. "A Company of Good Actors", 24 October 1925, p. 47. [*Playboy*]

Clarke, Austin. "Synge and Ireland", 29 August 1931, pp. 258-259. [Review of Daniel Corkery, *Synge and Anglo-Irish Literature*]

"Plays and Pictures: Three Operas at the Arts Theatre, Cambridge", 26 February 1938, p. 328. [Review of Vaughan Williams, *Riders to the Sea*]

" 'The Playboy of the Western World' at the Mercury", 4 February 1939, p. 169.

"Plays and Pictures: 'The Playboy of the Western World', at the Duchess", 4 November 1939, p. 644.

Pritchett, V. S. [Review of J. M. Synge, *Plays, Poems and Prose* (London, Everyman's Library, 1941)], 19 April 1941, p. 413.

Grigson, Geoffrey. "Books of the Day: Synge", 19 October 1962, pp. 528-529. [Review article of J. M. Synge, *Collected Works, Vol. I, Poems*, edited by Robin Skelton; J. M. Synge, *Four Plays and The Aran Islands*, edited by Robin Skelton]

Ellmann, Richard. "Deadly Merits", 20 March 1964, p. 461. [Review of *The Plays and Poems of J. M. Synge*, edited by T. R. Henn]

Donoghue, Denis. "Irish Texts", 16 September 1966, pp. 399-400. [Review of J. M. Synge, *Autobiography*, constructed by Alan Price; J. M. Synge, *Collected Works, Vol. II, Prose*, edited by Robin Skelton; *Irish Renaissance*, edited by Robin Skelton and David Clark]

The News of the World

"Amusements", 16 June 1907, p. 12. [*Playboy*]

The Observer

"At the Play: The Irish Season at the Great Queen-Street Theatre", 16 June 1907, p. 4. [*Playboy*]

Harrison, Austin. "A People's Drama: The Irish Plays at the Court Theatre", 13 June 1909, p. 6. [*Riders* and *Playboy*]

"At the Play: Court, Irish Plays and Players", 5 June 1910, p. 8. [*Deirdre*]

Robinson, Lennox. "The Abbey Theatre—II", 10 February 1924, p. 11.

Tynan, Kenneth. "Farce with Tears", 16 October 1960, p. 26. [*Playboy*]

The Outlook

"An Irish Satire", 8 June 1907, pp. 770-771. [Review of Maunsel edition, *The Playboy*]

D., T. B. "Irish Plays at the Court", 12 June 1909, p. 810. [*Riders* and *Playboy*]

Stair, Owen. "The Theatre: Irish Plays at the Court Theatre", 4 June 1910, p. 819. [*Deirdre*]

"A Great Irish Play and Some Irishmen", 9 December 1911, pp. 843-844. [*Playboy*]

"The 'Abbey' Movement", 12 April 1913, p. 513. [Review of Cornelius Weygandt, *Irish Plays and Playwrights*]

The Pall Mall Gazette

"The Abbey Theatre in Dublin: Mr. J. M. Synge's New Comedy Hissed", 29 January 1907, p. 10.

"Riot in a Dublin Theatre: Irishman's Play Hooted: An Insult to the Women of Mayo", 30 January 1907, p. 7.

"The Abbey Theatre Disorders: Why Society Boycotts the Institution", 31 January 1907, p. 7.

"The Irish National Theatre in London: A Mayo Problem Play", 11 June 1907, p. 4. [*Playboy*]

"Theatrical Notes", 24 June 1907, p. 1. [A note about demonstrations at the Great Queen-Street Theatre during the London performance of *Playboy*]

Wyllie, Bertie. " 'The Playboy of the Western World' ", 27 June 1907, p. 2. [Letter to the Editor, dated 26 June]

"The Abbey Theatre Company in London: 'The Playboy of the Western World' ", 8 June 1909, p. 5.

"The Abbey Theatre Company in London", 9 June 1909, p. 5. [*Well*]

"The Abbey Theatre Company at the Court", 18 June 1909, p. 5. [*Playboy*]

"The Irish Players at the Court", 1 June 1910, p. 5. [*Deirdre*]

"The Irish Players at the Court Theatre", 21 June 1910, p. 6. [Includes a brief, general discussion of the decadence of the Irish theatre. Synge, although not mentioned by name, is in the background]

"Reviews: A Playboy of the Western World", 16 January 1911, p. 4. [Review of Maunsel edition, *The Works*]

W., H. M. "Theatrical Notes: The Irish Players in New York", 11 December 1911, p. 4.

" 'The Playboy': Irish Company Arrested in America", 18 January 1912, p. 1.

"Mr. Bernard Shaw on American Gaels: The Real 'Play-Boys' ", 19 January 1912, p. 1.

The People

"Music and the Drama: Court, The Irish Players", 5 June 1910, p. 4. [*Deirdre*]

The Planet

Farrer, Reginald. "Drama: A Miscellaneous Lot", 22 June 1907, pp. 13-15. [*Riders*, p. 14]

Public Opinion

"A Picture of Human Grief", 21 June 1907, p. 774. [Review of Maunsel edition, *The Aran Islands*]

The Queen

"Irish Drama at the Great Queen Street Theatre", 15 June 1907, p. 1119. [*Playboy*]

The Radio Times

Stephens, James. "I Remember J. M. Synge", 23 March 1928, pp. 590 and 611. [The Talk of the Week, No. 10]

The Referee

Palamede. "Irish Plays", 16 June 1907, p. 3. [*Playboy*]

Mordred. "The Irish Theatre: Dublin at the Court", 13 June 1909, p. 2. [*Playboy* and *Well*]

Mordred. "The Irish National Theatre", 5 June 1910, p. 2. [*Deirdre*]

"Dramatic Gossip: A New Sensation", 11 June 1911, p. 2. [*Playboy*]

Reynolds's Newspaper

"The Irish National Theatre", 16 June 1907, p. 4. [*Playboy*]

The Saturday Review

Beerbohm, Max. "Some Irish Plays and Players", 9 April 1904, pp. 455-457. [*Riders* and *Shadow*. Reprinted in *Around Theatres*, II, 402-407]

[Poor Synge Is Dead], 27 March 1909, p. 388.

"Pat". "The Irish Mind in Modern Print", 27 March 1909, pp. 396-397.

Beerbohm, Max. "Irish Players", 12 June 1909, p. 748. [*Shadow* and *Riders*]

Dunsany, Lord. " 'Deirdre of the Sorrows' ", 4 June 1910, pp. 719-720.

MacCarthy, Desmond. "The Irish National Theatre", 18 June 1910, pp. 782-783. [*Playboy*]

"An Irish Dramatist in His Own Country", 28 January 1911, pp. 114-115. [Review of Maunsel edition, *The Works*]

P[almer]., J[ohn]. "The Extra-Occidental Theatre", 25 February 1911, pp. 236-237.

[A Paragraph on Shakespeare and Synge at Stratford-on-Avon], 6 May 1911, p. 540.

Morrison, G. E. "The Irish Players at Stratford", 20 May 1911, p. 616. [Letter to the Editor, dated 17 May]

P[almer]., J[ohn]. "The Irish Players", 10 June 1911, pp. 705-706. [*Playboy*]

Inkster, Leonard. "The Irish Players", 17 June 1911, p. 746. [Letter to the Editor, dated 13 June]

P[almer]., J[ohn]. "The Acting of the Irish Players", 24 June 1911, pp. 770-771. [Refers to Inkster's letter of 17 June 1911, p. 746]

McNulty, Edward. "The Irish Players", 24 June 1911, p. 777. [Letter to the Editor, dated 14 June 1911]

R., S., Ed. [Editor's reply to Edward McNulty's letter of 24 June], 24 June 1911, p. 777.

Fay, F. J. "The Irish Players", 1 July 1911, p. 17.

Inkster, Leonard. "The Irish Players", 1 July 1911, p. 17. [Letter to the Editor, dated 27 June 1911; a reply to John Palmer's article of 24 June 1911, pp. 770-771]

Ervine, St. John G. "The Playboy of the Western World", 8 July 1911, pp. 48-49. [Letter to the Editor, dated 29 June 1911; a reply to Mr. Edward McNulty's letter of 24 June 1911, p. 777]

McNulty, Edward. "Synge—'The Ragman'", 8 July 1911, p. 49. [Letter to the Editor, dated 26 June 1911; a reply to Editor's note following McNulty's letter of 24 June 1911, p. 777]

Hone, J. M. "A Memory of 'The Playboy'", 22 June 1912, pp. 776-777.

Palmer, John. "The Success of the Irish Players", 13 July 1912, pp. 42-43. [Review article of P. P. Howe, *J. M. Synge: A Critical Study*]

Hamilton, Cicely. "Drama: 'The Playboy of the Western World'", 6 August 1921, pp. 177-178.

Gore-Browne, Robert. "The Theatre: Plays Sacred and Profane", 8 November 1930, p. 592.

The Sketch

S., E. F. "The Stage from the Stalls", 19 June 1907, p. 300. [*Playboy*]

The Speaker

Duncan, Ellen. "The Irish National Theatre", 26 January 1907, pp. 496-497.

The Spectator

"The Work of J. M. Synge", 1 April 1911, pp. 482-483. [Review article of Maunsel edition, *The Works*]

"Some Books of the Week: *In Wicklow, West Kerry, and Connemara* and *The Aran Islands*", 4 May 1912, pp. 725-726. [Review of Maunsel edition]

De Blacam, Hugh. "A New School in Ireland", 18 July 1931, p. 89. [Review of Daniel Corkery, *Synge and Anglo-Irish Literature*]

Greene, Graham. "Stage and Screen: The Cinema", 20 December 1935, p. 1028. [Review of an independent film version of Synge's *Riders to the Sea*, played by the Abbey Theatre Players]

O'Donnell, Donat [Conor Cruise O'Brien]. "Mother's Tongue", 14 August 1959, p. 201. [Review of David H. Greene and Edward M. Stephens, *J. M. Synge, 1871-1909*. Reprinted in *Writers and Politics* (1965)]

Montague, John. "Un-English Urges", 7 December 1962, pp. 898-900. [Review of J. M. Synge, *Collected Works, Vol. I, Poems*, edited by Robin Skelton]

Burgess, Anthony. "Enemy of Twilight", 22 July 1966, p. 124. [Review article of J. M. Synge, *Collected Works, Vol. II, Prose*, edited by Alan Price]

Anderson, Patrick. "Down Among the Nuts", 9 August 1968, pp. 196-197. [Review article of J. M. Synge, *Collected Works, Vols. III and IV, Plays*, edited by Ann Saddlemyer]

The Sphere

S., C. K. "A Literary Letter", 9 February 1907, p. 126.

178   SYNGE: PUBLISHED CRITICISM

"A Literary Letter: The Works of John M. Synge", 22 April 1911, p. 96. [Review of Maunsel edition, *The Works*]

The Sporting Times

"Things Theatrical: 'Deirdre of the Sorrows' ", 4 June 1910, p. 4.

The Stage

"Irish Plays in London", 13 June 1907, p. 9. [*Playboy*]

"Provincial Production: 'Deirdre of the Sorrows' ", 20 January 1910, p. 23.

"Irish Plays: 'Deirdre of the Sorrows' ", 2 June 1910, p. 16.

The Standard

"A Much Criticised Irish Play", 11 June 1907, p. 9. [*Playboy*]

"Irish Plays: Intellectual Drama at the Court Theatre", 10 June 1909, p. 7. [*Playboy, Riders* and *Shadow*]

"Irish National Theatre", 31 May 1910, p. 8.

The Star

"John Millington Synge", 2 June 1909, p. 2.

Douglas, James. "Books and Bookmen: The Poems of John M. Synge", 24 July 1909, p. 2. [Review article of Cuala Press edition, *Poems and Translations*]

C., G. "Court Theatre: 'The Sorrows of Deirdre' ", 31 May 1910, p. 2.

Douglas, James. "Books and Bookmen: Mr. Montague's 'Dramatic Values' ", 11 February 1911, p. 2. [Review of C. E. Montague, *Dramatic Values*. See paragraph three]

Douglas, James. "Books and Bookmen: The Works of Synge", 18 February 1911, p. 2. [Review article of Maunsel edition, *The Works*. Most of the discussion concerns *Deirdre*]

The Sunday Times

Grein, J. T. "Great Queen-Street: 'The Playboy of the Western World', and 'Spreading the News' ", 16 June 1907, p. 4.

Grein, J. T. "Premieres of the Week: (3) Court, The Irish Plays", 13 June 1909, p. 4. [*Well*]

Grein, J. T. "The Dramatic World: (1) Court, 'Deirdre of the Sorrows' ", 5 June 1910, p. 6.

T. P.'s Weekly

M[acDonagh]., T[homas]. "J. M. Synge: Irish Dramatist, Writer, Poet", 9 April 1909, p. 469.

Gibson, Ashley. "The Irish Players", 10 June 1910, p. 723. [Major article on Synge, *Deirdre* and *Playboy*]

B. "The Irish Players", 16 June 1911, p. 744. [*Playboy*]

Lintot, Bernard. "At Number I, Grub Street", 18 August 1911, p. 201.

Lintot, Bernard. "At Number I, Grub Street", 22 September 1911, p. 361.

Bristowe, Sybil. "Mr. W. B. Yeats: Poet and Mystic", 4 April 1913, p. 421.

The Tablet

[Review of Francis Bickley, *J. M. Synge and the Irish Dramatic Movement*], 2 November 1912, pp. 687-688.

Robertson, Anthony. "The Irony of Synge", 1 February 1964, p. 130. [Review of *The Plays and Poems of J. M. Synge,* edited by T. R. Henn]

The Times

"Great Queen-Street Theatre: 'The Playboy of the Western World' ", 11 June 1907, p. 11.

"Obituary: Mr. J. M. Synge", 25 March 1909, p. 13.

"The Irish Plays", 12 June 1909, p. 8. [*Well*]

"Royal Court Theatre", 31 May 1910, p. 12. [*Deirdre*]

"Court Theatre", 4 June 1910, p. 12. [*Playboy*]

"The Abbey Theatre: Its Origins and Accomplishments", 17 March 1913 (Irish Number), p. 15.

Yeats, William Butler. " 'The Playboy': Action of the Liverpool Police", 1 December 1913, p. 66. [Letter to the Editor, dated 29 November]

Yeats, William Butler. "The Playboy at Liverpool", 4 December 1913, p. 12. [Letter to the Editor, dated 2 December]

" 'The Playboy of the Western World': Revival at the Court", 26 July 1921, p. 8.

"Synge Revival at the Royalty: 'The Playboy of the Western World' ", 13 October 1925, p. 14.

"Arts Theatre Club: Three Irish Plays", 26 October 1928, p. 14. [Shadow]

"Criterion Theatre: 'The Playboy of the Western World' ", 29 October 1930, p. 12.

"J. M. Synge", 1 March 1932, p. 10. [Review of Samuel Synge, Letters to My Daughter]

"Six Other Islanders", 16 September 1965, p. 14. [Review of The Autobiography of J. M. Synge, constructed by Alan Price]

The Times Literary Supplement

"The Aran Islands", 28 June 1907, p. 202. [Review of Maunsel edition, The Aran Islands]

"The Works of J. M. Synge", 23 February 1911, pp. 73-74. [Review of Maunsel edition, The Works]

"J. M. Synge", 29 August 1912, p. 338. [Review of P. P. Howe, J. M. Synge: A Critical Study]

Kerby, Paul. "The Source of a Plot", 7 July 1921, p. 437. [Undated letter to the Editor, concerning Shadow]

Brighouse, Harold. "The Source of a Plot", 15 July 1921, p. 453. [Undated letter to the Editor, concerning Shadow]

Renwick, W. L. "The Source of a Plot", 22 July 1921, p. 469. [Undated letter to the Editor, concerning Shadow]

Bloxam, R. N. "The Source of a Plot", 29 July 1921, p. 484. [Undated letter to the Editor, concerning Shadow]

"Synge and Irish Life", 23 July 1931, p. 578. [Review of Daniel Corkery, Synge and Anglo-Irish Literature]

"Recollections of Synge", 10 March 1932, p. 171. [Review of Samuel Synge, Letters to My Daughter]

Alspach, R. K. "Synge's 'Well of the Saints' ", 28 December 1935, p. 899. [Undated letter to the Editor, concerning the sources for *Well*]

"Forty Years of Irish Drama, Yeats, Synge and Lady Gregory: From the Visionaries to the Realists", 13 April 1940, pp. 182, 186.

"The Tinker", 14 February 1942, p. 79. [Review of L. A. G. Strong, *John Millington Synge*]

"Books Received: [Notice of Jan Setterquist, *Ibsen and the Beginnings of Anglo-Irish Drama, I. John Millington Synge*]", 10 April 1953, p. 242.

"Playboy of the Irish Stage", 19 June 1959, p. 370. [Review article of David H. Greene and Edward M. Stephens, *J. M. Synge: 1871-1909*]

"Books Received: [Notice of John M. Synge, *Riders to the Sea* and *The Playboy of the Western World*, with Introduction and Notes by E. R. Wood]", 11 August 1961, pp. 536-537.

"Strong Things", 2 February 1962, p. 74. [Review of J. M. Synge, *Translations*, edited by Robin Skelton]

"Books Received: [Notice of J. M. Synge, *Four Plays and The Aran Islands*, edited by Robin Skelton]", 16 March 1962, p. 190.

"Art of Collaboration", 26 October 1962, p. 824. [Review article of J. M. Synge, *Collected Works, Vol. I, Poems*, edited by Robin Skelton]

"Opinionated Playgoer", 9 January 1964, p. 28. [Review of F. L. Lucas, *The Drama of Chekhov, Synge, Yeats, and Pirandello*]

"Scanning the Playboy", 6 February 1964, p. 101. [Review of *The Plays and Poems of J. M. Synge*, edited with an Introduction and Notes by T. R. Henn]

"Mad Ireland", 22 December 1966, p. 1190. [Review of *Irish Renaissance*, edited by Robin Skelton and David R. Clark; J. M. Synge, *Collected Works, Vol. II, Prose*, edited by Alan Price]

"The Nun's Surrender", 8 August 1968, p. 852. [Review of J. M. Synge, *Collected Works, Vols. III and IV, Plays*, edited by Ann Saddlemyer]

"The 'Ascendancy' Writer", 2 July 1971, pp. 1-2. [Review article of Robin Skelton, *J. M. Synge and His World, The Writings of J. M. Synge*, and *Remembering Synge* (A Poem in Homage for the Centenary of his Birth, 16 April 1971); J. M. Synge, *Some Sonnets from "Laura in Death" after the Italian of Francesco Petrarch; My Wallet of Photographs* (The Collected Photographs of J. M.

Synge, arranged and introduced by Lilo Stephens); James Kilroy, *The "Playboy" Riots; The Synge Manuscripts* in the Library of Trinity College, Dublin]

To-Day

L., R. W. "The Passing Show: Ireland and the Play", 6 April 1904, p. 264. [*Riders* and *Shadow*]

The Tribune

"Literature and the Arts: The World's End", 6 May 1907, p. 2. [Review of Maunsel edition, *The Aran Islands*]

"An Irish Play", 21 May 1907, p. 2. [Review of Maunsel edition, *The Playboy*]

A., W. "The Irish Actors: 'The Playboy of the Western World' ", 11 June 1907, p. 7.

A., W. "The Irish Actors", 12 June 1907, p. 7. [*Riders*]

Truth

[Review of *The Playboy of the Western World*], 19 June 1907, p. 1524.

The Universe

B., S. " 'The Playboy' ", 19 April 1907, p. 15. [Review of Maunsel edition, *The Playboy*]

The Weekly Sun

P., W. F. "Mr. Yeats and Some Others", 15 June 1907, p. 3. [Review of *The Playboy* and a discussion of the right of the artist to be heard]

The Weekly Times/The Times Weekly Review

"Public Amusements: Court Theatre, 'The Playboy of the Western World' ", 5 June 1910, p. 4. [*Playboy* and *Deirdre*]

"Public Amusements: Court Theatre, 'Riders to the Sea' [and] 'In the Shadow of the Glen' ", 19 June 1910, p. 4.

"The Green Wears Well", 11 October 1962, p. 13. [Brief review of J. M. Synge, *Collected Works, Vol. I, Poems,* edited by Robin Skelton].

The Westminster Gazette

W., J. "Great Queen Street", 11 June 1907, p. 2. [*Playboy*]

W., J. "Irish Plays at the Court Theatre", 8 June 1909, p. 2. [*Playboy*]

W., J. "Royal Court Theatre", 10 June 1909, p. 3. [*Shadow* and *Riders*]

S., E. F. " 'The Tinker's Wedding' at the Afternoon Theatre", 12 November 1909, p. 3.

S., E. F. "The Irish National Theatre Society", 31 May 1910, p. 4. [*Deirdre*]

"Reviews: John M. Synge", 4 February 1911, p. 4. [Review of Maunsel edition, *The Works*]

MANCHESTER (England)

The Daily Dispatch

"Irish Plays: 'The Playboy of the Western World' at the Gaiety", 23 November 1909, p. 4.

" 'Deirdre of the Sorrows': First Manchester Performance of J. M. Synge's Last Play", 21 April 1910, p. 3.

"Books of To-Day: Synge, The Durbar, and Lancanshire", 7 October 1912, p. 3. [Review of Francis Bickley, *J. M. Synge and the Irish Dramatic Movement*]

The Manchester Catholic Herald

H. " 'The Playboy of the Western World' ", 27 November 1909, p. 1.

The Manchester Chronicle

"Irish Plays: Notes on Nationalism at the Gaiety Theatre", 16 February 1909, p. 2. [*Shadow*]

"More Irish Plays: Pathos and Comedy at the Gaiety", 17 February 1909, p. 3. [*Well*]

"At the Theatres: The Irish Players at the Gaiety", 23 November 1909, p. 3. [*Playboy*]

The Manchester Courier

"Manchester Amusements: Gaiety Theatre", 16 February 1909, p. 8. [*Shadow*]

"Gaiety Theatre: Grave and Gay", 17 February 1909, p. 9. [*Well*]

"Manchester Amusements: Gaiety Theatre", 23 November 1909, p. 10. [*Playboy*]

"Gaiety Theatre: 'Deirdre of the Sorrows' ", 21 April 1910, p. 12.

"Manchester Amusements: Gaiety Theatre, 'Riders to the Sea' ", 21 February 1911, p. 12.

"Gaiety Theatre: 'In the Shadow of the Glen' ", 24 February 1911, p. 12.

The Manchester Evening News

"The Irish Players: A Remarkable Production at the Gaiety Theatre", 17 February 1909, p. 7. [*Well*]

"Amusements: Irish Plays at the Gaiety", 23 November 1909, p. 6. [*Playboy*]

"Irish Players at the Gaiety Theatre", 21 April 1910, p. 6. [*Deirdre*]

The Manchester Guardian

[Masefield, John]. "The Irish National Theatre", 2 January 1905, p. 3.

E., O. "National Theatre Society: Performances in Dublin", 10 April 1907, p. 12. [A brief discussion of Synge's poetic and ironic prose]

M., A. N. "Gaiety Theatre: The Irish Plays", 16 February 1909, p. 7. [*Shadow*]

A., J. E. "Gaiety Theatre: The Irish Plays", (London edition), 17 February 1909, p. 7. [*Well*]

M., C. E. "Gaiety Theatre: The Irish Plays", (London edition), 18 February 1909, p. 4. [*Riders*]

"The Death of Mr. J. M. Synge", (London edition), 25 March 1909, p. 6.

"Our London Correspondence: Mr. Synge's Work in London", (London edition), 25 March 1909, p. 6.

"Mr. J. M. Synge", (London edition), 25 March 1909, p. 7. [Obituary, and lead article]

C., P. "The Irish Company in London", (London edition), 8 June 1909, p. 7. [*Playboy*]

C., P. "More Irish Plays in London", (London edition), 11 June 1909, p. 14. [*Riders* and *Shadow*]

M., A. N. "Gaiety Theatre: 'The Playboy of the Western World' ", (London edition), 23 November 1909, p. 9.

A., J. E. "Gaiety Theatre: The Irish Plays", 25 November 1909, p. 10. [Some brief remarks on *Riders*]

A., J. E. "Gaiety Theatre: 'The Playboy of the Western World' ", 19 April 1910, p. 11.

M., C. E. "Gaiety Theatre: Synge's 'Deirdre of the Sorrows' ", 21 April 1910, p. 6.

"The Works of Synge", (London edition), 19 January 1911, p. 4. [Review of Maunsel edition, *The Works*]

A., J. E. "Gaiety Theatre: A New Play by Lady Gregory", 24 February 1911, p. 11. [Suggests Synge influenced Lady Gregory]

M[ontague]., C. E. "The Workmanship of Synge", 24 June 1912, p. 5. [Review of P. P. Howe, *J. M. Synge: A Critical Study*]

[Review of Francis Bickley, *J. M. Synge and the Irish Dramatic Movement*], (London Edition), 8 October 1912, p. 4.

NEW HAVEN (Connecticut, U.S.A.)

The New Haven Evening Register

"May Censor the Irish Players", (Last edition), 6 November 1911, p. 1.

"Delightfully Artistic Are Irish Players", (Last edition), 7 November 1911, p. 13. [*Shadow*]

NEW YORK (U.S.A.)

The Daily People

F., L. C. "Music and Drama: The Irish Players", 3 December 1911, p. 2. [*Playboy*]

The Evening Mail

"Stop Irish Play, Is Plea to Mayor", 28 November 1911, pp. 1 and 3.

"How Bad Is 'The Play Boy of the Western World'?", 28 November 1911, p. 8.

The Evening Sun

"J. M. Synge", 2 April 1909, p. 8. [Obituary article]

Yeats, J. B. "John Synge: Some Recollections by an Irish Painter", 3 April 1909, p. 6. [Letter to Editor, dated 2 April]

"Books and Their Makers: John Synge", 24 April 1909, p. 6.

Yeats, Jack B. "J. M. Synge", 20 July 1909, p. 4. [Article dated Dublin, 8 July]

"News of the Theatres: Lady Gregory's Statement on the Irish Players", 17 November 1911, p. 10.

"A Reading from 'The Playboy' ", 20 November 1911, p. 10.

"Big Police Guard for Irish Play", 28 November 1911, pp. 1 and 7.

"But the Play Was Produced", 28 November 1911, p. 6. [Editorial]

"News of the Theatres: 'The Playboy' as a Play, Not as a Riot", 29 November 1911, p. 8.

"Bernard Shaw on the Irish Players", 9 December 1911, pp. 4-5.

"Shaw Jests at Philadelphia", (Final edition), 18 January 1912, p. 1.

The Evening Telegram

"On Both Sides of the Footlights", 24 November 1911, p. 10. [*Well*]

"Irish Lawyers Ask Mayor to Stop Play Which Caused Riot", 28 November 1911, p. 1.

"Mayor Decides Irish Play Is Quite Harmless", 29 November 1911, p. 2.

The Evening World

"Irishmen Protest to the Mayor Against the 'Playboy': Irishmen Urge Gaynor to Stop Performance of Play That Caused Riot", (Final edition), 28 November 1911, pp. 1-2.

"Gaynor's Censor Gives 'O.K.' to Irish Players", (Final edition), 29 November 1911, p. 1.

Darnton, Charles. "The New Plays: Irish Players Act 'The Playboy' with Spirit", (Final edition), 29 November 1911, p. 9.

The Gaelic American

"Dublin Revolts Against a Vile Play", 16 February 1907, pp. 1 and 2. [Includes extracts from "The Abbey Theatre: 'The Playboy of the Western World' ", *The Freeman's Journal* (Dublin), 28 January 1907, p. 10; A Western Girl. (Letter to the Editor, dated 27 January), *The Freeman's Journal* (Dublin), 28 January 1907, p. 10; B., T. F. "From the Point of View of Art", *The Freeman's Journal* (Dublin), 31 January 1907, p. 8. (Letter to the Editor, dated 30 January); "The Abbey Theatre", *Sinn Féin* (Dublin), 2 February 1907, p. 2]

"The Protests Continued", 16 February 1907, p. 2.

"W. B. Yeats Prosecutes", 16 February 1907, p. 2.

"Yeats Meets His Critics", 2 March 1907, p. 2.

"An Un-Irish Play", 23 September 1911, p. 2.

"Irish Players Well Received in Boston", 30 September 1911, pp. 1 and 10.

"Irishmen Will Stamp Out the Playboy", 14 October 1911, pp. 1 and 10.

"Stamp Out the Atrocious Libel", 14 October 1911, p. 4. [Editorial on *Playboy*]

"Condemns 'The Playboy' ", 14 October 1911, p. 10.

"Boston Gives It the Cold Shoulder", 21 October 1911, pp. 1 and 10.

"Paints the Playboy in Glowing Colors", 21 October 1911, pp. 1 and 10. [The title of the article refers to W. B. Yeats]

"Ordure and Art in Drama", 21 October 1911, p. 4. [Editorial]

"Gaelic Society Protest", 21 October 1911, p. 10.

"High English Approval", 21 October 1911, p. 10.

"Miss O'Reilly Objects", 21 October 1911, p. 10.

"Synge's Monstrosity", 21 October 1911, p. 10.

"Condemns the Playboy", 28 October 1911, p. 2.

"Yeats Cables Tale of Glorious Victory", 4 November 1911, pp. 1 and 10.

"Boston Irishmen Protest", 4 November 1911, p. 10.

"Philadelphia Gets Ready", 4 November 1911, p. 10.

"Protests of No Avail", 11 November 1911, pp. 1 and 8.

"Lady Gregory's Moral Victory, Moryah", 11 November 1911, p. 4. [Editorial]

"Condemn 'The Playboy' " 11 November 1911, p. 8.

Kelly, G. B. "Dr. Gertrude Kelly's View: Synge's Plays Are, Pathologically Considered, the Emanations of Diseased Mind", 18 November 1911, p. 1. [Letter to the Editor, dated 11 November]

"Yeats's Anti-Irish Campaign", 18 November 1911, p. 4. [Editorial]

"The 'Sun' Loyalist's Ravings", 25 November 1911, p. 4. [Editorial]

"New York's Protest Against a Vile Play", 2 December 1911, pp. 1 and 8. [Accompanied by anti-*Playboy* cartoon, p. 1]

"Playboy Dead as a Nail in a Door", 9 December 1911, p. 1. [Accompanied by anti-*Playboy* cartoon]

"Jew Papers and Irish Readers", 9 December 1911, p. 4. [Editorial]

"Truth and Fiction in the 'Sun' ", 9 December 1911, p. 4. [Editorial]

"An Honest American View", 9 December 1911, p. 5. [Extract from "Music and Drama: 'The Playboy of the Western World' ", *The New York Evening Post*, 28 November 1911, p. 9]

"MacManus Raps the Play", 9 December 1911, p. 5. [Reprint from MacManus, Seumas. "Seumas M'Manus Raps 'The Playboy' ", *The New York Times*, 27 November 1911, p. 11]

"Tart Reply to Yeats", 9 December 1911, p. 8.

"Bernard Shaw's Greatest Masterpiece", 16 December 1911, pp. 2 and 7. [The "famous" Shaw article in which Shaw interviews himself]

Iveragh. "Protesters Were Right", 16 December 1911, p. 3. [Undated letter to the Editor sent to *The World*, but not published by that newspaper]

O'Leary, Jeremiah. "An Irish-American's View", 16 December 1911, p. 3. [Letter to the Editor, dated 5 December]

"The 'Outlook's' Stupid Article", 16 December 1911, p. 4. [Editorial]

"Shaw Gives Himself Away", 16 December 1911, p. 4. [Editorial]

"The 'Evening Post' Commended", 16 December 1911, p. 5. [Reprint of An Irish-American, "The 'Playboy' Again", *The New York Evening Post*, 1 December 1911, p. 8 (Letter to the Editor, dated 29 November)]

Moran, Bernard T. "Mayo Man Disowns Them", 16 December 1911, p. 7. [Letter to the Editor, dated 8 December]

"Yeats Doesn't Chew Sawdust Any More", 23 December 1911, pp. 1 and 8.

Ceud Tiene. "Gossip from Chicago", 23 December 1911, p. 8.

"Denial from Irish Girls", 30 December 1911, p. 5. [Three letters to the Editor appear under this title. The letters are signed by the following: (1) Robinson's "Oversight" (2) Lennox Robinson (3) Sarah Allgood, Eileen O'Doherty, Cathleen Nesbitt, Maire Nic Shiubhlaigh, Eithne Magee]

"Condemn 'The Playboy' ", 6 January 1912, p. 2.

"The 'Evening Sun's' Impudent Lie", 6 January 1912, p. 5. [Editorial]

O'Leary, Jeremiah. "O'Leary Answers Quinn", 14 January 1912, p. 3. [Sums up anti-*Playboy* arguments]

"Philadelphia Spanks 'The Playboy' ", 20 January 1912, pp. 1 and 7.

" 'The Playboy' Reviewed", 20 January 1912, p. 7. [Extract from "The Playboy of the Western World: Confounding Drama with Pastoral Poetry", *The Dramatist* (Easton, Pa.), III (January 1912), 224-225]

"Pennsylvania Air Bad for 'Playboy' ", 27 January 1912, pp. 1 and 8.

"Lady Gregory's Inane Talk", 27 January 1912, p. 4. [Editorial]

"Chicago Doesn't Want 'Playboy' ", 3 February 1912, p. 1.

"Didn't Please Pittsburgh", 3 February 1912, p. 2.

"The 'Playboy's' Poor Defender", 3 February 1912, p. 4. [Editorial]

"Author of 'The Playboy' ", 10 February 1912, p. 2.

"Obdurate Lady Gregory", 10 February 1912, p. 3.

"Even Smalley Slaps It", 17 February 1912, p. 2. [Reprint of George W. Smalley, "Censors Here and Abroad", *New York Tribune*, 11 February 1912, Section One, p. 9.]

"Last of 'The Playboy' ", 17 February 1912, p. 2.

"Synge Not a Genius", 16 March 1912, p. 3.

"The Playboys at Home", 30 March 1912, p. 2.

"A Crazy 'Playboy' in Boston", 30 March 1912, p. 4. [Editorial]

"Yeats Slanders American Irish", 30 March 1912, p. 4. [Editorial]

"Loyalists Welcome the Playboys", 13 April 1912, p. 4. [Editorial]

The Globe and Commercial Advertiser

"New Plays That Open Next Week", 25 November 1911, p. 5. [*Playboy*]

"Col. Roosevelt To See Play That Provoked Riot", 28 November 1911, pp. 1-2. [*Playboy*]

McNally, Augustin. "Dramatic Reviewers at Odds Over Synge's Work, 'The Playboy of the Western World' ", 28 November 1911, p. 7.

Sherwin, Louis. "Dramatic Reviewers at Odds over Synge's Work, 'The Playboy of the Western World' ", 28 November 1911, p. 7.

" 'Playboy' Harmless Is McAdoo's Report", 29 November 1911, p. 1.

Sherwin, Louis. "Irish Players in 'Riders to the Sea' ", 7 December 1911, p. 8.

The Irish-American

Hackett, J. D. "Correspondence", 7 October 1911, p. 4. [Letter to the Editor, dated 1 October]

"The Imported Irish Drama", 7 October 1911, p. 4.

Brogan, A. J. "Abbey Theatre Players: 'The Playboy of the Western World' ", 14 October 1911, pp. 1 and 4.

"Irish Plays (?)", 14 October 1911, p. 4. [Editorial]

Fox, Michael. "Gaelic League Addresses Yeats", 21 October 1911, p. 4. [Undated letter to the Editor]

Kelly, Gertrude B. "The Alleged Irish Players", 18 November 1911, p. 4. [Letter to the Editor, dated 11 November]

"The Vagabonds", 2 December 1911, p. 4. [Editorial]

O'Leary, Jeremiah A. "The Press and 'The Playboy' ", 9 December 1911, p. 4. [Letter to the Editor, dated 7 December]

The Irish World and American Industrial Liberator

"Gaelic Notes: The Stage Irishman", 2 March 1907, p. 7. [Editorial on *Playboy*]

"So-Called Irish Players on the Wrong Track", 2 September 1911, p. 7.

"Condemn the 'Irish' Players", 14 October 1911, p. 2, col. 2.

Gallagher, J. F. "The Carrion Crows of Stageland", 14 October 1911, p. 7.

"An 'Irish' Play and Its 'Irish' Players", 14 October 1911, p. 7.

Brogan, P. H. "The Boston Mayo Men's Benevolent Association Repudiate the Foul Libel on Their Country", 21 October 1911, p. 7. [Undated letter to the Editor]

Fox, Michael, and T. J. Brennan. "The New York Gaelic Society Denounce 'The Play Boy' ", 21 October 1911, p. 7. [Undated letter addressed to W. B. Yeats]

"Further Opinions of the 'Irish' Players", 21 October 1911, p. 7.

"Cúrsaí an Tsaoghail", 28 October 1911, p. 7.

Larkin, F. O'Neill. "F. O'Neill Larkin Pronounces the 'Playboy' a Despicable Picture of Irish Life", 28 October 1911, p. 7.

Mullen, Thomas A. "Shocking Travesty", 28 October 1911, p. 7.

"Scathing Denunciation Accorded 'Irish' Players by an Appointed Committee", 28 October 1911, p. 7.

Jordan, Michael J. "Course, Vulgar, Brutal", 4 November 1911, p. 7. [*Playboy* in Boston]

Philpott, A. J. "Taken Too Seriously", 4 November 1911, p. 7. [*Playboy*]

Dwyer, Daniel J. "Not a Single Redeeming Feature", 11 November 1911, p. 7. [Undated letter to the Editor]

"The Irish Pagans", 11 November 1911, p. 7.

MacCarthaig, Gearoid. "A Shameless and Mercenary Crew", 11 November 1911, p. 7.

" 'Irish' Plays Condemned at the Capital", 18 November 1911, p. 7.

Kelly, Gertrude B. "A Good Advice: 'Boycott the Box Office' ", 18 November 1911, p. 7. [Letter to the Editor, dated 11 November]

"The Un-Irish Players in New York", 25 November 1911, p. 7.

"The 'Irish' Players", 2 December 1911, p. 3.

"Rebuking Indecency", 2 December 1911, p. 4. [Editorial on *Playboy*]

"Drive Him Off the Stage", 9 December 1911, p. 1. [Large cartoon depicting the lady "Erin" with whip in hand chasing the "Decadent Irish Playwright" from the stage]

"A Dreary Failure", 9 December 1911, p. 4. [Editorial on *Playboy*]

"Cúrsaí an Tsaoghail", 9 December 1911, p. 7.

"Four Reasons for Condemning the Irish Players", 16 December 1911, p. 5.

"Irish Players Condemned on All Sides", 16 December 1911, p. 5. [Includes reprints from "Music and Drama: 'The Playboy of the Western World' ", *The New York Evening Post*, 28 November 1911, p. 5; "Irish Players Consist Largely of Humbug", *The Brooklyn Daily Eagle*, 24 November 1911, p. 6. Also includes the following letter: Sutton, John P. "In Their True Light", *The Irish World and American Industrial Liberator* (New York), 16 December 1911, p. 5. (Undated letter addressed to the Editor of the Lincoln, Nebraska, *State Journal*)]

McGurin, James. "From President Irish-American Literary Society", 16 December 1911, p. 5. [Letter to the Editor, dated 4 December]

Moran, Bernard T. "Well Qualified to Speak", 16 December 1911, p. 5. [Letter to the Editor, dated 8 December]

Sutton, John P. "In Their True Light", 16 December 1911, p. 5. [Undated letter addressed to the Editor of the Lincoln, Nebraska, *State Journal*]

"Cúrsaí an Tsaoghail", 16 December 1911, p. 7.

The Journal of Commerce and Commercial Bulletin

"The Irish Players Quicken", 24 November 1911, p. 5. [*Well*]

"Irish Players Hooted in 'The Playboy' ", 28 November 1911, p. 5.

"The Irish Players in Two New Plays", 5 December 1911, p. 5. [*Riders*]

"Two New Comedies by Irish Players", 16 December 1911, p. 5. [*Shadow*]

The New York American

"Riot at Irish Players Fails to Stop Drama", 28 November 1911, pp. 1 and 6.

The New York Call

"Drama: J. B. Yeats to Read 'The Playboy of the Western World' ", 14 November 1911, p. 3.

Mailly, William. "Drama: 'The Well of the Saints' ", 25 November 1911, p. 4.

Mailly, William. "Irish Players Face Riot", 28 November 1911, pp. 1-2.

Mailly, William. "Drama: 'The Playboy of the Western World' ", 29 November 1911, p. 4.

Mailly, William. "Drama: 'Riders to the Sea' ", 6 December 1911, p. 4.

Mailly, William. "Drama: 'The Shadow of the Glen' ", 18 December 1911, p. 3.

The New York Commercial

"Music and Drama: Irish Players Interesting in 'The Well of the Saints' ", 24 November 1911, p. 2.

"Police Aid Irish Players to Produce Synge Drama", 28 November 1911, p. 1. [*Playboy*]

"New Plays of Week", 28 November 1911, p. 2. [*Playboy*]

The New York Dramatic Mirror

"A Rousing Playboy Riot: Unparalleled Disorder at the Maxine Elliott Theatre", 29 November 1911, pp. 7 and 11.

"Maxine Elliott's—Irish Players: *The Playboy of the Western World*", 6 December 1911, p. 6.

"Maxine Elliott's—Irish Players: *Riders to the Sea*", 13 December 1911, p. 7.

"Maxine Elliott's—Irish Players: *The Shadow of the Glen*", 20 December 1911, pp. 6-7.

The New York Evening Journal

McConaughy, J. W. "The New Play", 24 November 1911, p. 27. [*Well*]

"Police to Guard Irish Players in Drama To-night", 28 November 1911, p. 1.

"Censor Reports on Irish Play's Fitness To-day", 29 November 1911, p. 3.

The New York Evening Post

"Books and Reading", 13 August 1909, p. 4. [Review of Cuala Press edition, *Poems and Translations*]

"Music and Drama: The Irish Players", 24 November 1911, p. 9. [*Well*]

Benjamin, M. W. "The Irish Play", 28 November 1911, p. 8. [Undated letter to the Editor]

"Music and Drama: 'The Playboy of the Western World' ", 28 November 1911, p. 9.

An Irish-American. "The 'Playboy' Again", 1 December 1911, p. 8. [Letter to the Editor, dated 29 November]

"Drama at Home and Abroad: Synge and 'The Playboy' ", 2 December 1911, p. 6.

"Music and Drama: Irish Players", 5 December 1911, p. 9. [*Riders*]

Sherman, Stuart P. "Literary News and Reviews: John Synge", 11 January 1913 (Saturday Supplement), p. 6. [Review of J. W.

Luce and Co. edition, *The Works;* P. P. Howe, *J. M. Synge: A Critical Study*]

The New York Herald

"Shaw Play That London Barred Makes No Ripple Here", 24 November 1911, p. 12. [*Well*]

"Irish Play Leads to Riot and Fierce Battle of Men and Women with Police", 28 November 1911, p. 1.

"Thoughtful Like 'Playboy of the Western World' ", 28 November 1911, p. 13.

"Mayor Gives Irish Play a Clean Bill", 30 November 1911, p. 13.

"Plays and Players: Events of the Week at Theatres and Opera", 3 December 1911, Section 3, p. 9. [*Playboy*]

"Irish Players in New Roles", 5 December 1911, p. 9. [*Riders*]

The New York Herald Tribune Book Review

Ferguson, De Lancey. "John Millington Synge and the Great Period of the Irish Renaissance", 19 April 1959, p. 5. [Review of David H. Greene and Edward M. Stephens, *J. M. Synge, 1871-1909*]

The New York Freeman's Journal

"A Pagan Irish Drama", 2 September 1911, p. 4.

"Against the 'Playboy' ", 14 October 1911, p. 7.

"Arouses Storm of Protest in Boston", 21 October 1911, p. 2.

"A Scurrilous Misrepresentation", 21 October 1911, p. 2.

"Condemned on All Sides", 28 October 1911, p. 3.

"Those 'Irish' Pagans", 11 November 1911, p. 8.

"A Dreary Failure", 9 December 1911, p. 8. [*Playboy*]

"Condemn 'Irish' Players as Immoral, and Blasphemous", 23 December 1911, p. 2. [Includes extracts from "Music and Drama: 'The Playboy of the Western World' ", *The New York Evening Post*, 28 November 1911, p. 9; and from "Irish Players Consist Largely of Humbug", *The Brooklyn Daily Eagle*, 24 November 1911, p. 6]

"Four Reasons for Condemning the Irish Players", 23 December 1911, p. 2.

Sutton, John P. "In Their True Light", 23 December 1911, p. 2. [Reprint of a letter Mr. Sutton addressed to the Editor of the Lincoln, Nebraska, *State Journal*]

McGurin, James. "Synge's Indecent Production", 23 December 1911, p. 3. [Letter to the Editor, dated 4 December]

Moran, Bernard T. "A Calumny on a God-Fearing People", 23 December 1911, p. 3. [Letter to the Editor, dated 8 December]

The New York Press

"Lady Gregory Recounts Labors of Abbey Players: Defends Playboy, by Synge", 20 November 1911, p. 7.

G., J. C. "Shaw and Synge Plays Done by Irish Actors", 24 November 1911, p. 10 [*Well*]

"Audience in Riot Hurls Potatoes at Irish Players: Disturbers Call Play an Affront to Erin", 28 November 1911, pp. 1-2.

"Theatre Rioters Quickly Expelled: Roosevelt in Audience", 29 November 1911, p. 10.

The New York Times

"Lady Gregory Here With Irish Players", 20 November 1911, p. 11.

"Irish Players as Wild Westerners", 24 November 1911, p. 13. [*Well*]

"Irish Players Fear No Riot", 26 November 1911, Part 1, p. 15.

"Acting of the Irish Players", 26 November 1911, Part 7, p. 2.

MacManus, Seumas. "Seumas M'Manus Raps 'The Playboy'", 27 November 1911, p. 11.

"Riot in Theatre Over an Irish Play", 28 November 1911, pp. 1 and 3. [*Playboy*]

"The Play and the Acting", 28 November 1911, p. 3. [*Playboy*]

Montrose, Kitty. "The 'Playboy' Riot", 29 November 1911, p. 10. [Letter to the Editor, dated 28 November]

"The 'Playboy' Row", 29 November 1911, p. 10. [Editorial]

"Topics of the Times: Falsity Not the Grievance", 30 November 1911, p. 12. [Editorial]

"Approves 'The Playboy' ", 30 November 1911, p. 13.

"How Ireland Turned from Politics to Playwriting", 3 December 1911, Part 5 (Magazine Section), p. 5. [An interview with Lady Gregory]

"Irish Play Row in Philadelphia", 16 January 1912, p. 8.

"Topics of the Times: At Least Better Than Riot", 19 January 1912, p. 10. [Editorial]

Atkinson, Brooks. "The Play: Playboying the Western World", 3 January 1930, p. 20.

"The Play: Synge and Lady Gregory in the Abbey Theatre Bill", 21 October 1932, p. 25. [*Playboy*]

"Abbey Players Gain Free Choice of Bills", 14 August 1934, p. 15.

The New York Times Book Review

Untermeyer, Louis. "The Late J. M. Synge", 17 April 1909 (Saturday Review of Books Section), p. 247. [Article dated 14 April]

"The Genius of Synge's 'Playboy' ", 1 October 1911, p. 584. [Review of the John W. Luce and Co. edition of *The Playboy of the Western World*]

"Synge, The Firebrand", 3 December 1911, (Holiday Book Number), pp. 759-760. [Review of J. W. Luce and Co. edition, *The Works;* in particular, *Riders to the Sea*, *The Tinker's Wedding* and *In the Shadow of the Glen*]

Braithwaite, William Stanley. "A Study of Synge", 15 September 1912, Part 6, p. 501. [Review of P. P. Howe, *J. M. Synge: A Critical Study*]

Reynolds, Horace. "Synge's Plays and the Irish Stage", 14 April 1935, Section 6, p. 2. [Review of Random House edition, *The Complete Works*]

Mercier, Vivian. "How Did the Miracle Come About?", 19 April 1959, pp. 5 and 20. [Review of David H. Greene and Edward M. Stephens, *J. M. Synge: 1871-1909*]

The New York Tribune

"The Drama: The Irish Players in Plays by Bernard Shaw and J. M. Synge", 24 November 1911, p. 7. [*Well*]

"Irish Players Act 'Playboy' in Riot", 28 November 1911, pp. 1-2.

W., A. "The Drama: Synge's 'Playboy of the Western World' at Maxine Elliott's Theatre", 28 November 1911, p. 7.

" 'Playboy' Repeated: Disorder Is Slight", 29 November 1911, pp. 1 and 7.

W., A. "The Drama: Synge's 'Playboy of the Western World' at Maxine Elliott's Theatre", 29 November 1911, p. 7. [*Playboy*]

W., A. "The Playgoer: The 'Playboy' of Synge and the Playboys of New York", 3 December 1911, Part 5, p. 6.

W., A. "The Drama: Pieces by Synge, Shaw and Lady Gregory Acted by Irish Players", 16 December 1911, p. 7. [*Shadow*]

Smalley, George W. "Censors Here and Abroad", 11 February 1912, Section 1, p. 9. [*Playboy*]

The Outlook

"The Irish Play of To-Day", 4 November 1911, pp. 561-563.

"The Irish Players in New York", 2 December 1911, p. 801. [A brief comment about *Riders*]

Roosevelt, Theodore. "Introduction", to "The Irish Players", 16 December 1911, p. 915.

Quinn, John. "Lady Gregory and the Abbey Theatre", 16 December 1911, pp. 916-919.

The Sun

Yeats, W. B. "Irish 'Paganism' ", 8 October 1911, Section 1, p. 8. [Letter to the Editor, dated Boston, 6 October]

Yeats, W. B. "Aims of the Irish Theatre", 18 November 1911, p. 12.

"Irish Actors in a New Bill: They Appear in Dramas by Shaw and Synge", 24 November 1911, p. 7.

Conway, James P. "A Justification of Synge's Study of One Side of the Irish Character", 25 November 1911, p. 8. [Letter to the Editor, dated 24 November]

White, John T. "Complaint of an Old Irishman Who Admits That He Is Sensitive", 25 November 1911, p. 8. [Letter to the Editor, dated 23 November]

"News of the Theatres: The Irish Players To Be Seen in the Much Discussed 'Playboy' ", 26 November 1911, Section 3, p. 6.

"Plays of the Irish Actors: Revelations of Synge and G. B. Shaw", 26 November 1911, Section 3, p. 6. [*Well* and *Playboy*]

" 'Playboy' Mobbed: 40 Thrown Out", 28 November 1911, pp. 1-2.

" 'The Playboy' as Drama", 28 November 1911, p. 2.

"Throw Out 7 at 'Playboy': While Roosevelt Drowns Hisses with Applause", 29 November 1911, pp. 1-2.

"Play That Made the Trouble: Impressions of 'The Playboy of the Western World' ", 29 November 1911, p. 2.

An American Who Was Present. "All but the Widow Quinn Deserve the 'Hook' ", 30 November 1911, p. 6. [Letter to the Editor, dated 28 November]

Ardis. "Protest of an Unsubjugated Race", 30 November 1911, p. 6. [Letter to the Editor, dated 28 November]

F., L. "The Consputation of Synge: 'Manifestation' at the Performance of 'The Playboy' ", 30 November 1911, p. 6. [Letter to the Editor, dated 28 November]

H., M. "Voice of the Ironist", 30 November 1911, p. 6. [Letter to the Editor, dated 28 November]

Houston, Herbert S. "Futile Stupidity", 30 November 1911, p. 6. [Letter to the Editor, dated 28 November]

Kelly, Michael. "The Play's Moral Deformity", 30 November 1911, p. 6. [Letter to the Editor, dated 28 November]

Perry, Talbot. "Sensitive Plants", 30 November 1911, p. 6. [Letter to the Editor, dated 28 November]

Quinlan, Patrick L. "Warm Words from 'A Real Irishman' ", 30 November 1911, p. 6. [Letter to the Editor, dated 28 November]

T., H. "What's All This Pother", 30 November 1911, p. 6. [Letter to the Editor, dated 29 November]

Williams, Michael. "Lord, Confound Each Surly Hiss-ter", 30 November 1911, p. 6. [Letter to the Editor, dated 28 November]

" 'The Playboy' Stays", 30 November 1911, p. 7.

"More About the Playboy: John Synge's Much Discussed Play and Its Hero", 3 December 1911, Section 3, p. 5.

"New Irish Players", 5 December 1911, p. 9.

"Irish Players Held on Immorality charge", 18 January 1912, p. 1.

" 'The Playboy of the Western World' and the Trouble It Made", 28

January 1912, Section 4, p. 7. [Full page article, with photographs of actors]

Clark, Barrett H. "Hot on the Trail of One John M. Synge", 28 July 1918, Section 6 (Books and the Book World), p. 4.

The World

"Aim of Irish Players to Reproduce on Stage True Effect of Nature", 26 November 1911, Section M (Metropolitan Section), p. 6.

"Riot in Theatre: Irish Players Are Driven Off Stage", 28 November 1911, pp. 1-2.

"Says It Is True and Searching Study", 28 November 1911, p. 2.

" 'Broth-of-a-Boy Is Real Libel'—Shaw", 29 November 1911, p. 3.

"Critic Roosevelt Sees Six Ejected from Irish Play", 29 November 1911, p. 3.

"Mayor Hints at Press Agent Work", 29 November 1911, p. 3.

"300 More Rioters Could Not Get In", 29 November 1911, p. 3.

"Let Us Elevate the Stage", 29 November 1911, p. 10. [Editorial]

" 'Playboy' Can Still Play", 30 November 1911, p. 11.

De Foe, Louis V. " 'The Playboy', Despite Its Foes, Gives Synge a Place in Ireland's Hall of Fame", 3 December 1911, Section M (Metropolitan Section), p. 6.

NORWICH (England)

Eastern Daily Press

"Our London Letter", 11 June 1907, p. 6. [*Playboy.* See paragraph eight]

NOTTINGHAM (England)

The Nottingham Guardian Literary Supplement

"Short Notices", 30 April 1907, p. 3. [Short notice about Maunsel and Co. edition, *The Playboy*. See top of col. 3]

OXFORD (England)

The Isis

Mathurin. "Theatre Notes: The Irish Plays", 8 June 1907, pp. 396-397. [*Playboy*]

H., J. E. "Irish Plays and Players in London: An Appreciation and a Criticism", 12 June 1909, pp. 429-431. [*Well* and *Shadow*]

The Oxford Chronicle

"The Irish Theatre: Performances in Oxford", 7 June 1907, p. 7. [*Playboy*]

"The Irish National Theatre in Oxford: The Genius of J. M. Synge", 18 June 1909, p. 7.

"The Genius of J. M. Synge", 5 July 1912, p. 7. [Review of P. P. Howe, *J. M. Synge: A Critical Study*]

The Oxford Review

"The New Theatre", 6 June 1907, p. 2. [*Playboy*]

"New Theatre: The Irish Players", 15 June 1909, p. 3. [*Playboy*]

The Oxford Times

"The New Theatre", 8 June 1907, p. 12. [*Playboy*]

"The Irish Players at the New Theatre", 19 June 1909, p. 10. [*Playboy*]

PARIS (France)

Journal des Debats

Filon, Augustin. "Le Réveil de l'âme celtique", 19 April 1905, p. 1.

Phalange

Florence, Jean [Professor Blum]. "Le Théâtre irlandais", 20 January 1911, p. 52.

Le Temps

Millet, Philippe. "Un Théâtre irlandais", 23 January 1912, pp. 4-5. [Playboy]

Kemp, Robert. "Le Théâtre de J. M. Synge", 23 and 24 May 1942, p. 3.

PAWTUCKET (Rhode Island, U.S.A.)

The Evening Times

"Theatrical Attractions This Week in Pawtucket and Providence Playhouses: Providence Opera", 31 October 1911, p. 4. [Shadow]

"No Protest Against Irish Comedy Play", 1 November 1911, p. 8.

PHILADELPHIA (U.S.A.)

The Evening Bulletin

"Disturbers Held for Theatre Row: Say 'Playboy' is Unfair", 16 January 1912, pp. 1 and 10.

"At the Theatres: Adelphi—The Irish Players", 16 January 1912, p. 9. [Playboy]

"Irish Play Halted by More Disorder", 17 January 1912, p. 1.

" 'Playboy' Actors Are Under Arrest", 18 January 1912, p. 3.

"The Tomfoolery at the Adelphi", 18 January 1912, p. 6. [Editorial]

" 'Playboy' Actors Held for Court", 19 January 1912, p. 1. [Includes a front page photograph of five actresses from the Irish Players]

" 'Playboy' Decision Is Expected To-day", 20 January 1912, p. 2.

" 'Playboy' Decision Expected", 22 January 1912, p. 3.

"Irish Actors Freed by Order of Court", 23 January 1912, p. 1.

The Evening Telegraph

"Plays and Players: Irish Players in 'The Playboy' ", 13 January 1912, p. 5.

"Police Scent Plot in Disturbance at Adelphi Theatre", 16 January 1912, pp. 1 and 2.

O'Connor, Dr. J. H. "Fall Short of Purpose", 16 January 1912, p. 2. [Letter to the Editor dated 16 January 1912]

"At the Theatres: 'The Playboy' on the Stage", 16 January 1912, p. 11.

Plays and Players. "Decomposed Eggs Hurled at Actors Shown at Hearing", 17 January 1912, pp. 1 and 12.

[A Germantown Citizen]. "Opinion of Many", 17 January 1912, p. 12. [Undated letter to the Editor. Replies to Dr. J. H. O'Connor's letter of 16 January]

"Cough and One Hiss During Irish Play", 18 January 1912, p. 3.

"Irish Play Decision Withheld by Court", 19 January 1912, pp. 1 and 3.

"Judge Gives Playboy Clean Bill of Health", 23 January 1912, pp. 1 and 2.

The North American

"Who's Who on Philadelphia's Stage This Week: Irish Actress Likes America", 14 January 1912, Section 3 (News section), p. 4.

C., H. T. "Pertinent Comment on Plays and Players", 14 January 1912, Section 3 (News section), p. 6.

"Cops Throw Out 29, Arrest 2, and Check a Riot at Irish Play", 16 January 1912, pp. 1 and 8.

"Irish Players in Two Dramas at Adelphi", 16 January 1912, p. 8.
[*Playboy*]

"Irish Play Is Again Halted by 'Riots'; Police Arrest 14", 17 January 1912, pp. 1 and 6.

"Under Arrest; Irish Players Triumph in Criticised 'Playboy' ", 18 January 1912, pp. 1 and 9.

"Fourth Production of 'Playboy' Goes Finely", 19 January 1912, p. 2.

" 'Well of the Saints' by the Irish Players", 19 January 1912, p. 2.

"Irish Players Appear in a 'Court Comedy': No Decision", 20 January 1912, p. 3.

C., H. T. "Pertinent Comment on Plays and Players", 21 January 1912, Section 3 (News section), p. 6.

"Hibernians Denounce Irish Players' Work", 22 January 1912, p. 2.

"Irish Players Freed, Also the Disturbers", 24 January 1912, p. 8.

The Philadelphia Evening Item

"Disturbers Held for Theatre Row", (Latest Night Extra), 16 January 1912, p. 1.

" 'The Playboy' Is Presented", (Latest Night Extra) 16 January 1912, p. 2.

"Thirty Ejected from Theatre", (Latest Night Extra), 16 January 1912, p. 8.

"Irish Players Test the Law", (Latest Night Extra), 19 January 1912, p. 1.

"Irish Players in 'Well of the Saints' ", (Latest Night Extra), 19 January 1912, p. 2.

" 'Playboy' Actors Discharged", (Latest Night Extra), 23 January 1912, p. 1.

The Philadelphia Inquirer

The Call Boy. "The Call Boy's Chat", 14 January 1912, Section 3 (Special Feature section), p. 6. [*Well*]

"Four Novelties on Theatrical Roster: Adelphi", 14 January 1912, Section 3 (Special Feature section), p. 7.

"Halt Performance of Playboy with Hoots and Yells", 16 January 1912, pp. 1 and 4.

"13 Are Arrested: Accused of Riot at Irish Drama", 17 January 1912, pp. 1 and 2.

"Riots in Theatres", 18 January 1912, p. 8. [Editorial]

"Editorial Comment: One View of the Playboy", 19 January 1912, p. 8. [Extract from Darrell Figgis, "The Art of J. M. Synge", *The Forum* (New York), XLVII (January 1912), 55-70]

"Decision Reserved by Judge Carr on Playboy's Status", 20 January 1912, pp. 1 and 2 .

The Call Boy. "The Call Boy's Chat", 21 January 1912, Section 3 (Special Feature section), p. 6. [*Playboy* riots and a review of *Well*]

"Judge Dismisses Suit on 'Playboy' ", 24 January 1912, p. 11.

The Philadelphia Press

"Lady Gregory Defends Play", 7 January 1912, p. 10.

"New Playbills: The Playboy of the Western World, Adelphi—Irish Players", 14 January 1912, Part 4, p. 6.

"Irish Play Causes Riot at Adelphi", 16 January 1912, p. 1.

"Riot Again Halts Play at Adelphi", 17 January 1912, pp. 1 and 2.

"Court to Pass on Status of Irish Play", 20 January 1912, p. 3.

Davin, John F. "A Critic of the 'Playboy' ", 24 January 1912, p. 6. [Letter to the Editor, dated 21 January]

Wister, Jones . "Lady Gregory's Ideas of Elevating the Stage", 24 January 1912, p. 6. [Letter to the Editor, dated 22 January]

The Philadelphia Record

"Bernard Shaw Caustic: Says a Lost Tribe of Israel [American Gaels] Governs American People", 9 January 1912, p. 10.

"Local Playbills for This Week: Adelphi—'The Playboy' ", 14 January 1912, Part 4 (Real Estate section), p. 6.

"Failed to Stop Irish Players: Riotous Demonstration Nipped in Bud and the 'Playboy' was Successfully Given", 16 January 1912, p. 12.

"Rotten Eggs for Irish Players: Riotous Demonstration Greets Second Production of the 'Playboy' ", 17 January 1912, pp. 1 and 4.

"New Attack on Irish Players", 18 January 1912, p. 1.

"Warrants Are Served On the Irish Players", 18 January 1912, p. 1. [Includes a front page photograph of five actresses from the Irish Players]

" 'Playboy' Undisturbed: Peace Reigns at Final Performance of the Irish Comedy", 19 January 1912, p. 10.

"Legal Fight Over 'Playboy' Farce: Three Witnesses Declare Production Immoral", 20 January 1912, p. 4.

"Stage Topics of the Moment: Those Irish Ructions", 21 January 1912, Part 4, p. 6.

The Philadelphia Sunday Item

"Adelphi: Irish Players in Repertoire", 14 January 1912, p. 13. [*Playboy*]

"Irish Players in Synge Comedy", 14 January 1912, p. 13. [*Well*]

The Public Ledger

"The News of the Week in the Philadelphia Theatres: Adelphi—The Irish Players", 14 January 1912, Fourth Section, p. 7. [*Playboy*]

"Riot Starts When 'Playboy' Appears", 16 January 1912, p. 1.

" 'Playboy' Is Seen at the Adelphi", 16 January 1912, p. 7.

"Eggs and Pie Fly at Irish Players", 17 January 1912, p. 1.

"Warrant Served on Irish Players", 18 January 1912, p. 1.

"Riotous Criticism", 18 January 1912, p. 10. [Editorial; also includes a cartoon about the riots]

"Irish Players in Three Clever Plays", 19 January 1912, p. 2. [*Well*]

" 'Playboy' Presented Without Disturbance", 19 January 1912, p. 2.

"Shaw Pokes Fun at Philadelphia", 19 January 1912, p. 2.

"Irish Players in Fight for Freedom: Priests Object to Play", 20 January 1912, pp. 1-2.

" 'Playboy' Decision Not Yet Rendered", 21 January 1912, p. 2.

"Irish Players Win Decision in Court: 'Playboy' Not Immoral", 24 January 1912, p. 2.

"The Irish Actors", 24 January 1912, p. 10. [Editorial]

PROVIDENCE (Rhode Island, U.S.A.)

The Evening Bulletin

"Protest Against Irish Play Made to Commissioners", 30 October 1911, pp. 1 and 3.

"Irish Play Will Be Produced Here Despite Protest", 31 October 1911, p. 1.

Young, F. H. "At the Theatres: Providence Opera House", 31 October 1911, p. 11. [*Shadow*]

"Lady Gregory Tells of Drama", 31 October 1911, Second Section, p. 1.

" 'Playboy' Given Without Change", 1 November 1911, p. 1.

Young, F. H. "Irish Players Win Applause", 1 November 1911, Second Section, p. 8. [*Riders* and *Playboy*]

Young, F. H. "Irish Players Win Applause to End", 2 November 1911, Second Section, p. 7. [*Well*]

The Evening News

"What Is Going on in the Local Theatres: Opera House", 31 October 1911, p. 3. [*Shadow*]

" 'Playboy of the Western World' Will Be Given", 31 October 1911, p. 8.

"At the Play Houses: Opera House", 1 November 1911, p. 4. [*Playboy*]

The Evening Tribune

"Local Opposition to Irish Play", 30 October 1911, p. 2.

"Protested Irish Play Will Be Presented", (Last edition), 31 October 1911, p. 1.

"Theatrical Offerings of Wide Variety This Week", (Last edition), 31 October 1911, p. 9. [*Shadow*]

"Police Made Complete Preparations for a Riot", (Last edition), 1 November 1911, p. 1.

"More Clever Work by Irish Players", (Last edition), 1 November 1911, p. 3. [*Riders* and *Playboy*]

"Irish Players Close Engagement", (Last edition), 2 November 1911, p. 3. [*Well*]

The Providence Journal

"Lady Gregory Tells of Drama", 31 October 1911, p. 2.

Young, F. H. "At the Theatres: Providence Opera House", 31 October 1911, p. 8. [*Shadow*]

Young, F. H. "Irish Players Win Applause", 1 November 1911, p .11. [*Riders* and *Playboy*]

Young, F. H. "Irish Players Win Applause to End", 2 November 1911, p. 6. [*Well*]

The Providence Sunday Journal

"At the Theatres: The Irish Players", 29 October 1911, Third Section, p. 10.

SAINT LOUIS (Missouri, U.S.A.)

The Saint Louis Daily Globe-Democrat

"Gaelic Life and Character", 12 February 1911, Part I, p. 11. [Review of Maunsel edition, *The Works*]

SEOUL (Korea)

The Korea Daily News

"Remarkable Scenes in a Dublin Theatre", 16 March 1907.

SHEFFIELD (England)

The Sheffield Guardian

C., G. "The Bookshop: John M. Synge", 26 May 1911, p. 12.

SOUTHPORT (England)

The Southport Guardian

"Books of the Day: John Millington Synge", 23 October 1912, p. 11.
[Review of Francis Bickley, *J. M. Synge and the Irish Dramatic Movement*]

VIENNA (Austria)

Neue Freie Presse

Trebitsch-Stein, Marianne. "Literaturblatt: Ein Beitrag zur Geschichte des irischens Theaters", 13 April 1913, pp. 31-34.

WASHINGTON D.C. (U.S.A.)

The Evening Star

"Amusements: Belasco", 14 November 1911, p. 12. [*Well*]

The Sunday Star

Johnson, Philander. "The Theater", 19 November 1911, Part II, p. 2.
[*Playboy*]

The Washington Herald

"Asks Fair Play for Plays and Irish Players", 13 November 1911, pp. 1 and 3.

J., A. M. "At the Theatres: The Belasco—The Irish Players", 14 November 1911, p. 9. [*Well*]

" 'The Playboy' Seen at the Belasco", 16 November 1911, p. 7.

The Washington Post

G[raves]., R[alph]. "Offerings at Local Theaters This Week: Belasco —The Irish Players, in Three Plays", 14 November 1911, p. 5. [*Well*]

Graves, Ralph. "Savage Standard for Grand Opera To Be Maintained", 19 November 1911, Magazine Section, p. 2. [*Playboy*]

The Washington Times

"Irish Plays Are Insult to Race, Catholics Say", 12 November 1911, pp. 1 and 8.

The Aloysius Truth Society. "Aloysius Truth Society Bitterly Denounces Irish Plays after Special Committee Sees 'The Playboy' at the Belasco", 16 November 1911, p. 10.

Murdock, Julia. "Julia Murdock Fails to See Anything Offensive in the Irish Players' Production of 'The Playboy of the Western World' ", 16 November 1911, p. 10.

White, George. "Criticizes Review of Irish Players", 18 November 1911, p. 8. [Undated letter to the Editor]

INDEX

A., 158
A., J. E., 185
A., M., 95
A., W., 182
Abbey Theatre (and Irish National Theatre), 20, 31, 32, 34, 36, 37, 41, 43, 46, 47, 48, 49, 52, 62, 103, 105, 113, 119, 124, 126, 128, 134-160 *passim*, 165, 167, 168, 171, 173-185 *passim*, 197, 198, 201, 202, 209
Abbey Theatre Debate (Yeats vs. rioters, 4 February 1907), 40, 74, 137, 140, 144, 147, 150, 154, 155, 157, 158
Adams, J. Donald, 19, 61
Adelman, Irving, 11
Aeschylus, 21, 31, 47, 62, 98
Aesthetic Theory, 50
Agate, Captain James E., 61, 87
Allen, Beverly S., 41
Allgood, Sara, 161, 189
Aloysius Truth Society, The, 210
Alspach, R. K., 181
Altick, Richard D., 21
American Who Was Present, An, 199
Anderson, Maxwell, 21, 62
Anderson, Patrick, 177
Andrews, Charlton, 19
Andrews, Irene Dwen, 41
Another Irishman, 145
Anouilh, Jean, 31
Aran Islands, The, 21, 48, 91, 98, 99, 103, 107, 108, 109, 119, 154, 164, 165, 172, 175, 177, 180, 181, 182; J. W. Luce and Co. edition, 21, 43, 91, 103; Maunsel and Co. edition, 48, 91, 119, 154, 164, 165, 175, 177, 180, 182; Tauchnitz edition, 91
Aran Islands, The, 44, 46, 49, 98
Archer, William, 95, 170, 171
Ardis, 199
Armstrong, William Arthur, 19
Arnold, Sidney, 95
Atkinson, Brooks, 197
Aufhauser, Annemarie, 19, 33, 75, 81, 87
Aughtry, Charles Edward, 19
Avis, 155
Ayling, Ronald, 13

B., 179
B., M. P., 158
B., S., 182
B., T. F., 141, 146, 149, 187
Babler, O. F., 11
Baker, Blanch M., 11
Barnes, T. R., 41
Barnet, Sylvan, 57
Barnett, Pat, 41
Bateman, Reginald, 19
Bateson, F. W., 12
Baugh, Albert C., 21
Baughan, E. A., 166, 167
Bauman, Richard, 41
Bazalgette, Léon, 107
Beeching, H.C., 101
Beerbohm, Max, 75, 81, 175
Bellinger, Martha Fletcher, 19
Benjamin, M. W., 156, 194
Bennett, Charles A., 19
Bennett, James O'Donnell, 132, 133
Bentley, Eric Russell, 41, 95
Bergholz, Harry, 95
Berman, Morton, 57
Bessai, Diane E., 61
Bewley, Charles, 41
Bibliographies, 11-12, 96-106 *passim*, 136, 152, 163, 164, 175, 177, 186
Bickley, Francis Lawrance, 2, 19, 21, 28, 33, 37, 41, 42, 52, 57, 93, 95, 103, 120, 135, 162, 164, 167, 168, 171, 179, 183, 185, 209
Biggers, Earl Derr, 126
Biography, 13-18, 43
Birmingham, George A., 41
Birrell, Francis, 6, 171
Blaghd, Earnán de.
  See Blythe, Ernest.
Blake, Warren Barton, 13, 19, 20, 41
Blissett, William, 61
Block, Haskell M., 20
Bloxam, R. N., 180
Blum, Professor. See Florence, Jean.
Blythe, Ernest (Earnán de Blaghd), 95
Bookseller, The, 162
Borel, Jacques, 61
Boucicault, Dion, 140
Bourgeois, Maurice, 1, 2, 11, 12, 13, 20, 37, 41, 52, 57, 61, 68, 75, 81, 85, 87, 93, 95, 97, 102, 103, 107,

211

Hillebrand, Harold Newcomb, 99
Hind, Charles Lewis, 45
Hoare, Dorothy Mackenzie, 26, 58
Hoare, John Edward, 26, 27, 77, 82, 88
Hodgson, Geraldine E., 99
Hogan, John Joseph, 27
Hogan, Patrick A., 142
Hogan, Robert, 15, 27, 45, 58, 65, 88, 100
Holbrooke, Mr., 165
Holloway, Joseph, 14, 27, 45, 58, 65, 88, 100, 140
Homer, 4
Hone, Joseph M., 15, 17, 63, 65, 73, 99, 113, 176
Honig, Edwin, 45
Hornblow, Arthur, 65
Horniman, A. E. F., 139, 140, 144 150, 154, 155, 158
Hortmann, Wilhelm, 27
Houghton, C. H., 152
Houston, Herbert S., 199
Howarth, Herbert, 27, 45
Howe, Percival Presland, 21, 27, 28, 31, 34, 37, 46, 49, 50, 51, 52, 58, 65, 66, 77, 82, 85, 88, 91, 92, 99, 164, 166, 167, 180, 185, 195, 197, 201
Huckleberry Finn, 69
Hudson, Lynton, 27
Hueffer, Ford Madox (Ford Madox Ford), 66
Hughes, Herbert, 172
Huneker, James, 27, 46
Hunt, Hugh, 99
Hurbut, Gladys, 65
Huscher, Herbert, 27, 46
Hyde, Douglas, 42, 63

Ibsen, Henrik, 3, 19, 25, 38, 41, 53, 59, 61, 70, 78, 82, 86, 89, 95
Ichikawa, Sanki, 107
In the Shadow of the Glen, 81-83, 98, 99, 101, 105, 119-132 *passim*, 137, 138, 140, 145, 148, 153, 155, 160, 161, 163, 164, 165, 169, 170, 172, 175, 178, 180, 182-186 *passim*, 193, 194, 197, 198, 201, 202, 207, 208
In Wicklow, West Kerry and Connemara (and *The Congested Districts*), 92, 177
Influences, French, on Synge, 19, 33, 41, 46, 47, 51, 75, 81, 87, 89, 96, 103, 181
Inglis, Brian St. John, 99
Inkster, Leonard, 176
Introductions to Editions, 107-109
Ionesco, Eugène, 19, 25

Irish National Theatre. See Abbey Theatre.
Irish Peasant, Folk Drama, and Stage Irishman, 20, 21, 25, 27, 31, 47, 62, 72, 95, 96, 105, 145, 147, 154, 159, 161, 191
Irish Players, 28, 31, 33, 38, 41, 44, 46, 52, 71, 122-130 *passim*, 132, 151, 156, 163, 164, 166, 167, 169, 173, 174, 176, 184, 186, 187, 191, 192, 194-208 *passim*; Arrest of Irish Players (Phila.), 151, 157, 166, 174, 186, 189, 197, 199, 203-208 *passim*
Irishman, 151
Irishwoman, An, 142
Iveragh, 189

J., A. M., 210
J., D. J., 141
J., M., 134, 135
J., P., 120
Jackson, Holbrook, 27, 171
Jacobs, Willis D., 46
Jacques, 148, 151
Jacquot, Jean, 44
James, Henry, 93
James, W. P., 167
Jameson, Storm, 28
Jeffares, Alexander Norman, 28, 40, 99, 104, 106
Jesus Christ, 68
Jiménez, Juan Ramón, 108
Jiménez, Zenobia Camprubí de, 108
Jingle, 164
Jochum, Klaus Peter S., 11
Johnson, Lionel, 45
Johnson, Philander, 209
Johnson, Wallace H., 66
Johnston, Denis, 25, 28, 46, 66, 77
Jonson, Ben, 29, 47, 66
Jordan, John, 46
Jordan, Michael J., 123, 191
Joyce, James, 46, 47, 71, 76, 77, 97, 99, 100, 104
Justitia, 140, 143

K., P. M. E., 158
K., T. M., 172
K., T. W., 140
Kain, Richard Morgan, 46, 66
Kaul, R. K., 28
Kavanagh, Patrick, 5, 46, 100
Kavanagh, Peter, 2, 28, 97, 100
Keane, Michael, 150
Keating, John, 33
Kelly, Blanche Mary, 28
Kelly, (Dr.) Gertrude B., 188, 191, 192
Kelly, Michael, 199

218 INDEX

220 INDEX

Evening News, The, 207
Evening Tribune, The, 207
Providence Journal, The, 208
*Providence Sunday Journal,
The,* 208
Seoul (Korea)
Korea Daily News, The, 208
Sheffield (England)
Sheffield Guardian, The, 209
Southport (England)
Southport Guardian, The, 209
St. Louis (Missouri, U.S.A.)
*St. Louis Daily Globe-Democrat,
The,* 208
Vienna (Austria)
Neue Freie Presse, 209
Washington, D.C. (U.S.A.)
Evening Star, The, 209
Sunday Star, The, 209
Washington Herald, The, 210
Washington Post, The, 210
Washington Times, The, 210
Nic Shiubhlaigh, Máire.
See MacSiubhlaigh, Máire
Nicoll, Allardyce, 31
Non-Dramatic Prose Works, 91-92
Nordman, C. A., 31, 59, 68, 78, 82,
86, 88
Obituaries, 52, 101, 119, 120, 121,
136, 137, 139, 140, 144, 148, 150,
151, 154, 155, 159, 166, 175, 178,
179, 185, 186
O'Brien, Conor Cruise
(Donat O'Donnell), 48, 63, 177
O'Brien, Edward J., 108
O'Brien, Maurice N., 31
Observer, 148
O'Byrne, J. K., 151
O'C., S., 149
O'Callaghan, 134, 135, 136
O'Casey, Sean, 25, 26, 28, 36, 44,
46, 47, 68, 69
O'Connor, Brother Anthony Cyril,
16, 31, 59, 68, 78
O'Connor, Eily, 134, 135, 137
O'Connor, Frank, 32, 48, 68
O'Connor, Dr. J. H., 203
O'Conor, Norreys Jephson, 48
O'Cuisín, Seumas
(James H. Cousins), 158
O'D., D., 160
O'D., D. J., 68
O'D. Power, Victor, 145
O'Dempsey, Michael, 154
O'Doherty, Eileen, 189
O'Donnell, Donat.
See O'Brien, Conor Cruise
O'Donnell, James Preston, 101
O'Donoghue, David James, 16, 143,
147, 150, 151

O'Donovan, Michael Francis,
See O'Connor, Frank
O'Faolain, Sean, 12, 48, 152
O Faracháin, Roibeárd.
See Farren, Robert
O'Grady, L. C., 143
O'Hagan, Thomas, 32, 48
O'Hannay, Rev. J., 154
O'Hegarty, P. S.
(P. S. O h-Eigeartaigh), 12, 32,
152, 157
O h-Eigeartaigh, P. S.
See O'Hegarty, P. S.
O'L., J. J., 144
Old Parnellite, An, 141
O'Leary, Jeremiah A., 189, 191
O'Leary, John, 106
O'Leary-Curtis, W., 143, 147
O'Mahony, Mathew, 32
O'Mangain, H. C., 143
O Maoláin, Micheál, 142
Omicron, 171
O Neachtain, Eoghan, 149
O'Neill, Eugene, 22, 47, 104
O'Neill, George, 49, 148
O'Neill, James J., 144
O'Neill, Maire, 7, 14, 113, 152
O'Neill, Michael J., 15, 16, 27, 45,
58, 65, 88, 100, 101
Onófrio, Lilia d', 32, 78
Oppel, Horst, 63
O'Reilly, Miss, 188
Orel, Harold, 59
O'Riordan, Conal, 89
Orpen, Richard, 63
Orpen, William, 63
O'Ryan, Agnes, 32
Oryza, 143
O'Shaughnessy, James, 130
O'Síocháin, P. A. (Sheehan, Patrick
Augustine), 49, 91
O'Sullivan, Denis, 140
O'Sullivan, Seamus, 101
Ottaway, D. Hugh, 78
Ouine, Sean, 120
Ould, Hermon, 78
Owen, Alice G., 49

P., 169
P., A., 167
P., H. T., 124
P., W. F., 182
Page, Curtis C., 16, 78
Palamede, 175
Palmer, Arnold, 167
Palmer, Helen H., 12
Palmer, John, 102, 176
Parker, Derek, 94
Parnell, Charles Stewart, 27, 45
Passages Referring to Synge *en*

Tindall, William York, 37
Tinker's Wedding, The, 85-86, 103, 124, 165, 166, 167, 171, 183, 197; J. W. Luce and Co. edition, 19, 21, 30, 43, 85; Maunsel and Co. edition, 85
Tobin, Michael, 37
Tomas, 151
Townshend, George, 37
Toye, Francis, 169
Tracy, Robert, 109
Trebitsch-Stein, Marianne, 209
Trevor, William, 170
Trewin, John Courtenay, 37, 104, 169
Triesch, Manfred, 12, 17, 113
Trinity College, Dublin, 12
Trividic, C., 37
Tucker, S. Marion, 43
Tupper, James W., 37
Turner, Edward Raymond, 104
Turner, W. J., 72
Twain, Mark, 69
Two Tigers, The, 89
Tyler, Gary R., 11
Tynan, Kenneth, 173

Ua Broin, G. C., 142
Ua F., R., 52
Ua Fuaráin, Eoghan, 37, 52
Ua Muineacháin, P. S., 141, 146
Ulanov, Barry, 37
Ungvári, Tamás, 109
Untermeyer, Louis, 72, 197
Ussher, Percy Arland, 52, 104

Van Doren, Carl Clinton, 37
Van Doren, Mark, 37
van Hamel, A. G., 4, 52
Van Laan, Thomas F., 79
"Vedette", 169
Vendler, Helen Hennessy, 104
Vernon, Frank, 79
Visitor from Tzardom, A, 145
Völker, Klaus, 17, 37, 60, 72, 79, 83, 86, 89
Vox Populi, 143

W., A., 198
W., H. M., 174
W., J., 183
Wade, Allan, 40, 54, 113
Walbrook, Henry MacKinnon, 4, 72
Walker, Biron, 48
Walker, Mary.
    See MacSiubhlaigh, Máire
Wall, Mr., 137, 138, 139, 150, 159
Waller, A. R., 45
Walley, Harold Reinoehl, 72
Ward, Alfred Charles, 37, 72, 153

Ward, Sir A. W., 45
Wareing, Alfred, 27
Warner, Alan, 52
Warnock, Robert, 38, 79
Watkins, Ann, 38, 52
Watson, Ernest Bradlee, 38
Watt, Homer A., 79
Watt, William, 26
Wauchope, George Armstrong, 38
Webb, Clifton, 74
Webb, Geoffrey, 38
Weiss, Samuel A., 38
Weldon, A. E. (Brinsley McNamara), 104
Well of the Saints, The, 87-89, 102, 105, 109, 119-140 *passim*, 145, 148, 154, 161, 163, 164, 172, 174, 175, 179, 181, 184, 185, 187, 193-210 *passim*
Wells, Henry W., 104
Western Girl, A, 140, 146, 187
"Western Peasant, The", 147
Weygandt, Cornelius, 38, 41, 46, 52, 104, 164, 168, 173
Wheeler, A., 143
When the Moon Has Set, 89
Whitaker, Thomas R., 72
White, George, 210
White, Herbert Oliver, 38
White, John T., 198
Whiting, Frank M., 38
Whitman, Charles Huntington, 38
Wieczorek, Hubert, 72
Wild, Friedrich, 94
Wilde, Percival, 105
Williams, Harold, 38, 53
Williams, Michael, 199
Williams, Raymond, 2, 7, 38, 53
Williams, Rowan, 32
Williams, S. C., 122, 123
Williams, Vaughan, 169, 172
Williamson, Audrey, 72
Willock, Sophie.
    See Bryant, Sophie (Willock)
Wilson, Edmund, 4, 105
Wilson, Lawrence, 44, 77, 81, 113
Wister, Jones, 205
Wood, Alfred Charles, 30
Wood, Edward Rudolf, 73, 79, 181
Wood, Frederick T., 94
Woods, Anthony S., 53
Wordsworth, William, 96
Works, The, G. Allen and Unwin, revised collected edition (1932), 20; J. W. Luce and Co. edition, 21, 27, 30, 43, 50, 51, 194, 197; Maunsel and Co. edition, 30, 33, 34, 36, 44, 50, 52, 53, 119, 122, 130, 138, 154, 162, 164, 165, 166, 167, 169, 171, 172, 174, 176, 177,